CORBYNISM

A Critical Approach

SOCIETYNOW

SocietyNow: short, informed books, explaining why our world is the way it is, now.

The *SocietyNow* series provides readers with a definitive snapshot of the events, phenomena and issues that are defining our twenty-first century world. Written by leading experts in their fields, and publishing as each subject is being contemplated across the globe, titles in the series offer a thoughtful, concise and rapid response to the major political and economic events and social and cultural trends of our time.

SocietyNow makes the best of academic expertise accessible to a wider audience in order to help readers untangle the complexities of each topic and make sense of our world the way it is, now.

CORBYNISM: A CRITICAL APPROACH

MATT BOLTON

University of Roehampton, UK

AND

FREDERICK HARRY PITTS

University of Bristol, UK

United Kingdom – North America – Japan – India
Malaysia – China

Emerald Publishing Limited
Howard House, Wagon Lane, Bingley BD16 1WA, UK

First edition 2018

Published under exclusive licence by Emerald Publishing Limited

Reprints and permissions service
Contact: permissions@emeraldinsight.com

British Library Cataloguing in Publication Data
A catalogue record for this book is available from the British
Library

ISBN: 978-1-78754-372-0 (paperback)
ISBN: 978-1-78754-369-0 (E-ISBN)
ISBN: 978-1-78754-371-3 (Epub)

ISOQAR certified
Management System,
awarded to Emerald
for adherence to
Environmental
standard
ISO 14001:2004.

Certificate Number 1985
ISO 14001

INVESTOR IN PEOPLE

CONTENTS

First Liberalism is identified with Capitalism;
then Liberalism is made to walk the plank;
but Capitalism is no worse for the dip, and
continues its existence unscathed under a new alias.

—Karl Polanyi

PREFACE

At the time of writing, this is the first book to set itself the sole task of taking Corbynism seriously and critically as a semi-coherent set of ideas. It has been impossible to keep up with the books on Jeremy Corbyn's leadership of the Labour Party or the wider Labour left published over the course of the period in which we were developing the arguments and analyses presented here. But these books provide somewhat different angles on the topic – placing Corbyn in the context of the longer history of the Labour left, examining the practical political programme or movement attached to him, or casting him as the antihero in the triumph-against-adversity tale of how an unambitious backbencher was thrust into the political limelight – and as such speak for themselves.[1]

This book, on the other hand, adds to this existing and still-growing literature a slightly more conceptual, analytical and abstract objective. This is, in short, to provide the reader with a critical orientation towards the foundations and implications of the rapidly germinating but theoretically deep-rooted intellectual world of Corbynism. It does not exhaustively document every aspect of this new, evolving and diverse worldview, but sets out some pointers for debate and critique from a circumspect left perspective. It will be up to others to make claims to give the definitive account of, or have the final word over, what Corbynism is and where it is going. No doubt this book will be joined and possibly

outpaced by others – not to mention events themselves, which
is always a danger of writing history on the hoof. Our aim
here is simply to generate theoretical resources and create
intellectual space for 'good conversation' about Corbynism
and the consideration of its consequences and alternatives.[2]

All good intentions aside, at first glance this book may
come across as two academics using abstract critiques to
browbeat party members from the sidelines. But this does
not quite capture where we are coming from. Both of us supported Jeremy Corbyn in the 2015 leadership election. One
of us was even involved in setting up and coordinating a local
Momentum group. We were both able to set aside our initial
reservations about the political milieu Corbyn sprung from,
specifically with regard to its positions on foreign policy and
the prevalence of conspiracy-theory critiques of capitalism
and imperialism.[3] We celebrated instead the greater good his
leadership election victory represented: a Labour Party finally with the left in the driving seat, and a burgeoning 'social
movement' sitting behind it, right at the heart of UK politics.

But as that first year went on, Momentum meetings dete-
riorated into sectarian power struggles, the same faces turned
out in the same number to knock doors, and CLP meetings
consisted of shell-shocked centrists and little more. There
was a growing disconnect between the rhetoric – particularly
online – and the reality. We had both been, on and off, active
in and around the Labour Party and wider labour movement
since the late noughties, playing small roles in party and movement life. We had spent these years wishing for the left to take
the reins, and with Corbyn what once felt a generational task
seemingly happened overnight. But the impact appeared to
be confined to our online lives. In our everyday experience of
party activity the 'movement' seemed a spectral and largely
untransformative presence. By the local elections of 2016, the
campaign on the ground was still manned by the very same

older members and 'moderates' who elsewhere were being disparaged, ridiculed and sneered at by the increasingly combative social media crowd.

The gap between the grand claims being made by the more vocal Corbyn supporters – that this was an unprecedented 'social movement' which was about to reshape British politics forever – and our concrete experience of it grew ever wider. This was exacerbated by Corbyn's performance in Parliament, the seeming absence of any political strategy beyond abstract moralising, and the general chaos surrounding his leadership. A nadir was reached during the referendum on the UK's membership of the EU. Corbyn followed party policy by campaigning for Remain, but a lack of enthusiasm for the European project was palpable throughout.

The blame for the referendum result cannot be pinned on Corbyn alone. But stacked against him was the fact that voters were unsure of Labour's stance right up until the day of the vote, and his call for the immediate invocation of Article 50 on the morning of the result.[4] This proved to be the final straw for the Parliamentary Labour Party (PLP). Members of Corbyn's Shadow Cabinet resigned *en masse*, and MPs passed a vote of no confidence in his leadership. The expectation was that Corbyn would resign. Labour's poll ratings, already shaky, dropped through the floor. Yet Corbyn refused to step down, citing the mandate he had been given the year before from the party membership.

It was at this point that we became convinced enough of our growing doubts about the Corbyn project to voice them in a series of online articles and blogposts.[5] Here we critiqued some of the claims being made on behalf of the Corbyn movement and compared them to the underwhelming reality we had experienced during the first year of his leadership. We pointed to the emptiness of its pseudo-populist rhetoric, its appeal to a 'people' that did not exist, the moralising,

apolitical nature of the platform, the abject failure of the
Labour contribution to the Remain campaign, and the
seemingly unsurmountable splits both within the PLP and the
broader Labour membership. We feared that Brexit heralded
the triumph of the Faragean hard-right across Britain, a
prospect which was only made more likely by the elevation of
the anti-migrant Theresa May to Prime Minister.

We had initially dismissed the question of Corbyn's 'electability' on the grounds that Corbynism was necessarily a long-
term project, for which it was worth sacrificing two or even
three elections for the sake of some future leftwards 'hegemony'. But at the time we started engaged critically with Corbynism, electability appeared to assume a new urgency owing
to the radically changed political stakes of failure. A Labour
electoral collapse post-Referendum would allow a Conservative administration high on nativism and authoritarianism to
unilaterally redraw the British polity in its own image. We
thus – somewhat naively – called for a negotiated settlement
in which Corbyn would hand over the reins to a soft-left candidate able to overcome the schisms in the PLP and allow
Labour to mount an effective challenge to May's Conservatives. Although opening ourselves up to the inaccurate but
amusing accusation of being, as one anonymous Twitter wag
had it, 'Marxists4OwenSmith', we were far from alone in our
analysis.[6] Many of those who counted themselves as amongst
Corbyn's most enthusiastic supporters reached similar conclusions – most famously Owen Jones, the *Guardian* columnist.[7]

Corbyn triumphed in a second leadership election against
Owen Smith in September 2016, and the case seemed closed.
Yet there had been something unsettling about the paranoid
defensiveness and personalised invective exhibited by some
of Corbyn's support during the so-called 'coup.' During this
period, virtually the entirety of the PLP were regularly cast as
wicked 'Blairite' conspirators, intent on Corbyn's destruction

so as to follow their true 'Tory-lite' agenda. At one point
Paul Mason, the Corbyn-supporting journalist, argued that
Corbyn-critical Labour MPs constituted 'the final defence
line of the 1%,' apparently the only thing standing between
neoliberal capitalism and the emergence of socialism.[8] The
increasingly toxic and divisive atmosphere began to cast a
different light on the central tenets of the Corbyn movement
itself. Regardless, we continued campaigning for the Labour
Party at a local level, our concerns kept largely to ourselves.

Commentary suspended, in the 2017 General Election we
pounded pavements door-knocking and delivering leaflets
alongside, nationwide, thousands of Corbyn-enthused volunteers working with the 'moderate' old guard. This experience conclusively proved that substantial parts of our past
critique were wrong. And they were wrong because the two
events which we, and many others, thought spelled disaster
for the Corbyn project – the Brexit vote and the split in the
PLP – proved to be its saving grace. The EU Referendum
had polarised the electorate (or revealed its polarisation) in
an unprecedented manner. This dichotomy was then intensified by May's extraordinarily sectarian attitude to the post-
referendum period, which saw Remain voters – 48% of the
country – labelled 'citizens of nowhere' and 'saboteurs' con-
spiring against the 'will of the people.' Our assumption was
that the irrational populist energies unleashed by the Brexit
campaign signalled that the political moment was racing
away from Corbynism. In fact, as we shall see, the opposite
was the case. The Brexit vote was the making of Corbynism,
the necessary precondition of its success. The same is true of
the PLP split and the challenge to Corbyn's leadership. Far
from heralding the collapse of Labour as an electoral force,
the so-called 'coup' against Corbyn activated his slumbering
support in a manner that had been utterly absent during
the previous twelve months. And even though it ebbed away

in the intervening period, the energy of the second Corbyn leadership campaign reappeared in the General Election campaign.

For other left critics like Owen Jones, the 2017 election result settled any doubts about Corbyn's 'electability,' 'competence' or 'strategy.' Our position, meanwhile, was somewhat different. Our initial criticisms were, like Jones', focused not on disagreements over policy but on the electoral and political risks of sticking with a failing leadership at a time of rising nativism and constitutional crisis. But in the course of making that argument, and in the discussions and debates that followed, these initial doubts developed into a deeper and more fundamental critique of the Corbyn worldview as a whole.

Once we had taken a step back and surveyed the theoretical underpinnings of that worldview, it became clear that the question of its electability was increasingly moot. There were clear resonances between the platform that was gradually being built around Corbyn's leadership – based on a hyper-personalisation of politics and capitalism itself, a sectarian atmosphere of denunciation and delegitimization of internal critics, ambivalence towards the EU and transnational institutions, a tendency towards Manichean conspiratorial thinking, and a programme of economic nationalism – and that of the populist currents gaining prominence across the globe. There was no longer any reason to suspect that Corbynism could not also chime with voters here.

This book picks up this thread and runs with it, exploring how the claims Corbynism's intellectual and political coalition makes about itself conflict with the theoretical and practical consequences of the way it sees the world. What this shows is that rather than embodying a radical challenge to the current trajectory of global capitalism, Corbynism in fact reflects wider societal, ideological and political-economic shifts that bring it closely in-step with an increasingly 'post-liberal' political environment. This, we suggest, is the source of its actual and potential success as a movement today.

In making this argument, the book is therefore the product of a long process of critique and self-criticism. When we have cause to criticise those who focused all their attention on Corbyn's lack of 'electability' rather than analysing the content of his worldview, we are as much admonishing ourselves as anyone else. On the other hand, given that both of us have participated in various parts of the Marxisant left and anti-austerity movements which ended up forming Corbynism's base, we are arguably more familiar with the theoretical perspectives informing much of the new Labour membership than many critics in the traditional press. This may be news to some on the right, but with a few notable exceptions, most of the Corbyn base and its core of intellectual leading lights are not Militant-esque 'Trots' or 'Stalinists'. Rather what theoretical formation they possess will likely rest in in leftist backgrounds in some respects much like ours, influenced by non-aligned Marxisms, libertarian forms of socialism and communism, Italian autonomism, and the British New Left, as well as newer ideas around so-called 'accelerationism.' This is a heady and powerful mix of new thinking that has tremendously reinvigorated the intellectual resources of the UK left. But part of our argument here is that underpinning each of these is a form of rather old-fashioned orthodox Marxism, and it is through this shared inheritance that the connection is made with the more traditional Bennism represented by Corbyn himself.

Our own analysis, meanwhile, draws from a heterodox current of Marxian theory which holds no truck with the teleological economic determinism that characterises so much of even the most sophisticated orthodox theories. Nor does it

proclaim Marx a prophet, or insist that there is a readymade
political programme to be cribbed from Marx's work, that
just needs to be at last put into practice in the 'correct' way
for everything to be made right with the world. Rather, this
understanding of Marx sees his work as primarily a critical
tool, a means to examine and interrogate the society in which
we live, and to grasp the abstract forms which force us to
exist by means of labour, commodities and money. This is
politically thin gruel compared with the lavish promises of
eternal harmony and red plenty which are the province of
proponents of 'fully automated luxury communism' and the
like. But it is a perspective which, like Marx himself, takes its
cues from the world as it is, seeking to work through the real
contradictions which run through society, rather than wishing them away in the name of the perfected society to come.

~~~

We would like to take this opportunity to thank everyone who
helped in bringing this book to fruition. Philippa Grand and
the team at Emerald for their encouragement and patience;
in alphabetical order Lewis Coyne, Jennifer Evans, Jack Grif-
fiths, David Hirsh, Siobhan McAndrew, Paul Thompson, Jack
Watkins and Jon Wellington for their thoughts, feedback and
encouragement, large and small, on various iterations and
presentations of bits and pieces associated with the book, for
which all the usual disclaimers apply; and finally our partners
and children for the support and inimitable brand of respite
the latter offered as we slogged away in the final stages. We
would also like to thank the organisers and participants of
the Political Studies Association Political Marketing Group
Meeting 'Political Marketing and the Future of the Labour
Party' at the University of Salford on the 20th October 2017,
where we test-ran some of the arguments presented here.
Some of the arguments presented in the book appear in a

different form as an article in *British Politics*, for which we would like to thank the editors and anonymous reviewers.[9] Finally, this book is dedicated to the memories of Moishe Postone and Robert Fine, both of whom passed away whilst we were in midst of writing. We did not know them personally, and we make no claim as to whether they would agree with our conclusions, but without their work this book may well have not existed.

Introduction

TAKING CORBYNISM SERIOUSLY

In this book we set out to take Corbynism seriously, on its own terms. We take it seriously as a set of ideas and practices above and beyond Jeremy Corbyn, but necessarily existing through him – and therefore unthinkable without an understanding of the man himself and his image. Taking it seriously means that we do not see Corbynism as something which only acts upon society from without. Rather Corbynism needs to be grasped as a part of that society, as an expression of certain things about the way society works and how it understands itself. In this book we provide a critical overview of the fragmentary and sometimes diverse theoretical basis of Corbynism, moving beyond utilitarian debates over 'electability' to challenge common threads around which the movement's grasp of capitalism, class and geopolitics coheres.

It was the failure of Corbyn's critics, both within the Labour party and without, to subject the political and theoretical content of the 'Corbyn worldview' to proper scrutiny – rather than merely patronising, deriding or romanticising it – which led to the paroxysms of shock and contrition felt throughout British politics following the 2017 election result. In this book, we seek to remedy that failure through the examination of the core tenets of Corbynism that have hitherto escaped systematic analysis. In so doing we show how the economic protectionism and foreign policy isolationism which constitutes the core of Corbynism is expressed through a politically ambivalent critique of capitalism as a 'rigged system'. We explore how these aspects chime with broader political and economic shifts in a post-2008 crash, post-Brexit, post-Trump world. We argue that Corbynism's resonance with a wider 'populist turn' goes some way to explain the success of the movement thus far.

As such, unlike many of the critiques that have followed in the wake of Corbyn's ascendancy, our contribution adopts a critical approach to Corbynism from the left. This book does not treat Corbyn and the left-intellectual milieu that has coalesced around his leadership with scorn, nor caricatures it as a dismal alliance of 'Trots,' naïve cultists, bourgeois falafel-munchers and the 'thick as pigshit.'[1] Instead, we seek to place it in context by tracing the theoretical roots of the Corbyn worldview. Drawing on a tradition of critical Marxist thought, we move beyond the mainstream conversation about Corbyn's electability or unsuitability, contextualizing and clarifying Corbynism's intellectual origins – stated or not – in wider left politics and theory. Although polling is still a little sluggish for Corbyn himself compared to where a party leader might expect to be in the circumstances, Corbynism as a political movement is now undeniably in the ascendency, and conceivably on the verge of power.[2] This proximity to government makes a critique of the intellectual underpinnings of both Corbyn and the wider movement constructed around him a pressing matter. Critique is necessary for the further development of left strategies that can escape some of the problematic aspects of Corbynism outlined here, with or without Corbyn himself.

Indeed, this is not a book about Jeremy Corbyn per se – although, for reasons we will go on to discuss, it is not possible to consider Corbynism without Corbyn himself at the helm. Corbyn's personal demeanour, his manner of speaking and dress, and the particular trajectory of his political career were all crucial factors in the rise of Corbynism, even if the ideas and worldview that he has come to represent cannot be reduced to his person. In particular, we focus on how his reputation for moral exceptionalism – of being forever on the 'right side of history' – has proven to be a vital political tool in overcoming the internal contradictions that run through the movement. At times, then, Corbyn's personal views or history of political activity are highly relevant to the consideration of the 'ism' constructed around him. But, on occasion, we will talk more of Corbyn not as a person with his own thoughts and ideas, but as a kind of cipher for a wider political moment, a vehicle for more meaning that his slender frame can reasonably carry. In essence, then, this is a book about *Corbynism* – to which the inevitable objection might be raised: what is Corbynism, and is it possible to speak of a coherent 'ism' of that name?

Against us is the possibility that, in linking so-called 'Corbynism' to other manifestations of a more general populist shift, we provide evidence that Corbynism does not deserve its own 'ism', precisely because it is merely one iteration of a broader trend. Furthermore, the specificity of Corbynism as a standalone 'ism' is infringed by the fact that much of the worldview we intend to critique is drawn from modes of analysis which have been a mainstay of traditional leftist and orthodox Marxian thinking for much of the twentieth century. But we keep to the use of 'Corbynism' as a term precisely because the rise of Corbyn has distilled many of those leftist tendencies into their purest form and placed them at the centre of British politics in a way that is unprecedented in British political history. And, in the person of Corbyn and Corbyn alone, an additional ingredient is added that seems capable of temporarily suspending the contradictions of these tendencies, striking a political concord that carries a dynamic populist pitch at the ballot box. Therefore, in this book we map the contours of a certain orientation to questions of class, history and political economy that has taken root in many quarters of the UK left, rather than exhaustively documenting its every flow and ebb.

Even though Corbyn may be too convenient an alibi for the movement that carries his name to successfully carry on once he has gone, it is important nonetheless to reckon with the possibility that 'Corbynism' can outgrow, outlast and out-live the tenure of Corbyn himself as leader. But the only way to do this is to delve deeper into the complex of political and economic thinking that provides its foundations and lines of flight. In part this book is a contribution to constructive contention over its future path at a time where the invigor-ating intellectual and political energies Corbyn's leadership unleashed find themselves constrained by their conditions of organisational survival resting on the suppression of contra-diction and contestations.

THE COMPONENTS OF CORBYNISM

We can clarify the target of our critique, both in terms of per-sonnel and ideology, along a few axes. The Corbyn movement comprises a variety of different strands of the British left, each of which have fed into Corbynism something of their own theoretical and rhetorical constitution. It is the diversity and often conflicting commitments of the project that, if anything, gives it the potential to germinate alternatives, but crucially, it is the relative strength within Corbynism of divergent ele-ments that defines its character at any one time.

Firstly, and most prominently in terms of organisation and leadership, we have the 'trad Left' strand represented by

Corbyn himself, Shadow Chancellor John McDonnell, strategist Seumas Milne, head of the Unite union Len McCluskey and advisor Andrew Murray. Typically, but with inevitable exceptions, this wing mixes 'Bennite' economic nationalism and what we describe as 'personalised' forms of anti-capitalism with Leninist central party planning. Alongside this are forms of reflexive 'anti-imperialism,' 'anti-Americanism' and 'anti-Zionism' drawn from the 1960s 'New Left'. Institutionally, it holds a historical and today largely residual proximity with the embalmed official Communist Party, who maintain a pro-Corbyn position largely outside the Labour Party.[3] Momentum has become a vital battleground of competing factions from within this aging Bennite and Leninist left, albeit augmented by younger activists with a thirst for new ideas, among them a politics of grassroots social reproduction- in short, how we live and look after ourselves and others- so far squeezed out by hard-left political hackery.[4]

This older current meets a new and youthful 'postcapitalist' techno-utopian wing epitomised by figures such as Paul Mason, *Novara Media*'s Aaron Bastani and *Inventing the Future* authors Nick Srnicek and Alex Williams, as well as a newly-established think-tank, the Autonomy Institute.[5] Degrees of difference notwithstanding, this 'accelerationist' perspective unites with the older tradition around an understanding of capitalism, technology and historical development derived from the more deterministic elements of Marx, in the postcapitalist case fed through the readings of neo-Marxists like Antonio Negri.[6] Here the arc of history unfolds in the favour of the forces of production against outdated relations of production challenged by the hegemony-building of new and revolutionary political subjectivities – whether workers or Mason's multitudinous 'networked individuals'.[7] The utopianism of a 'fully automated luxury communism' has come to infect mainstream policy thinking within the Labour Party, not least in proposals for a universal basic income and the harnessing of automation and artificial intelligence to restructure the relationship with work.[8]

Beyond these two leading political and intellectual strands we see the presence of many splinters, communities, and groupuscules that do not fit into either category and whose theoretical conceptualisations or practical activity find, for whatever reason, somewhat less of an uptake in defining the contours of what Corbynism is and can be at the present moment. What is interesting is how this takes in a broad sweep of not only the far-, hard- and ultra-left but also picks off compliant elements of the centre- and soft-left in its increasingly disorganised and directionless forms.

Where Trotskyists do play a prominent role in the Corbynist intellectual and political coalition it is not always in the way the popular imagination of 'Trot entryists' [sic] would readily permit.[9] The Socialist Workers Party (SWP) and the Socialist Party hold little real sway over Corbyn or Corbynism, in spite of the creeping irony that the more anti-authoritarian wings of the latter have gradually stepped into the party line on issues like Brexit. That said, Stand Up To Racism, an anti-racist organisation which doubles as a 'front' for the SWP – now held in contempt by much of the wider left after accusations of rape against a leading member were whitewashed following a sustained campaign of victim-blaming – has received personal support from both Corbyn and members of the Shadow Cabinet.[10] More significant are the Alliance for Workers' Liberty, whose heterodox and 'third-campist' Trotskyism has become an increasingly assertive and critical presence through their activity in the 'left Remain' Another Europe group and the Labour Campaign for Freedom of Movement.[11]

Beyond this on the Marxian left there are autonomist and libertarian leftists, principally represented in the group Plan C, who have had some involvement with the broader Corbynist intellectual and political environment. This has principally been through channels such as *The World Transformed* festival that now constitutes a permanent conference 'fringe' – presumably pending the full transformation of the party into a social movement.[12] There is some admixture here with the old-school cultural studies Compass soft-left who today throw their lot in with Corbyn on the basis of a Gramscian politics geared around the pursuit of hegemony.[13] Occasionally issuing calls for a 'Progressive Alliance', it is perhaps best represented by cultural theorist Jeremy Gilbert.[14] There is another overlap between the cultural studies soft-left and the accelerationist appeal for a 'Mont Pelerin Society of the left', expressed in a forthcoming book by Gilbert and Alex Williams, *Hegemony Now*.[15] At the very edge of this strand of the Corbyn milieu is found low-key buzz around the concept of 'Acid Corbynism'.[16] Derived from the late Mark Fisher's unfinished work on 'Acid Communism', its recuperation of hippiedom and celebration of dance culture ranks among the most stimulating outlets for the political energies of Corbynism, if somewhat tenuously connected to the wider movement.

Other communities, too, are bubbling up. Of a similarly 'cultural' bent, owing in equal parts to Chairman Mao and Raymond Williams, is the more traditionally and self-consciously intellectual Marxist and anti-imperialist *New Socialist*. Distinguished by its theoretically-informed long-form polemics and editorials, its analyses often sit quite comfortably within the 'trad-left' section of Corbyn's support identified above.[17]

Around certain issues, most notably Brexit – or 'Lexit' in its 'left' complexion – we also see the development of an intellectually distinct 'Polanyian' left preoccupied with a vision of 'Full Corbynism' based around the defence of national sovereignty in matters of trade, currency and economy policy against the forces of international neoliberalism.[18] In line with this protectionist standpoint, this latter tendency has also driven the development of a Corbynist localism based around the so-called 'Preston Model' of local procurement and municipal trade.[19]

Of late, the more heterodox elements of the Corbyn intellectual coalition have taken a backseat to the party's Stalinist-style political operators – in the case of Seumas Milne and Andrew Murray, a literal description – schooled in the smoke-filled rooms of Bennite and Leninist union and party life. Such machinations have reverberated through the party and the Momentum grouping, frequently masquerading as the implementation of 'true' direct democracy. Most infamously, Momentum ensure their delgates adhered to the leadership's line by voting down a debate about Brexit at the 2017 party conference.[20] There was also, at the very beginning of Corbyn's reign, the introduction of e-plebscites of the membership to circumnavigate resistant MPs on issues where members can be trusted to follow the leadership's line, such as the proposal to provide tactical air support to ground forces fighting ISIS in 2015.[21] Needless to say, this has not been used since on issues like the UK staying in the European Single Market, where the membership is squarely against the leadership.[22]

Whilst the struggle for the party's structure is an inevitable consequence of Corbyn's ascendancy, at times this substitutes for a struggle over the party's mind. This applies equally to all sides, with Corbynskeptics as incapable of creating a convincing and intellectually coherent alternative as Corbynists are of grappling the substantial contradictions in their own projects- and others still wedged between them, politically conflicted but working within the uneasy political settlement that has always somehow characterised Labour Party life. This book is thus a contribution to this working through of contradictions on all sides of the organisational and political dividing lines within Labour.

In what follows, we will concentrate in the main on the first two stands of Corbynism: the Bennite left and the post-capitalist utopians. This is not only because they have the clearest, most established and most internally coherent worldview, but also because they interrelate in unexpected ways which have been fundamental to the development of Corbynism thus far. Despite slight differences of historical context and the polyvalent stresses they place on different prime movers of social change, there are certain commonplaces that construct a rhetorical and political unity between the diverse components of the Corbynist intellectual coalition. Analytically these revolve around a naturalised understanding of capitalist society, which feeds into a singular, unidirectional and essentially Manichean vision of history in which innately 'good' forces – whether the 'working class,' the 'forces of production,' 'anti-imperialist' nation-states, 'postcapitalist' potentialities or 'the people' – are somehow constrained by 'bad', with change regarded as a question of removing those barriers.

A QUESTION OF POPULISM

The specificity of Corbynism, as we define it, is that the more 'trad-left' parts of its worldview are enriched by something contemporary, the strand of left populism that posits the revolutionary power of a popular '99%' against the domination of an all-powerful '1%.' It is this addition which has opened the path for possible success in the present historical moment. This is due to the resonance of such a politics with a changing global landscape in which populisms of the right and left display a dynamic, utopian appeal based on the shared conviction that the political and economic malaise of the post-2008 crash era can be directly traced to the moral failings of an international elite, whose contempt for the rest of society finds economic expression in falling median wages, deindustrialisation, and precarious work.

'Populism' is a notoriously slippery concept. There is much disagreement within the literature as to whether it is merely a style of politics which can be freely and harmlessly utilised on certain occasions by political parties within the bounds of liberal democratic norms, or whether it is a form of anti-politics which marks a decisive break with those norms, and thus poses a serious threat to the institutional structure of liberal democracies.[23] As such, defining this or that political movement as populist is not simple, particularly when the question of direct comparisons between 'left' and 'right' forms of populism is raised. That said, there are some key characteristics which, put together, do result in a minimally-coherent concept of populism. This concept, we suggest, does apply to Corbynism. In this we follow Chantal Mouffe, the leading theorist of left populism, who is in no doubt that Corbynism should indeed be characterised as such.[24]

For Mouffe, the central determinant of a populist project is the creation of a stark division between an 'us' and a 'them.' She argues that a successful populist political movement must bring together different social groups under the banner of a collective identity, a 'we' which in defining itself as such produces a 'political frontier' against the collective enemy, those who are not included within that 'we.' In Mouffe's telling, it was Corbyn's success in piecing together such a 'we' and opposing it to a 'them' that underlay Labour's performance in the 2017 election.

In addition to this binary divide, Jan-Werner Müller argues that the 'logic of populism' entails 'a particular moralistic imagination of politics.' It is 'a way of perceiving the political world that sets a morally pure and fully unified…people against elites who are deemed corrupt or in some other way morally inferior.'[25] The central criterion through which the moral are distinguished from the immoral is one that we will see repeatedly throughout the book – productiveness. Populist rhetoric, whether of right or left provenance, routinely pits a 'pure, innocent, always hardworking people…against a corrupt elite who do not really work.' From this moralistic, productivist perspective, the unproductive – whether at the top or bottom of society – are regarded as undermining the internal solidity of the 'we.' Corbyn's routine condemnations of a 'rigged system' deliberately set up by 'elites' in order to hold back the ordinary 'wealth creators' fits neatly into this category.

Populism is often associated with the idea of a demagogic, authoritarian leader in the mould of a Donald Trump, Recep Tayyip Erdogan or Viktor Orbán. The genial – if rather thin-skinned when challenged – figure of Corbyn certainly sits uneasily in this company. But it is precisely the incessant focus on Corbyn's unassuming personal goodness, which we discuss in Chapters 2 and 3, and the structural role his ascribed persona has played in the development and success of the movement as a whole which marks him out as a populist leader. The notion that Corbyn himself sits in a moral realm high above the tainted institutions and processes of liberal democracy and the corrupt 'establishment' is fundamental to the approach to politics adopted by the Corbyn movement. The perception of Corbyn's personal moral exceptionalism is not, then, merely a tool or trope to be cynically instrumentalised for other ends, but is the foundation upon which the entire project is built.

In considering the complex of ideas that constitutes Corbynism, it is not our intention to make predictions of every single potential policy shift which may or may not be imposed upon the leadership by the wider left milieu, because they simply cannot be identified in advance, subject to the happenstance of a radically shifting political landscape. Indeed, we are open to the possibility that by the time this book is read, some of the positions we criticise – say, on Europe – may have shifted in a more favourable direction. But rather than attempt to keep pace with these changes or host within these pages hostages to fortune, the aim of this book is to abstract from the vagaries of an increasingly high-stakes political game some overriding theoretical principles and positions that have remained constant and core in the Corbyn project. What we set out to do in this book, therefore, is to delineate the coordinates of the default positions taken by the core Corbyn leadership team, and the more theoretically fecund elements which surround it – neither of which, up to now, have been subject to any serious or systematic critical appreciation as a defined set of ideas. It is, we think, time to give Corbynism credit where it is due as equal to, or more than, the sum of its hastily assembled parts.

OUR PERSPECTIVE

Alternatives to these strands of Corbynism from within Labour have been in short supply. There are active non-Corbynist or Corbyn-critical lefts with which our perspective shares points in common, in part if not in whole. Some of these sit largely within Labour – such the party's traditional social democratic or 'soft' left, or the internationalist and often post-Trotskyist 'decent left'.[26] Among the latter there are also Corbynites who stand against the leadership position on Brexit, oppose any concession to racists and xenophobes on immigration, question a protectionist economic strategy, and show solidarity with those subject to brutal regimes abroad.[27] On the other hand, some of the alternative perspectives to Corbynism sit squarely outside the Labour Party – such as the extraparliamentary and 'anti-national' ultra-left, who have used the space afforded by refusal to participate in electoral politics to articulate and promote uncompromising and uncompromised critiques of the direction of the Corbyn project and the wider coincidence of a 'red-brown' alliance operative across the Anglophone far right and left.[28]

What brings these two perhaps unlikely bedfellows together – the social democratic and ultra-left – with our perspective, and distinguishes them from the main Corbynist current, is the recognition (implicit or explicit) of the inherently contradictory and negative character of capitalist social relations. While the approach taken to those relations varies enormously between the two – with the libertarian ultra-left seeking to abolish them in their entirety, and the internationalist social-democratic wing resigned to working through the contradictions without resolution – both acknowledge in practice, if not always in theory, the extent to which the abstract forms of capitalist society (money, production, commodities, labour, value) dominate all aspects of life within it. In both cases, social conflict is understood as being a historical, rather than ontological, phenomena. Contradiction is treated as something running *through* capitalist society as a whole, rather than being imposed upon it from the outside. Mediation – by both political or economic forms – is viewed as an inescapable moment of social and political life, the only means through which we can currently exist, for good or ill.

For the Bennite and postcapitalist wings of Corbynism by contrast, here betraying again their shared roots in orthodox Marxism, contradiction and social conflict are grasped as the result of external constraints imposed upon a social force itself regarded uncritically as innately 'good' – whether it is the 'working class,' the productive forces, or postcapitalist potentiality. The arrival of the good society therefore entails the eradication of contradiction through the removal of those 'bad' forces which hold it back – the capitalist class, international finance, or the relations of production – whether through the subsumption of the economy into the state, giving workers control of production, or full automation. Here there are again clear theoretical parallels with the populist insistence that social conflict can be immediately resolved through the formation of a unified 'people,' whose triumphant rise to 'hegemony' enables the expulsion of the 'them' held to be responsible for society's troubles. In each case, the historical source of social contradiction is left untouched. As such, the path is laid for powerful narratives of betrayal and conspiratorial resentment when the impossible demands for resolution cannot be met within a set of social relations that remains essentially unchanged – if not increasingly authoritarian attempts to make a stubbornly unyielding reality fit the theory.

It is worth noting at the outset that this unsteady synthesis of ultra-left total critique and more modest social democratic compromise, teamed with other aspects of a revisionist and heterodox Marxism, is unlikely to leave even readers sympathetic with our perspective entirely happy with the result. That is perhaps an inevitable consequence of an attempt to face head-on the problem of existing within a society in which survival depends upon mediation through the very social forms that make that survival a struggle. Rather than bullishly insisting that this contradiction can be immediately overcome, and those social forms wiped away 'as if with a sponge,' we acknowledge the gravity and seeming intractability of the situation, and the risks carried by premature and false claims of resolution.[29] Nevertheless, in order to head off some potential criticisms from the start, we will begin negatively, from what our perspective is *not* – and this relates to a looming presence in the intellectual life of the Labour Party predating by some distance Project Corbyn: Blue Labour.

~~~

In a 2017 essay for the *New Statesman*, Jonathan Rutherford argues that the only realistic philosophical alternative to Corbynism within the Labour Party is Blue Labour.[30] Rutherford, an academic and advisor to risen and fallen stars of the dormant Labour right like Chuka Umunna and Rachel Reeves, admirably contributes to ongoing attempts to take

Corbynism seriously as an identifiable set of ideas.[31] But in this book we show how Rutherford's posing of a stark choice between the two does not sufficiently address how both tendencies express wider philosophical points of convergence on the contemporary left, particularly around so-called 'post-liberalism', the nation, the people and how these relate to the state.[32] Selling readers on the assumption that there is no alternative, Rutherford obscures the true extent to which it is possible to articulate a real political-philosophical alternative to both Blue Labour and Corbynism based on a countervailing set of ideas sourced from within the left but not presently among its mainstream: a 'critical Marxist' alternative we begin to delineate here.

Blue Labour arose as a political tendency within the Labour Party towards the end of the Brown premiership. Associated with the academic and peer Maurice Glasman, and latched onto sporadically by numerous ambitious gadflies of the party's centre and right, Blue Labour argues that the latter period of the Blair-Brown government saw Labour lose touch with what was presented as its traditional support base, socially conservative 'white working class' voters in small towns and post-industrial cities.[33] Labour, it was argued, had become the party of globalisation and metropolitan liberalism, pushing for an ever-more centralised state, free markets and mass immigration. It had prioritised 'abstract values' and universalist principles of equality and rights over the particular communal bonds of mutual reciprocity, local identity, and national, familial and religious ties that characterised 'white working class' communities.[34] Today, Blue Labour ascribes the former set of opposing principles to Corbynism, an association the critique we present in this book exposes as strange and wilful.

Rutherford's critique centres, as does ours, on the confluence between the more traditional left strands of Corbynism and the forms of postcapitalist and accelerationist thinking which have rapidly gained hegemonic status within the left intellectual milieu around Corbyn's leadership. Rutherford argues that the first – based on a Bennite programme of nationalisation and state-directed production – was merely another reiteration of the 'command and control, tax and spend politics' that has befallen Labour since 1945. While the latter, self-styled 'postcapitalist' wing is more favourable to the kind of participatory politics that Blue Labour champions, its focus on the development of automated technology and the end of work, as well as its supposedly metropolitan liberal and public sector character, has led to a hollowed-out and asocial form of abstract universalism which is pushing Labour ever further away from the ethical and cultural traditions which have held both British society and the labour movement itself together for generations. This is a claim we contest.

The choice between Corbynism and Blue Labour is a deceptive one, between two visions based upon strikingly similar misreadings of the same set of issues: people, nation, Brexit and so-called 'post-liberalism'.[35] Both Corbynism and Blue Labour see the world in essentially national terms. Both sense opportunity in Brexit to reinstate the sovereignty of the nation-state against global capital and international capital.[36] In line with this identification of popular and national sovereignty, both Corbynism and Blue Labour talk of a 'people'- and this 'people', when invoked within the boundaries of a single polity in which state and society are conflated, cannot but be national. Moreover, as if to highlight the starting points they share with nativist right, both Corbynism and Blue Labour back controls on or an end to freedom of movement. Illustrating the overlap on these issues, adherents of both viewpoints are represented in the recently-launched 'Full Brexit' campaign for a hard 'Lexit'.[37] And, finally, both Corbynism and Blue Labour, in their own respects, embrace the possibilities of a new 'post-liberalism.'[38]

Corbynism and Blue Labour each draw, to some extent, upon divergent legacies of the Marxist tradition. Corbynism, in its Bennite and postcapitalist inflections, draws from an economistic, determinist one; Blue Labour from a more humanist, ethical variety.[39] Our approach, on the other hand, sees each pole as constitutive of the other: the conceptual and the material, the political and the economic, 'nature' and 'society', mediating one another in a contradictory whole. Here, what is social appears as nature, and what is 'natural' can only exist through social forms.

In this book we argue that capitalism is distinguished from other modes of organising society by a series of socially-constituted contradictory forms through which everyone, rich or poor, is compelled to live – commodities, value, money and labour. The central contradiction of capitalist society is that our survival is dependent upon the continuous production of the very forms which dominate us. The particular relationship between 'the economy' and the political sphere which characterises capitalist society is one result of the dominance of these abstract forms which mediate our existence. To argue that 'economic development' or 'production' determines everything else throughout history – or that the future development of productive capacity will inevitably lead to a communist utopia – is to mistake one of the consequences of a particular mode of social organisation for its cause. Without cognisance of the compulsions and contradictions deriving from the specific way that social interaction is mediated in capitalist society – compulsions and contradictions which run through the entirety of that society, rather than being imposed on one part of it by another, or from somewhere outside altogether – it is very easy for critics of capitalism to misrepresent the object of critique, and thus for that critique to aim at the wrong target. There are better and worse forms through which life in capitalist society can be mediated, and a 'truncated' critique which mistakes the symptoms of capitalism for the disease itself can easily lead to regressive outcomes, from authoritarian state capitalism to antisemitic nationalism and theocratic fascism.

Stripped of the security supplied by historical determinism, there is no guarantee that a critique of capitalism will lead in a progressive direction. It is this belief which motivates this book's qualified defence of the formal, impersonal structures of the rule-based liberal order. In our view, the institutions and forms of democratic liberalism that were built out of the ashes of the Second World War – pluralist elections, the rule of law, transnational cooperation, negotiated frameworks of trade – cannot be regarded, in the manner of cruder Marxisms, merely as a cynical means of cloaking oppression, a 'rigged system' purposively set up by elites to dupe the people. Rather than seeing the institutional framework of bourgeois liberal democracy as an obstacle blocking the road to socialism, which must be removed in the name of the society to come, we instead recognise it as the 'insufficient but bloody necessary' foundation of any emancipatory project.[40]

This is not because we are unaware of the very real flaws and inequalities within that system, but because it remains both the precondition for any emancipatory movement and the strongest bulwark against something much worse. This belief influences our approach to the epochal question of the gradual degeneration of democratic institutions by a global populism which condemns them (from both left and right perspectives) as 'liberal' and 'centrist,' and thus essentially worthless. This analysis culminates in a consistent but idiosyncratic Marxian position that seeks to defend the small gains of liberal society from their ill-fated overhaul in an age of extremes. Increasingly this means defending liberalism from those who would claim to be its defenders, as politicians who once flaunted their cosmopolitan credentials now wrap

themselves in national flags in a doomed attempt to stave off
the populist onslaught by mimicking it.

Our critique has at its heart a commitment to what
Michael Walzer identified in the aftermath of Donald Trump's
election victory as the 'historical task of the left in the present
period'.[41] This has three prongs. Firstly, 'a sharp leftist analysis and critique of what's going on' with the rise of authoritarian right-populist regimes across the globe. Secondly, writes
Walzer, 'the practical political work of the next few years is
all too obvious; it is the defensive version of standard left
activism. We have to defend what's left of the gains of post-
Second World War social democracy.' Thirdly, the left must
recognize that 'fighting from the left isn't all we have to do.'
Rather, 'the dangers we face today are not dangers only to the
achievements of the left', but to liberal society as a whole. As
such, the third historical task of the left in the present period
is to 'help hold the center.' Focusing on 'the defense of civil
liberties and civil rights', this operates from the conviction
that 'the survival of a vital center is also the precondition of
an active left'. Here Walzer captures something crucial for
the present conjuncture. Competing tendencies in the Labour
Party – the 'post-liberal' right included – like left and right
the world over, luxuriate in the flames licking at the sides of
liberal society. In so doing the left fails to recognize the extent
to which the world they want to win rests upon the legal and
political relations liberalism guarantees.

What this call to hold the centre exposes is how far Corbynism, in common with so-called 'post-liberal' critiques like
that of Blue Labour plays fast and loose with the liberal certainties on which subjective forms of class struggle and social
democracy are contradictorily based. In common with its
critics some strands of Corbynism treat with circumspection
allegedly 'abstract' rights through which the rule of law guarantees and contains concrete forms of struggle. Rhetorically,

this shores up the power of an isolationist nation-state at precisely the time where genuinely internationalist understandings of human association are needed to counteract the rise of authoritarian national populism.

Corbynism cannot be understood without seeing its relation to Brexit and Trump on the right, and those movements on the left which seek to ride the binary divisions of the national-popular moment to progressive ends. A comparison of these shared philosophical and political tendencies – Corbynism and Blue Labour among them – on key points at stake in twenty-first century capitalism uncovers a series of unexamined shibboleths which run through the worldview of the contemporary left, uniting even those factions which regard themselves as being implacably opposed. It is the comparison of Corbynism with its wider political context that this book, for the most part, is devoted to.

WHAT FOLLOWS

In what follows we do not propose to go into significant empirical detail around the political economic shifts that have spurred the rise of Corbyn. Nor do we interrogate every detail of how Corbynism proposes to address this political economic context. We take an alternative tack expressed in two key features of our critical analysis. On one hand, our aim is to elucidate the *essential* characteristics of Corbynism as a political orientation. Rather than engage in a micro-analysis of the specifics of Labour's policy platform (although there will be some brief detours), we want to outline and critique the general worldview which motivates such a platform in the first place. Similarly, we are preoccupied not so much with the specificities of capitalism at any given time as its essential characteristics as a particular form of social organisation. These two

concerns overlap, insofar as the policies put forward by Corbyn's Labour are fundamentally shaped by the particular way
that the left milieu from which his leadership has emerged
understands the way that capitalist society is organised.

Our argument is based upon a fundamentally different
analysis of what capitalism is and how it works to that which
characterises the dominant strands of Corbynism. To this end,
we adopt the critique of 'worldview Marxism' found in the
work of theorists connected to the 'New Reading of Marx'
such as Michael Heinrich, Moishe Postone and Werner Bonefeld.[42] Our return to Marx is founded upon our insistence that
the *critique* (as opposed to a 'Marxist' correction) of political
economy remains the most dynamic tool to analyse both capitalism as a social form, and the traditional 'left' worldview
which has developed within it. It is with this in mind that the
book takes Corbynism seriously both as an expression of a
certain kind of society, and as a way of comprehending that
society in theory and, by extension, practice.

In Chapter 1 we explain Labour's surprisingly strong performance in the 2017 General Election, with the party gaining
30 seats and depriving Theresa May of her majority, a result
which flew in the face of almost every prediction. We suggest
that the key to understanding this remarkable turn of events
lies in the process by which 'the deficit' became a dead letter
in British politics, and the affordances this granted the Labour
Party to make progress on the basis of a Corbynist agenda.
Tracing the story of the deficit's rise and fall uncovers a number of important insights about the origins and character of
the present political turbulence in the UK, and Corbynism's
position in it. In particular, it reveals the crucial role played
by the initial austerity narrative itself, showing how its crude
'we're all in it together' productivism, as well as its anti-austerity opposition, acted as the forerunner of the populist currents
that were to follow in its wake and eventually subsume it.

Chapter 2 focuses on the role that Corbyn's personal reputation for unshakeable moral integrity and political prescience – a man who has forever been on 'the right side of history' – has played in the development of Corbynism as a whole. It shows how the moral mythology that surrounds Corbyn as an individual was rooted in the collapse of the Bennite 'hard left' tradition of the Labour Party in the early 1990s, and the subsequent process of romanticisation of that tradition, and of Benn himself, that followed, particularly in the wake of the hard left's leadership of the opposition to the invasion of Iraq in 2003.

In Chapter 3, we show how Corbyn was the beneficiary of this process of dehistoricisation and depoliticisation, as it fed into the 'Year Zero' narrative that was built around his candidacy for the Labour leadership and which carried over into the General Election itself. The chapter argues that the faith in Corbyn's personal integrity is such that the actual content of his programme – a national-populist platform of economic protectionism, twinned with a crude 'two campist' isolationist foreign policy – has long been left unexamined by his critics and the wider liberal-left. This absence of scrutiny, accompanied by a process in which certain scenes from Corbyn's lengthy political career have been turned into modern day parables, has been crucial both in piecing together an electoral coalition, and preventing certain tensions and contradictions within the movement itself from rising to the surface.

In Chapter 4, we seek to counter this romanticised, historically-revisionist version of Corbynism by examining the theoretical premises of the Bennite tradition which have been carried over into its successor. We do this by comparing the 'Alternative Economic Strategy' proposed by Benn as a solution to the crisis of British capitalism in the mid-1970s to the 'Alternative Models of Ownership' document commissioned by John McDonnell in 2017. This comparison sheds some light on the ambivalence shown by the Labour leadership towards the prospect of a 'hard Brexit' – withdrawal from the European Single Market and the customs union. We situate this in relation to contemporary visions of the state, and specifically the nation-state predicated on a turn away from left traditions of transnational solidarity. The chapter then contrasts the theory of capitalism which lies behind the Bennite-Corbyn vision of 'socialism in one country' to a critical Marxian understanding of capitalism as a historically-specific global system constituted by 'socially mediated labour.' We suggest that it is the failure to recognise the abstract forms of social domination produced by such a system that lies behind Corbynism's recent turn to the protectionist solutions espoused by nationalist movements on both left and right. The chapter spells out some of the possible malign consequences of such a turn.

In Chapter 5 we critically analyse Corbynism's mobilisation of the populist notion of the 'people', and the respects in which this stands in for a lack of class analysis that elides antagonistic relationships for a contradiction-free conceptualisation of how power will inevitably accrue to the popular subject. We suggest that an orthodox Marxist understanding of class, value and history leads Corbynism – both in its more traditional form, represented here by the work of Ralph Miliband, and its fresher postcapitalist iteration – to strategically miscalculate the possibilities for an incipient liberation present in the current state of things. The failure to recognise the negative, mediated and inherently contradictory character of class society – in which the activity undertaken by workers to ensure their daily survival produces the forms which come to dominate them – leads to the false presumption that social antagonism can be resolved through the production of a non-contradictory 'people,' protected from the pressures of the world market by the nation-state and technocratic fixes.

In Chapter 6 we explore how Corbynism is structured around a truncated critique of capitalist society as a 'rigged system,' that can easily lapse into a kind of conspiracy theorism. The chapter argues that the ease with which the 'rigged system' trope has passed along the political spectrum from Bernie Sanders to Donald Trump and then to Corbyn indicates a troubling political ambivalence. In both its right and left formulations, the 'rigged system' conceit does not grasp class and capitalism as antagonistic, mediated and contradictory social forms, but presents capitalist society as a relatively uncomplicated and natural process of production which has been hijacked by the illegitimate intervention of the 'wealth extractors,' international finance and the banking sector. We expose how this truncated critique of the 'rigged system' segues with similar ideas circulating around the rise of Trump and Brexit- for instance, opposition to 'globalism' and a retreat into the nation-state as the horizon of political activity. We show how it can spill over into antisemitic conspiracy theories, especially when combined with the reflexive 'two-campism' of contemporary forms of 'anti-imperialism.'

In the conclusion we first consider some of the responses to our arguments from various sections of the Corbynite left, particularly around the question of personalised critique, antisemitism and the Marxian character of our position. We then go onto explore some of the alternatives within and without Corbynism for the future of the left and the Labour Party in the UK. We critically examine how the optimism Project Corbyn sells its adherents proposes a false resolution of contradictions contemporary conditions cannot effect, arguing that postcapitalist utopia is not on its way and rather that a politics of pessimism can best match present realities and work with them practically. We suggest that, in an age of Trump, Brexit, and the rise of national populism, the left has a responsibility to hold the centre as well as dispute it.

We contend that the idea of a critical Marxism still represents a possible pole of difference around which both partisans and critics of Corbynism can orient themselves, while maintaining a critical fidelity to principles of internationalism, pluralist democracy and human rights.

~~~

Overall, this book advocates what Marx called the 'ruthless criticism of all that exists' as the only viable way for the left to continue its renewal, stressing that a critique of Corbynism is not exclusive of a critique of capitalism, and that to critique the latter is at the same time to critique the cornerstones of the former. No theoretical standpoint, including that of Corbynism, can free itself from its constitution in capitalist society, and ideas as such can be considered as the key to 'material' conditions rather than the conditions deterministically unlocking the ideas. Indeed, the essence of Marx's materialist method does not conclude that the ideas society holds about itself are simply a form of mystification. They are not merely a means to disguise the way that society really is, which must then be stripped away to reveal the underlying truth. Rather, a Marxist materialist method holds that to critique the ideas that society holds about itself is to simultaneously critique the social forms of which they are themselves an expression.[43]

1

EXPLAINING 2017: THE RISE AND FALL OF AUSTERITY POPULISM

In the days following the 2017 General Election, British politics was awash with *mea culpas*. Self-flagellating apologies poured out of every paper, news programme and political website. Channel 4 newsreader Jon Snow epitomised the general masochistic tone the day following the result: 'I know nothing. We, the media, the pundit, the experts, know nothing. We simply didn't spot it.'[1] And he had a point. Ever since Jeremy Corbyn's shock victory in 2015 Labour leadership contest, there was barely a pundit, psephologist or policy wonk who had not predicted electoral catastrophe. Yet it had not come to pass. On the contrary – Corbyn's Labour had gained 30 seats, deprived a once imperious Theresa May of her majority, and, perhaps most startling of all, had won 40 per cent of the popular vote. At a stroke a whole plethora of political truisms disintegrated: Corbynism was a 'movement' more clicktivist than canvasser, Corbyn himself was electorally toxic, Labour faced a 1931-style demolition and the total collapse of its Parliamentary presence. Notwithstanding that

Labour did not win, and will likely need an even bigger push to win next time, all had proven to be categorically wrong – even the clicktivism proved moderately successful.[2] Once the ritual humiliation was over, and the MPs who had opposed Corbyn from the start had swallowed their pride, some sheepishly joining in with the chants of 'Oh Jeremy Corbyn', the experts and analysts began to collect the shards of their shattered worldview and rearrange them in the light of this new situation. How was this result possible? What had we all missed?

It was not as if historical precedent had not backed up the catastrophist thesis. There was 1983 of course, the last time the programme of the so-called Labour 'hard left' had been put to the test in an election. Electoral carnage and seventeen years of opposition had followed. But there were more recent warning signs too. In 2015, Ed Miliband had risked a slight shift to the left, banking on an upswell of support amongst a 'squeezed middle' after five years of Conservative–Liberal Democrat public sector cuts. It seemed like a plausible move – which was why the election result, when it arrived, was such a body blow. Cameron and Osborne had sold the need for cuts off the back of the government deficit and debt run up in the aftermath of the 2008 global financial crisis. Their explanation for the crash and subsequent debt was that it was the direct result of Labour's 'overspending.' The only solution to such wasteful extravagance, they argued, was thus a severe bout of 'austerity', in which spending on public services would be progressively cut back until the government bank balance was back in the black. So successful was this narrative that Miliband had not been able to say a word during the 2015 campaign without the question of 'the deficit' being thrown at him. In order to try to fend off such attacks and carve out the space to be heard on his own terms, the very first page of his manifesto declared that not a single Labour pledge required a penny of extra borrowing. But even this display of neurosis was not enough. When polling day arrived, the Tories won their first majority for a quarter of a century.

Come 2017, and Labour's prospects seemed even worse. The vote to leave the European Union (EU) set alight the inferno of nationalism, imperial nostalgia and anti-migrant revanchism that UKIP leader Nigel Farage had long been stoking, bringing down the Cameron government with it. The new Prime Minister was Theresa May, whose stint as Home Secretary was best known for her desire to create a 'hostile environment' for migrants, including ordering a fleet of vans emblazoned with the injunction to 'go home' to drive around ethnically diverse areas of London. In the weeks following her ascension to power, May had attempted to capitalise on the nativist spring unleashed by Brexit – railing against cosmopolitan 'citizens of nowhere' whose loyalty was to the international flows of capital, commodities and labour rather than to the 'ordinary working class people' rooted in local communities.[3] She had interpreted the narrow 52–48% Leave victory in the most extreme way possible, promising Brexit voters that she would leave the Single Market in order to end the freedom of Europeans to live and work in Britain and restore a supposedly lost 'sovereignty' – whatever the cost. Her hopes of bringing the substantial UKIP vote into the Tory fold and gain a foothold in Leave-voting Labour seats seemed to have paid off by the time she called a 'snap' election in April 2017. May had built up a formidable lead in the polls. She had the vociferous and unanimous support of the rightwing press who, aroused at the prospect of 'hard Brexit', called for her to 'crush the saboteurs' and enact 'blue murder' on any opposition.[4]

The idea that a Labour Party led by Jeremy Corbyn – in the eyes of his critics inside and outside the party metropolitan, tax-and-spend, pro-immigration – could avoid electoral wipe-out in such unpropitious circumstances seemed implausible

even to some of his biggest supporters. Indeed, Len McCluskey, the head of the Unite union who had long been one of
Corbyn's most steadfast backers, claimed a month before
election day that keeping Labour's losses down to 30 seats
would constitute 'success.'[5] To make matters worse, Corbyn could not even claim to straightforwardly represent the
48% who had voted Remain, overwhelmingly concentrated
in cities and younger demographics – his core constituency.
Corbyn, like his mentor Tony Benn, had opposed British
membership of the EU for his entire career. From the Bennite
perspective, the EU was a 'bosses club' imposing neoliberal
strictures upon the British nation-state, particularly through
the political and economic infrastructure of the Single Market.[6] Corbyn's internal critics suspected that his lukewarm
campaigning during the referendum had its roots in this historic antipathy, which set him at odds with much of his own
base, particularly younger voters, as well as the party's own
democratically-decided policy.

This contradiction had been exacerbated by the post-
referendum support shown by both Corbyn and his Shadow
Chancellor John McDonnell for May's hardline position of
leaving the Single Market and the Customs Union – neither
of which had been mooted during the Referendum campaign. Corbyn thus seemed to have adopted what journalist
Stephen Bush described as a '0% strategy'.[7] His continued
support for immigration and free movement alienated the
52% who had voted Leave, while his insistence on leaving
the Single Market angered the 48%, both in terms of the economic consequences of such a drastic move, but also because
many viewed EU membership as an expression of an open-
minded, internationalist outlook. The combination of the deficit, immigration, and the nationalist energies unleashed by
the Leave vote seemed insurmountable. Even as the Labour
election campaign seemed to be gaining momentum and the

Tory effort very publicly falling apart, the conditions for Labour gains seemed so remote that they blinded everyone to what was happening on the ground.

Nearly everyone, at least. For the left's true believers, there was nothing surprising about the 2017 result when it came. It was what they had predicted for decades, if only someone had listened. Throughout the dark days of the Kinnock and New Labour eras, the so-called 'hard left' of the party had insisted that what the electorate was really craving was a no-holds-barred socialist party who would break with the neoliberal consensus and offer a real choice. When Labour lost elections as in 2015, this subterranean consensus suggested, it was not because they had moved too far to the left. It was because *they were not left enough*. Contrary to conventional wisdom, Miliband's problem was not that he failed to convince voters he took the issue of the deficit seriously. Nor was the bout of English nativism which Cameron had engendered (somewhat portentously, given what was to come) by raising the spectre of a Labour coalition with the Scottish National Party to blame. Rather Miliband's defeat could be explained by his failure to sufficiently differentiate Labour's platform from that of the Conservatives, falling back on what Corbyn himself described as an 'austerity-lite' manifesto.[8] This belief helped fuel Corbyn's victory in the leadership campaign following Miliband's resignation. More than anything else, Corbyn's rise was driven by Labour members' sheer frustration at Miliband's failure to forcibly challenge the Conservative's narrative around austerity and the deficit, and exasperation that none of the other candidates for Labour leader – all tarnished by association with the Blair-Brown years and lacking credibility in their claims to authenticity and charisma – seemed to recognise the urgency of doing so. If nothing else, so the theory went, at least Corbyn could be trusted to deliver an unadulterated anti-austerity message.

From this perspective, Corbyn's performance in the 2017 election had shown this analysis to be right all along. For his fans, a properly socialist leader had put forward a properly socialist manifesto, in the teeth of ferocious opposition both internal and external – and the result had been anything but calamitous. Labour had run an energetic, positive, smart campaign. Labour thrived off a cleverly leaked manifesto, a series of simple policies that set the pace on radio news bulletins, Corbyn's unflappable debate performances and regional television coverage of a constant series of city-specific rallies.[9] The quick-witted air war was backed up online and through unprecedented numbers of volunteers taking to the streets to engage potential Labour voters and getting them to turn out on polling day.[10] Through the courage of the leadership and the commitment of those pacing the streets and flooding social media, Labour had overturned the austerity consensus. They had refused to kowtow on immigration numbers, bow to Brexit nativism or scapegoat those on benefits, so the story went. They had stood up against the forces of reaction which were on the rise across the globe. And they had had won the support of 40 per cent of the electorate in doing so, against all odds. This was vindication.

A romantic tale, no doubt – and not without an element of truth. Certainly the disintegration of Cameron and Osborne's austerity narrative was the crucial factor in Corbyn's success. Two years previously the deficit had strangled Miliband's campaign at birth. It was the most powerful adversary in British politics, squeezing the life out of every other issue. And yet, astonishingly, in the 2017 campaign the words 'debt' and 'deficit' were barely mentioned.[11] It was fought instead on the basis of sentiment, emotion, culture and 'values'.[12] There can surely have been no issue which has suffered such a dramatic change in political fortunes in such a short space of time. More than anything else – more than

Momentum's sterling electioneering, more than the meme-makers pumping out jpgs and gifs, more than the fabled manifesto – it is the strange death of the deficit which holds the key to explaining Labour's remarkable performance in 2017.

AUSTERITY POPULISM

The collapse of the international banking sector in 2008, as credit markets seized up following the revelation of huge levels of toxic sub-prime debt throughout the system, over-turned three decades of economic wisdom. Governments who had vowed to give the financial markets a free hand were now called upon to bail out the banks to the tune of billions. Electorates around the world demanded answers. How had this happened? Who was responsible? For those competing for political power in the wake of the crash, the overriding priority was to construct a narrative that was able to explain the crisis to the public, justify a particular policy response, and pin the blame for economic disaster elsewhere. And no political narrative succeeded on all three counts to such an extent as that constructed by David Cameron, George Osborne and Nick Clegg, the leading figures in the Conservative–Liberal Democrat coalition government which came to power in 2010.

Austerity is often taken to have caused the contemporary rise of populism.[13] In retrospect, however, it is abundantly clear that austerity itself was a populist project – both in Chantal Mouffe's sense of the creation of a political frontier between 'us' and 'them,' and Jan-Werner Müller's notion of the hyper-moralisation of political discourse. How else to explain the sin-gularly odd way that Britain responded to the financial crisis? The Cameron government was far from the only one to react to the crash and their ballooning deficits by insisting on the need for a programme of austerity. But in no other country did the public don hairshirts with such gusto. As Owen Hatherley has noted, Britain was convulsed by a fit of 'austerity nostalgia' in the wake of the crisis – unleashing dark political energies Tom Whyman captured well in the coinage 'cupcake fascism'.[14] This mood was epitomised by the ubiquitous 'Keep Calm and Carry on' poster, which seemed to pine for 'an actual or imaginary English patrician attitude of stoicism and muddling through', the reprise of an age marked by make-do-and-mend thrift and 'hardiness in the face of adversity.'[15] It was as if the public actively welcomed the collapse of the economy, regarding it as an event which finally gave some meaning to a life waylaid by the cheap thrills of credit-fuelled consumerism and reality TV, a form of existence that suddenly felt as toxic as the junk bonds clogging up the balance sheets of banks around the world.

The austerity narrative was founded on an opposition between a national community of 'hardworking people' and a feckless underclass who had brought Britain to its knees – namely the 'scroungers', the benefit cheats, those too lazy to work and choosing to live off the largesse of the state.[16] In this telling, the financial crisis itself was essentially caused by the Labour government's reckless decision to rack up monstrous debts in order to fund the lavish lifestyles of their shiftless clientele. In contrast to this rotten coalition of bloated state, corrupt liberal-left political elite, and workshy scroungers, the Tories would instead take the side of the 'hardworkers', those willing to take responsibility for their own lives and roll up their sleeves to 'sort out Labour's mess'.[17] 'We're all in it together' was the cry, deliberately evoking the Churchillian spirit of wartime. The 'deficit' – and those responsible for it – was turned into a national enemy whose defeat, as in the Blitz, depended upon a heroic act of collective endurance, a momentous sacrifice of abstention in order to save the country, and indeed future generations, from financial ruin.

This was classic 'productivist' discourse. The economically active (the 'hardworking families', the inhabitants of 'alarm clock Britain') were presented as morally superior to the non-productive (the unemployed at the bottom, the state itself at the top), who are portrayed as a parasitic drain on the resources of the former. Britain's economic woes were the result of the non-productive being allowed to gain political and economic dominance over the productive, an imbalance that was both economically disastrous and morally reprehensible. 'Where is the fairness, we ask, for the shift-worker, leaving home in the dark hours of the early morning, who looks up at the closed blinds of their next door neighbour sleeping off a life on benefits?' George Osborne asked in his 2012 conference speech. 'When we say we're all in this together, we speak for that worker.'[18] The only solution to such a dire situation was to either force the non-productive minority to become productive themselves, through a ramped-up programme of 'workfare', or cut them off from any state subsidy whatsoever via savage benefit cuts and sanctions, consequences be damned. The implication was that public spending on services for the productive might once again be possible as soon as this parasitic excrescence was no longer allowed to deplete the vitality from society. Austerity was thus both economically necessary and morally right, an act of national rebirth in which the dregs of the old society would be cast off and the new rebuilt around the righteous desires of the productive.

It is doubtful whether Cameron and Osborne actually believed their claims of a causal relation between Labour welfare spending, the crash and the deficit. Indeed, in an interview in 2017, after he had left Parliament, Osborne admitted he did not.[19] The demonization of 'scroungers' and pinning the blame for the crash on the previous Labour government was a political manoeuvre designed to legitimate a broader strategy to cut public expenditure and fundamentally change

the relation of state to society. It set the template for what
was probably the most brazen lie in British political history a
few years later – the promise that leaving the EU would mean
£350m a week extra for the NHS, a pledge that was immediately recanted the morning after the vote to Leave.[20]

The difference between the two was that the austerity narrative retained its connection to matters of prosperity in the
last instance, even if that prosperity was by no means distributed evenly across society – whereas the Leave campaign's
claim was used to force through a policy which virtually every economist agreed would reduce Britain's economic well-
being. Thus in 2013, once his austerity policies looked like
they were seriously threatening to thrust the economy back
into recession, Osborne changed tack. He 'paused' austerity
by pushing plans for further cuts back into the next Parliament, stimulating a period of economic growth in the run-
up to the 2015 election.[21] The 'belt-tightening' rhetoric did
not change, but the policy did – which is not to say that the
'pause' provided any real relief for those still reeling from the
effects of the cuts already implemented, or reduced the impact
of those still to come. The point is merely that when it came
to the crunch, economic realism trumped the ideological narrative. While Cameron and Osborne were happy to utilise
populist tropes as a tool when necessary, their government
retained a core of general economic rationalism. The way in
which they went about managing the economy is up for dispute – but their attachment to principle of economic interest
itself is not.

The extent of Cameron and Osborne's bad faith matters
less than the extraordinary power generated by the concept
of austerity. It seemed to tap into a force that was far greater
than the trivialities of day-to-day politics. It drilled down
into deep-lying reserves of national sentiment and cultural
memory, conjuring up image after idealised image of a past

that had never actually existed, but whose retrieval was nevertheless held to unlock the door to an authentic life. The energy and intensity of this torrent of false nostalgia inevitably overwhelmed valiant technocratic arguments about the historically low cost of state borrowing, relative bond yields or interest rates. Charged with such cultural significance, the political and media debate around 'the deficit' could never have been one based on reasonable consideration of the various approaches to a post-crisis economy.

For all the criticism hurled at Ed Miliband and Ed Balls by Corbyn supporters for their supposed 'austerity-lite' programme, there was in truth no shortage of attempts to put forward alternative proposals to the Conservative–Liberal Democrat spending cuts, certainly in the first years of the coalition.[22] But worthy attempts to convince people that government finances were not the equivalent of a maxed out credit card, and Britain was not like Greece because it had control of its own currency singularly failed to cut through. In the popular imagination, the need to 'get the deficit down' was shot through with a moral urgency in the name of the. the 'hardworking families' who were striving to get the country out of 'Labour's mess'.[23] The idea that Corbyn would have fared any better at challenging this moral fable than Miliband during the coalition years radically underestimates the libidinal power generated by 'austerity nostalgia.'

Such emotional reactions are not those of a debate that is grounded in rationality, where ideas are dispassionately evaluated on the basis of their respective merits, as much as such a thing is possible. A political system in which the very existence of opposing arguments is regarded as being morally suspect is one that is already well on the way to populism. And so it would turn out – for the emotional tenor of the debate over austerity, in which opposing viewpoints were not merely disagreed with but banished from the realm of

acceptable discourse, was in hindsight a clear prefiguration of
the Brexit campaign itself. Therefore to argue that Miliband
failed to successfully challenge the austerity narrative because
soft left cowardice prevented him from breaking with an
'austerity-lite' platform is to get things the wrong way round.
It was rather the blanket delegitimisation of the anti-austerity
argument in the face of amoralistic fantasy of national self-
sacrifice that made it necessary to place deficit reduction at
the centre of his platform in the 2015 election.

It is by no means insignificant to what followed that the
anti-austerity movements which *did* make some impact in the
early years of the coalition – such as Occupy, UK Uncut and
the People's Assembly Against Austerity- drew on precisely
the same productivist tropes as that which they unsuccess-
fully opposed. Whereas for Cameron the parasitic elements
against which the 'hardworking' productive people had to be
united were in the main internal enemies – the unemployed,
those on benefits, the disabled, and the state itself, in its public
service guise at least – for the anti-austerity movement, the
threat was to be found on the global level, namely the international banking and financial system, and the global political
project of neoliberalism which had allowed that system to
dominate the rest of the economy.

To reduce this analysis – which achieved hegemonic status amongst the liberal-left in the wake of the crisis – to its
bare bones, the financial crash was caused not by state overspending but by a lack of state regulation of the financial and
banking sectors. This had enabled those sectors to make vast
amounts of profit from speculation on behalf of the '1%' at
the expense of the other '99%'.[24] The 'real economy' which
makes actual physical things had been undermined by the
power, greed and mathematical trickery of financial institutions, for whom money seemed to beget money, apparently of
its own accord.[25] While in the Cameron narrative, the crisis

had been caused by the moral failings of those too lazy to work, and a Labour government too lax to make them, here the crisis was understood as the result of the moral failings of the international financial elite, whose refusal to curb their own greed had brought the entire system down as a consequence. This had been compounded by a further moral failing, that of what John McDonnell routinely describes as the 'political choice' to impose austerity.[26]

From this perspective, austerity was not only a vicious, self-centred political decision made by and for the '1%', it was objectively irrational. The problem facing the economy was ultimately one of distribution. The greed of those in power had titled the balance of the economy too far towards the unproductive global 'elite' and away from those who actually do all the work. The crash, it contended, was the consequence. The contrast was often made to the post-war era of welfare capitalism, in which capital had far less freedom to roam the globe in search of profits, and the gap between the '1%' and the rest was much less pronounced. The shift from this form of capitalism – based on mass production and a Keynesian welfare state – to the financialised precarity of 'neoliberalism' in the early 1970s was regarded straightforwardly as the result of class warfare. The system of production, this suggested, had been taken over by a financial elite and distorted in such a way to place profits above social needs.

This analysis is by no means without merit. Neoliberalism as a strand of political-economic theory certainly does exist, with roots stretching back to early 1930s Germany.[27] The economy – in 'developed' countries at least – did become more financialised and less industrialised from the late 1970s onwards. The provision of public services was transformed to adhere to the tenets of 'market rationality.' And the trade union movement suffered a series of severe defeats, which ripped up the old corporatist model of Keynesian social democracy.

But, as Werner Bonefeld asserts, 'normative' critiques of neo-liberalism reject neoliberal *capitalism* only abstractly. They pose no questions about 'the character of capitalist wealth itself' – of which neoliberalism is only one expression. Instead they lash out at what is seen as a 'doctrine of narrow-minded economic interests,' in particular those of finance capital. By suggesting that neoliberalism has somehow 'corrupt[ed] capi-talism', they elide the extent to which neoliberalism is merely 'a theoretical expression of capitalism', and therefore miss the object of critique – capitalism itself – not only in theory but in practice too.[28] This perspective offers another way through the recent online debate, out of which no side stood smelling of roses, between the Labour right and left about the meaning and salience of the term 'neoliberalism', which has rumbled on at precisely the time its relevance is diminishing.[29]

By ignoring the core of what neoliberalism expresses, in the anti-austerity discourse the implementation of some neoliberal-inspired policies is routinely dehistoricised. It is ripped out of the context of the severe crisis of profitability that hit the 'good' welfare-Keynesianism in the late 1960s and demanded a change in the organisation of capitalist production. Such a dehistoricised perspective has no means to grasp the necessity of profit in a capitalist system – a necessity that applies just as much to workers, who rely upon the profitability of their employer as the guarantor of future work, as it does to indus-trialists or financiers. Profit is instead regarded as a political choice, imposed from above. Nor is the mutually constitu-tive relationship between 'productive' or 'real' industry and 'unproductive' finance recognised. Thus the pursuit of the restoration of growth, fictitious or not, through the 'neolib-eral' explosion of financial instruments, globalised trade and personal debt was not seen as emerging from the contradic-tions of the previous form of social organisation but rather transformed into an evil conspiratorial plan cooked up in Chicago, unleashed on an unsuspecting public, and held in place purely by ideology or military force. This has the effect of not only writing out of history both the economic failure of and popular resistance to the hierarchical strictures of Keynesian Fordism, but also flattens the substantial (and ongoing) developments within neoliberal government policy itself into a one-dimensional caricature which hides mores than it reveals. Moreover, it can result in a perspective which regards the forms of rule-based cosmopolitan liberalism which have accompanied a globalised economy as being merely an ideological cover for exploitation.

The logical conclusion to be drawn from the popular understanding of neoliberalism as form of conspiracy imposed via the 'Washington Consensus' and backed up by US military power is that the nation-state should use its powers to throw off the shackles imposed by the predatory practices of unproductive global finance and American imperialism, reject the rule-based cosmopolitan order of internationalism liberalism, embark on a programme of intensive economic intervention on a national level, and restore the 'real', 'productive' national industrial economy back to its rightful position.

As we shall see in Chapter 4, this was the programme proposed by Corbynism's ideological predecessor, Tony Benn, in the mid-1970s, and it remains central to the Corbyn worldview today. The risk of uncritically holding to this position is that any challenge to the transnational liberal order in the name of the nation-state appears to be an attack on 'neoliberalism' itself, and thus something to be welcomed. It is this conflation of cosmopolitanism with neoliberalism that explains to a great extent Corbyn's ambivalent response to both Brexit and even the election of Donald Trump – something we will explore in more detail in later chapters.

~~~

For all the differences of their conclusions, then, the central arguments of both the austerity narrative and its anti-austerity opponent ultimately rested on the same premises. The financial crash was caused by a wholly avoidable structural imbalance between the productive and unproductive sectors of society, an imbalance that was at best ignored and at worst encouraged by the practices of a corrupt political elite. The solution to the crisis was the restoration of proper order through a political programme which would take back power from the unproductive elements of society, and their political handmaidens. For Cameron, this took the form of ruthless benefit cuts, intensified workfare schemes and the slashing of public sector jobs. For the anti-austerity movement it meant the use of the state to stimulate the economy, put up barriers to the free movement of global capital and the end of predatory financial trickery. The implication of both arguments was that once those parasitic elements who had been draining the productive vitality from society were removed or tamed, everything would be fine. Both the austerity and anti-austerity narratives agreed that the primary cause of the 2008 crash was the errors, greed, laziness and corruption of identifiable groups and individuals. The difference was only in who was to blame.

THE STRANGE DEATH OF THE DEFICIT

How, then, did Corbyn's Labour manage to overcome the austerity impasse in 2017? For his supporters, there is no great mystery to unravel. An explicitly anti-austerity Labour party had delivered an explicitly anti-austerity message and won the argument.[30] Things turned out just as they had always said they would. From this perspective it was Corbyn's election as leader which marked the line in the sand. As we shall see, the idea that Corbyn represents a clean break with everything that has come before in Labour history has been absolutely crucial to his success from the moment of his entry into the leadership contest in 2015. But, in truth, the mysterious disappearance of 'the deficit' cannot be explained by the heroic persuasiveness of Corbyn and his army of supporters.

Firstly, as we have seen, contrary to the 'austerity-lite' mythology, there had been no shortage of attempts to challenge the austerity narrative during the early years of the coalition government. The problem was that few were listening. Secondly, despite all the rhetoric of a clean break with the craven compromises of the past, when it came to the question of the deficit Labour's 2017 manifesto did not in fact fundamentally alter the approach developed by Miliband and Balls two years earlier. Labour's 2017 manifesto was self-consciously presented as 'fully costed,' meaning it required no additional borrowing for day-to-day spending.[31] Furthermore, the manifesto promised that a Labour government would 'eliminate the current deficit' and ensure the national debt fell by the end of every term, in line with the self-imposed 'fiscal credibility rule' McDonnell had announced the previous year.[32] This was precisely the position that the left- Corbyn and McDonnell included- had decried as 'austerity-lite' in Miliband's 2015 offering.[33] And the reason why Corbyn and McDonnell had adopted this position was exactly the same as Miliband's: because they expected the austerity narrative to continue to dominate the economic debate. It was a preemptive measure taken to try to fend off the barrage of attacks they presumed were coming their way. If they had truly believed they had successfully overturned the consensus around debt and the deficit, why bother tying their own hands with a self-imposed 'rule'?

What was really remarkable about the 2017 election was the failure of that barrage of attacks to arrive – and the abject failure of those which did take aim at the figures in the manifesto to have any impact on the electorate. The 'fully costed' nature of Labour's manifesto was of the most speculative kind, based on radically optimistic projections of economic growth and tax revenues which would follow from the stimulus provided by government investment. These projections enabled Corbyn to make an array of voluminous spending pledges, with something on offer for virtually every section of society. Leaving aside the question of how likely Labour's economic predictions were to come true, it is inconceivable that this far-from-watertight 'fiscal rule' neutralised the issue of the deficit of its own accord, given that Miliband's much more rigorous attempt two years earlier had failed miserably to do so. Had 'the deficit' retained the same power as in 2015, it would have been the easiest task in the world to convince wavering voters that Corbyn's commitment to his 'fiscal rule' was a lie, that he had not the slightest interest in cutting the deficit, and that his big-spending programme of investment would drag the country back to financial ruin.

Such arguments were indeed made by Labour's opponents. Corbyn's manifesto would 'bankrupt Britain' bellowed the *Telegraph*.[34] 'Jeremy Corbyn's election giveaway is a magic money tree blowing a £300bn black hole in Britain's finances,' railed the metaphor-mixing *Sun*.[35] And yet, in stark contrast to the coalition era, it was now the Tories with the communication problem. Where once arguments about the merits of Keynesian counter-cyclical stimulus had fallen on stony ground, now it was precisely the opposite. It did not matter how much the right-wing press screamed of the purportedly dire consequences of Corbyn and McDonnell's spending plans. Something had changed. The austerity narrative had lost its bite. The Tory attacks on Labour's lavish spending sounded increasingly hollow, even half-hearted. Now it was those who continued to insist on the need for restraint who found themselves ignored, unable to land a punch on a man who should, in theory, have provided the easiest of targets.

The question of what lies behind the strange death of the deficit cannot, then, be answered by recourse to Corbyn's hard left heroism. Nor, in truth, was it simply a case of austerity fatigue, or the fact that the latest round of cuts at last began to affect wealthier demographics, particularly school funding (although these were both important factors). The truth of its demise is far stranger than such simplistic explanations suggest. And the key to understanding it is Brexit, not Corbyn. That is to say, in order to grasp the true, rather than mythic, role of Corbynism in this story we need to view it through the prism of Brexit.

~~~

The vote for Brexit was a moment of seismic, even revolutionary, importance in British politics; the point at which the increasingly tenuous connection between economic calculation and ideological narratives finally broke loose. The very ground of British politics seemed to collapse in the wake of the result. And for the past six years at least that ground had been austerity. Ever since the 2008 financial crisis, the Conservatives had presented themselves as the bulwark against economic ruin. In 2015, this argument had been rewarded with a majority. And yet just a year later, as an endless series of economists, business leaders and politicians lined up to predict the similarly dire consequences of leaving the world's biggest trading bloc, the result was the exact opposite. Warnings of self-inflicted economic catastrophe no longer registered. People refused to believe them – or worse, no longer cared. There was evidently something bigger at stake than mere economic well-being. A united British people were 'taking back control' from the 'elite', the 'experts', 'Brussels bureaucrats', 'the immigrants.' 'We want our country back' was the cry, and to hell with the economic consequences.

The Leave campaign itself sunk ever deeper into the swamp of pure reaction. Billboards threatened the imminent arrival of '76 million' Turks.[36] UKIP leader Nigel Farage apocalyptically claimed migration was pushing Britain to 'breaking point'.[37] A week before the vote, the rising tension culminated in the assassination of pro-EU, pro-migrant Labour MP Jo Cox by a neo-Nazi activist. He shot and stabbed her to death while shouting 'Britain First.' The shock success of the toxic Leave campaign in such circumstances split the country down the middle. Numerous attempts to categorise the split followed – old vs young, small towns vs big cities, 'authoritarian' vs 'liberal,' 'closed' vs 'open', 'the people' vs 'the elite.' Theresa May decided to adopt the latter frame, using the populist signifier of 'the people' to interpret the 52–48% vote for Brexit in the most hardline manner possible, making the reduction of immigration and withdrawal from the European Court of Justice her lead priorities. The extremity of May's position, her refusal to regard as legitimate the 48% who had voted to remain, in favour of a pure winner-takes-all majoritarianism, exacerbated the tribalism that the referendum campaign had unleashed. The electorate was polarised like never before, along lines which refused to fit into the old boxes of social status, occupation or income. Nor was it a division which could be overcome through rational debate or argument. The division was now one of identity, of morality – of *who we are* and *who you are not*.

Brexit recalibrated the political scales to such an extent that attempting to make a direct comparison between events before and after the referendum is a pointless exercise. Arguments which simply attribute Corbyn's success and Miliband's failure to their relative commitment to anti-austerity, without taking into account the intervention of Brexit, and the dramatic polarisation of the electorate that followed, are in this sense ahistorical. In 2015, Miliband was fighting on a terrain dominated by austerity and the perception of 'economic credibility'. By the time Corbyn entered the electoral fray in 2017, austerity was already dead. And it was Brexit, not Corbyn, that killed it.

But it is equally ahistorical to portray Brexit as an inexplicable and wholly irrational act of spontaneity, running against the grain of everything that had preceded it. Britain's populist turn, the triumph of identity over economic interest, did not come out of nowhere. The roots of British antipathy to Europe and anti-migrant racism go way back, of course. But in the short term, the path to Brexit was laid by austerity itself. The connection between Brexit and austerity is one that has been routinely made on the left, including by Corbyn himself the morning after the referendum, when he popped up on TV screens nationwide to suggest that the result showed 'many communities are fed up with cuts'.[38] In this reading Brexit is straightforwardly interpreted as a cry for help by those 'left behind,' lashing out at whatever target is at hand and using the EU as a proxy for austerity.[39] But this argument has no means to explain why Cameron could win the 2015 election on an explicitly pro-austerity platform and yet lose to a supposed anti-austerity backlash a year later. Nor can it explain why so many of the most pro-austerity Tory voters, particularly those in the affluent South East counties who had benefitted the most from rising house prices, were also the most pro-Leave.[40] There was no inevitable contradiction between the austerity narrative and Brexit – the two were perfectly compatible for many, perhaps most, voters.

And this compatibility, we suggest, was evident even in those areas in which a vote to Leave could perhaps be more legitimately read as a reaction to economic decline. Even if here, in the post-industrial towns of the North and the Midlands, the vote to Leave was a form of popular revolt against austerity, it was a revolt *based entirely on the logic of austerity itself*, not a rejection of it. It is only by recognising this that it becomes possible to see how 2017 was a 'post-deficit'

election not because the 'austerity' narrative had failed, or
had been defeated, but because it had succeeded only too
well. Significantly, Brexit emerged out of the confluence of the
two forms of productivist moral tales which had dominated
British politics since the crash – that used to justify austerity
and that used to resist it.

THE AMBIVALANCE OF '45

The brilliance of the Leave campaign in the EU referendum
lay in its ability to harness the combined power of both of
these analyses, holding them to their promises, pushing them
to logical yet mostly unforeseen conclusions, seamlessly incorporating them into the Brexit narrative. So successful has this
strategy been that it has left the pro-European wings of both
the austerity and anti-austerity movements floundering on
the sidelines of the post-referendum debate, impotently looking on as the charge to hard Brexit – defined as leaving the
European Single Market, and the Customs Union – takes its
seemingly inexorable course. And the reason for this chronic
inability to stage even the flimsiest of interventions is that any
attempt to do so from the basis of their previous positions
faces the prospect of the full weight of their own arguments
being thrown back at them in their new Brexit form.

The Leave campaign took the two forms of productivism
exhibited by the austerity and anti-austerity movements – one
aimed primarily at internal 'scroungers', the other at external
predatory forces – and merged them into one. Whereas Cameron had blamed the crash and justified austerity on the basis of
a supposed underclass of benefit cheats living off the largesse
of a Labour-run public sector, for the Leave campaign (and
the UKIP platform that proceeded it) the parasitic force which
had dragged Britain into economic crisis and years of austerity

was immigration, and, in particular (although by no means exclusively), immigration from the EU. In UKIP leader Nigel Farage's telling, everything from declining wages through to traffic-jammed motorways was ultimately down to immigration.[41] The housing crisis, unemployment, a lack of funding for the NHS, a shortage of school places, overcrowded trains – there was not a single issue facing Britain that could not be blamed on migrants. The implication of this argument – and, in truth, there was very little left implicit in it – was that just as for Cameron the eradication of the unproductive was the only way to restore the country to its former glories, so too would the cessation of immigration and the removal, forced or otherwise, of those who were no longer welcome enable the dark days of austere sacrifice to come to an end.

Like Cameron, UKIP and Leave certainly pinned a good share of the blame for this on the Blair-Brown government. But the real culprit was not internal but external – Britain's membership of the European Union. The free movement of people – a formal legal right to work and study that accompanies membership of the European Single Market, and which, as long as that membership is retained, is beyond the reach of any individual government – had, in the eyes of Farage and Leave, allowed 'uncontrolled migration' into the UK, drained the resources from British public services, and, contrary to the evidence, put downward pressure on the wages of British workers.[42]

The Leave campaign then skilfully combined the no-holds-barred nativism of this argument with the core of the anti-austerity narrative, in order to create a causal connection between the funding of public services and leaving the EU. The now-infamous claim that the British public was wasting '£350m a week' on EU membership, money that could be spent on funding 'our NHS instead', was aimed squarely at those who had felt the sharp end of austerity but for whom the full-fat nativism of Farage, Boris Johnson et al might prove a little too hard to stomach on its own. It was an argument that chimed with those put forward by the initially miniscule but increasingly influential 'Lexit' (left-wing Brexit) movement, an alliance of the traditionally eurosceptic Labour left and anti-EU trade unions and far left groups, some of whom had previously run a joint electoral platform under the inelegant moniker No2EU: Yes to Democracy.

The Lexit wing of the Leave campaign had its origins in the Bennite faction of the Labour left, the tradition within which Corbyn spent his formative political years. From a Lexit perspective, the EU and its unelected bureaucratic leaders had joined forces with other transnational organisations (everything from the IMF and World Bank through to NATO and the UN) to deprive the British nation-state of its power to protect its people against the ravages of predatory global finance. Here the Lexiteers found common ground with Farage, suggesting that the rules of the Single Market in particular were illegitimate restrictions on the sovereignty of the British nation-state, imposed by an alien power. These purported impositions included free movement, a limit on the amount of 'state aid' a national government can provide an ailing national industry, regulation of government procurement policy and, more generally, the broader legal and institutional structure of the European project as a whole.

Where they disagreed with the right of the Brexit movement was on the effect of those restrictions. For the right-wing Brexiteers, the EU was imposing socialism on Britain by the back door. For the Lexiteers, the EU was blocking the transition to socialism. In either case, as with austerity, the language and imagery of the Second World War was routinely used in order to present the struggle to leave the EU and restore British 'independence' as an extension of the fight against the Nazis. It is of no small significance that in 2003

Tony Benn himself portrayed attempts to leave the EU in anti-colonial terms, describing it as a 'national liberation struggle,' regarding it as a crucial part of the ongoing battle against 'international capitalism.'[43]

The Leave campaign's choice of 'our NHS' as the public service whose survival supposedly rested on withdrawal from the EU was by no means accidental. The NHS is the one state institution to inspire the same intensity of public affection as the idealised memories of wartime pluck which provided 'austerity populism' with its ideological power. This appeal had long been recognised by the anti-austerity movement. Ken Loach's film *The Spirit of '45*, which told the story of how the NHS and the rest of the welfare state was built out of the ruins of the Second World War, was merely the most high-profile attempt to divert the austerity narrative's nostalgia for the 1940s into channels more conducive for leftist politics.[44] Campaigns against the EU's proposed TTIP treaty with the United States similarly centred on forecasts of the leech-like attachment of parasitical American capital to the NHS that would follow.[45]

Such an approach not only failed to challenge the nationalist premises of the austerity argument, but in many ways strengthened it. Seen through a Faragean lens, the NHS became yet another example of British wartime exceptionalism, a national treasure constructed in the face of threats from alien forces. This framing of 'our NHS' left it wide open for reappropriation by the right. Indeed, the idea that a wave of 'health tourism' – in which foreigners fraudulently claimed health care in the UK – was responsible for the travails of the health service became common currency amongst right-wing papers in the run up to the EU referendum.[46] By making the survival of the NHS its central focus, the Leave campaign thus managed to invoke the 'spirit of '45' in both its left and right guises. It brought the productivist and exclusionary logics shared by the austerity and anti-austerity movements to a head.

The referendum was thus transformed into the means by which the various promises made by the two narratives were given concrete form. In both cases, the resumption of public spending was predicated on the expulsion of the alien outsider, whether in the form of the immigrant, the scrounger, the European Court of Justice, or the shadowy world of 'globalist' finance. 'The deficit' and 'the 1%' were powerful images, but they were intangible – the odd banker stripped of his knighthood aside – and it was precisely this intangibility that gave their personified representations a dangerous political dynamism that we will go on to consider in later chapters. Moreover, neither the deficit nor the 1% could be removed in a single moment of decision. The moment of reckoning never seemed to arrive. It was always just around the next corner. In contrast, for the Brexit tendency, the demonic power of the EU took corporeal form everywhere they looked – from the colour of the British passport to the relative bendiness of a banana, the weights on a market stall, to accents on the street – and came to step in as a placeholder, depending on where one stood politically, for both the deficit and the 1%. Raising the question of British membership in a referendum offered the prospect of a concrete decision to which the latter two abstractions could now be reduced. The Leave campaign thus brought the moment of truth back from the ever-receding horizon and planted it firmly in the here and now. Here, at last, was the chance to redeem the promises that had been made, the chance to remove every one of the externally-imposed restrictions that had been holding the national community of 'hardworking people' back and had necessitated austerity in the first place. A straight question, once and for all. In or out. Servitude or freedom. All it took was a tick in a box.

The Leave campaign's critique of the EU took on both aspects of the productivist analysis, top-down and bottom-up, adopted from left and right, and pushed them to, and beyond, their limits.

Together, this amounted to a formidable political arsenal, bringing together the strongest elements of both the austerity and anti-austerity narratives: an emotional appeal to cultural tradition, the moral righteousness of the productive, the sanctity of national sovereignty, anti-migrant nativism, conspiracist railing against 'global elites'. This was then employed in such a way as to explain the financial crash, failing public services and Britain's post-industrial malaise all at once. Against this, arguments based on topics as deathlessly utilitarian as the loss of a few percentage points of GDP or the smooth functioning of trans-European supply chains were doomed to fail. For the first time in decades, the notion of 'economic credibility' had lost its purchase as fantasies of 'control' took over, on both left and right. The utter failure of the endless warnings that Brexit amounted to an act of unprecedented act of national self-sabotage, combined with the fantastical promises from both right and left of the wondrous world to come once Britain had shaken off the dead hand of the EU, pushed British politics into new territory. Brexit ushered in a new era in which fantasies of national sovereignty or the 'will' of a dreamt-up 'people' overcame appeals to economic interest, whatever the cost, as the fragile connection between ideology and economic interest finally snapped in two.

'SOME THINGS MATTER MORE THAN MONEY'

One of the first and most famous public flauntings of this devil-may-care irrationalism over questions of economic interest came in an interview Farage gave to the BBC in 2014. There he stated that, where immigration was concerned, 'there are some things that matter more than money'.[47] Even in spite of the fact that more immigrants make the country richer, Farage would sooner be poorer. 'I do think the social side of this matters more than the pure market economics.'[48] In retrospect, it is clear that this statement marked a wider moment in which the politics of 'economic credibility' lost control of the ideological narratives that had been used to justify them. As noted above, Cameron and Osborne had been happy to sell public spending cuts as a project of national redemption in which 'we' were 'all in it together' against the collective foes of debt and unproductive 'scroungers.' But when it came to the crunch, they subordinated the fantasy of 'austerity nostalgia' to a form of economic reason, however disputable, that by implication recognised the relationship between the needs of capitalist reproduction and the reproduction of humans as labour power. Farage's statement, by contrast, openly questioned the centrality of economic calculation altogether, and with it the fraught dependency of humans upon such calculation.

Here the moral urgency of exclusion contained in the productivist fairytale was separated from the question of productivity itself. As such, while inspired by the racist desire to cleanse Britain of perceived outsiders, it opened up a plane of political possibility on which left and right coalesced in certain forms of thinking and acting. In some way, Farage's comment gave a glance of what a politics that prioritised things other than commodities, wealth and value could look like. In much the same way, the left tradition from which Corbynism springs also regards the relationship between the 'social side' and 'pure market economics' to be essentially contingent, a matter of will power rather than necessity. In this, Corbynism mirrors the obsession with 'taking back control' which underpinned the vote for Brexit, with the two movements even agreeing on the political agent needed to wrench back that elusive control – the nation-state. Both claim to be able to free society from the necessity of living through the economic forms of capitalism through the building of national barriers. Apparently different but strangely resonant, each shows the janus-faced indeterminacy of populism in an era of democratic crisis.

The reality is that the society they seek to build by strength of moral force alone cannot be found apart from in and through the economic forms dismissed as secondary concerns. Without wage-labour, money, the buying and selling of commodities, and economic growth, individuals in capitalist society cannot live – even while these same conditions grind us down. Rather than facing up to the unforgiving reality that in capitalist society the fulfilment of social needs and the need to make profit exist in an inseparable contradiction – the one impossible without the other, while constantly negating it – these critiques entertain a compensatory fantasy that the relation between the two is simply a matter of 'taking back control'. There is no escape from this conundrum, and this is what gives both Brexit and Corbynism their edge: impossibility, insatiability, irrepressibility. Once unbottled, such fantasies can no longer be stopped shut. In a topsy-turvy world where subjects act under conditions they cannot choose, where the attempt to satisfy needs create objective realities beyond their control, groundswells against the status quo can have unintended consequences. Left populisms in this sense are fully of a piece with those of the right. Emotional or irrational urges are unlocked as electoral assets with unpredictable outcomes that risk the liberal democratic certainties within which social democracy, for better or for worse, moves – particularly when impossible promises do not, and cannot, come true.

~~~

Austerity populism died on June 23rd 2016, killed by an uncontainable explosion of its own exclusionary logic. This logic was no longer merely an instrumental tool, cynically used by the government for its own ends. The polarising division between 'friends' and 'enemies,' those inside the tribe and those outside, now constituted the very foundation of British politics. As such, the political terrain had shifted irrevocably, and although few realised it at the time – least of all Corbyn's critics – all bets made in the previous era were off.

Political success now depended on the speed at which the new situation was recognised. Strange as it may seem now, given the torturous lethargy of her post-election reign, Theresa May was the quickest off the mark. The distinct brand of 'Erdington Conservativism' developed by her close advisor Nick Timothy seemed perfectly primed for the post-austerity, post-Brexit era.[49] Inspired by the 19th century Birmingham industrialist Joseph Chamberlain, Timothy's vision was founded upon an interventionist economic pro-gramme of infrastructure investment, the rejection of 'glo-balist' free trade in favour of protectionist tariffs to secure British industry, fierce Euroscepticism, a radical reduction in immigration, selective state education, and a laser-like focus on the apparently communal concerns of the so-called 'white working class' – traditional values, self-responsibility, patriot-ism, and law and order. There was an obvious overlap with both the message of the Leave campaign, as well as the creed of 'faith, flag and family' which had long been touted by the 'Blue Labour' wing of the opposition party- indeed, Lord Glasman took tea with Timothy in the early months of May's premiership.[50] As May walked into Downing Street for the first time as Prime Minister it seemed that her programme of economic and cultural protectionism was destined for hegem-onic status. On the steps of Number 10, she promised, in language clearly adopted from the anti-austerity wing of the Leave campaign, that her government would be 'driven not by the interests of the privileged few, but by yours' – the mil-lions of 'ordinary people' who were 'just about managing'.[51]

For most commentators (including ourselves at the time), the emergence of 'Mayism' seemed to signal the final demise of Corbynism.[52] The combination of anti-austerity economics, anti-globalist nationalism and anti-immigrant nativism in a post-Brexit, post-austerity world seemed invincible. In desperation, the Parliamentary Labour Party attempted to force Corbyn's resignation by putting up a series of Shadow Cabinet ministers to quit *en masse*. At the time, such despair seemed wholly appropriate. And yet, a more sober analysis would have revealed the strong correspondence between the new post-Brexit terrain and the protectionist economic and foreign policies long advocated by the Bennite 'hard left', of which Corbyn was both founding member and modern day heir. Far from Brexit destroying Corbyn's electoral chances, it is clear, in retrospect at least, that it was the indispensable precondition for his success. Brexit was not the sign of the political zeitgeist rushing away from Corbynism, as so many thought. It was precisely the opposite. By pushing the populist logic of both austerity populism and its anti-austerity cousin to their conclusion, and eradicating economic competence as a criterion for electoral success, Brexit cleared the ground for Corbynism's consolidation, simultaneously sublimating and abolishing the issue of the deficit through the fulfilment of its exclusionary promise.

The effect of Brexit was to send British politics into a space somewhere between fantasy and abyss in which Project Corbyn was perfectly primed to operate. The stuff of success in such a scenario is emotion, sentiment, identity, abstract concepts like national sovereignty and the will of a dreamt-up 'people,' with either a nativist or socialist inflection – or both. This was the kind of heady mix on which the 2017 election was fought. On both left and right a deranged optimism prevailed, in which faith in the future was all that was needed to bring it into being. This wishful thinking, seemingly at odds with the cold reality of forthcoming political isolation and economic decline, was exemplified both in the credulous Brexiteers convinced that Empire 2.0 was on the horizon, as well as the Corbynists who held in their man expectations apparently so high as to never be met. Farage's heresy resounded, and with it the dangerous insatiability of the abstract principles and unmeetable goals to which it opposed economic calculation. Ironically, for all her attempts to capture the revanchism of the Brexit campaign, it was Theresa May's failure to reach the required level of utopian exuberance which led to her underwhelming electoral performance. In such conditions, centring an election campaign upon the grey promise of 'stability,' and promoting policies as knotty and downcast as a change in the contributions to adult social care, was not enough for voters used to stronger stuff left and right to reward May with a majority.

Brexit thus opened up political space for Corbyn to construct an electoral platform of bold state intervention of the kind that had been wholly denied to Ed Miliband – as long as that platform came dressed in the protectionist colours of a post-liberal, isolationist nation-state, in which the free movement of people no longer held. Understanding how and why Corbyn was able to deal with the thorny issue of free movement while keeping his supporters onside, in a manner that was completely denied to his predecessor, is crucial to grasping the nature of Corbynism as a whole. And here we must turn to the figure of Corbyn himself. Without the advantage of Corbyn's reputation as a uniquely authentic man of principle, an impression shared across the political spectrum, Labour would not have been able to take advantage of the gap opened up by the collapse of the austerity narrative through the skilful neutralisation of the question of immigration. The next chapters will therefore trace the development of this Corbyn mythology, outlining the many ways in which it has been crucial to the rise of a Corbynism constructed around the man from a set of seemingly independent ideas, whilst simultaneously being dependent on him and him alone for its existence, survival, and unpredicted success.

2

THE PRECONDITIONS OF CORBYNISM: ON TWO-CAMPISM

Jeremy Corbyn might be regarded as the most openly and uncompromisingly pro-migrant leader in Labour's history. He had spent his political career on the backbenches campaigning for the rights of migrants and extolling the virtues of a multi-cultural society. His victory in the 2015 Labour leadership election was driven in part by his principled defence of migrants and the cultural and economic benefits that immigration has brought to Britain, in contrast to his vacillating predecessors and rival leadership candidates. In the fateful election campaign which preceded the leadership contest, Ed Miliband had made 'controls on immigration' one of his key manifesto pledges.[1] Labour had even put the phrase on an official mug. Those 'controls' would have prevented EU migrants from claiming benefits for two years after moving to the UK. This was widely, and no doubt correctly, seen as a craven attempt to appease those elements of the Labour vote tempted by the rising nativist tide that would eventually surge into the Leave campaign. For the left, both within Labour and without, the policy (and the mug) became a totemic symbol of Labour's moral decline. Diane Abbott, now Corbyn's Shadow Home Secretary, described both the policy and the mug as 'shameful.'[2] Corbyn himself said on the leadership campaign trail that the proposal to introduce immigration controls of any sort was 'appalling.'[3]

The impetus behind Corbyn's bid for the leadership derived from the Year Zero narrative which quickly sprung up around his campaign. If victorious, so this story went, Labour's supposedly irredeemably corrupt past – of which the immigration mug was the epitome – would be wiped out by a movement whose purity was guaranteed by that of its unassuming leader. Paradoxically, the same tale formed the basis of the main charge against him made by his internal critics. Here Corbyn was portrayed as a naïve idealist, a man who would put the purity of his principles before pragmatism.[4] He would rather turn Labour into a party of protest than make the compromises necessary for it to become a party of government.[5] For both friend and foe, the idea that Corbyn would cast aside his lifelong principles for the sake of electoral expediency seemed farfetched – doing so would, surely, undermine the very purpose of a Corbyn leadership.

And yet, in the 2017 election, the man who was elected precisely on the basis that he would not cede to pressure and impose 'controls on immigration,' fronted a manifesto pronouncing an end to the free movement of people from the EU – in real terms, the most right-wing policy on immigration the party had seen in generations. The truly remarkable thing about his scenario was that he did so while not only escaping censure from the left, but rather being cheered to the rafters. No other Labour leader would have been capable of such an achievement. Miliband was certainly not granted such generosity, his whole campaign clouded by the infamous mug and so-called 'Edstone' on which the demand for immigration controls was engraved. Examining this puzzling development reveals the extent to which the figure of Jeremy Corbyn himself has been indispensable to the success of Corbynism. Put any other left politician in his place – John McDonnell, Diane Abbott, George Galloway, Chris Williamson – and the contradictions that run through the project would have caused its collapse long ago. Corbyn himself is the glue that holds the thing together.

Or rather, it is a particular *image* of Corbyn that holds it together – that of the moral paragon: virtuous, righteous, incorruptible. Because, short of any longer-term strategic considerations in direct contradiction with the Corbyn movement's appeal to integrity over political expediency, the only way to explain why leftist activists were willing to put their opposition to immigration controls on hold in this instance, or why, in similar fashion, liberal Remain voters backed Labour despite their stance on Brexit being virtually identical to the Conservatives, is that they instinctively trusted Corbyn in a way they did not other politicians. And this trust, this absolute faith in his ethical infallibility, is something very specific to Corbyn on a personal level. It arises not merely from the words he says but his demeanour, his appearance, his way of speaking, the specific trajectory of his political career. Rather than Corbyn's refusal to shift from his steadfast principles being the deadweight dragging the party down, it was precisely the presumption that Corbyn was a uniquely principled politician which enabled him to make the strategic shifts necessary to piece together a successful electoral coalition.

But in truth, the argument in this chapter is not that Corbyn has utilised his image and the instinctive trust it generates in order to betray his principles- although, on immigration, this is indeed the case. It is, rather, that the assumption of his righteousness has prevented any serious examination of *what those principles actually are*. Corbyn's persona has wielded a

curiously depoliticising effect from the outset of his ascent to
the Labour leadership. It is striking to recall how rarely the
actual political content of Corbyn's beliefs or proposed programme has been put under any real scrutiny by his internal
rivals. Party critics fruitlessly tried and failed to convince his
recalcitrant supporters of the inevitability of electoral failure,
or brandished tales of organisational incompetence. But no
serious effort was spent actually critiquing either his ideas or
those of the political tradition in which he has spent his life.

The incessant focus on the inevitability of electoral disaster
meant that, on the one hand, Corbyn's critics failed to recognise the substantive aspects of Corbynism which dynamically
chime – for good or ill – with broader political and economic
shifts that had taken place over the previous decade. Had they
taken Corbynism seriously on its own terms, its resonance
with prevailing ideological and electoral tendencies in Britain
and beyond would have been much clearer and its success in
2017 much less surprising. On the other hand, the inordinate
attention given to utilitarian arguments about electability
based on the historical precedent of 1983 and 2015 eventually left Corbyn's opponents with nothing to say when the
predicted electoral disaster did not unfold.

It is certainly true that Corbyn has faced fierce and incessant opposition from the right-wing press. But this has
remained at the level of hysteria rather than analysis. Rather
than carefully scrutinising the historical context and real consequences of his actual political positions, the media routinely
presents Corbyn in such a caricatured fashion – accusing him
of 'dancing a jig' on his way to the Cenotaph, or of being a
paid Cold War informant – that any legitimate critique is lost
in the noise.[6] This failure to properly examine the political
content of the Corbyn programme, a direct consequence of
the bewitching power of Corbyn's personal reputation, has
therefore led to large swathes of the 'soft' and liberal-left

uncritically embracing what is essentially a programme of economic nationalism at home, and a simplistic Manichean 'two-campist' foreign policy abroad – whereby 'my enemy's enemy is my friend,' and the enemy is always 'the West,' regardless of particular circumstances.

The constant focus on the merits of Corbyn's personal character is not, then, merely an eccentric but inconsequential quirk shared by his more overenthusiastic supporters. It is a vital political tool, perhaps the most potent in his armoury. This chapter will first examine the practical benefits accrued to Corbyn by virtue of his symbolic status, showing how it helped him overcome the immigration conundrum which had scuppered Miliband's support amongst the left. It then traces the origins and development of Corbyn's saintly reputation, rooting this trajectory in the political collapse of Labour's 'hard left' following the rise of New Labour, and in particular the disintegration of that wing of the party led by Corbyn's personal mentor, Tony Benn. We will examine how Benn himself was elevated to the status of moral exemplar through a radical process of depoliticization prefiguring that which would prove to be so crucial to the rise of Corbynism. In particular, we suggest that Benn and Corbyn's role in opposing the 2003 Iraq war was vital to this process.

THE IMMIGRATION CONUNDRUM

Corbyn undoubtedly deserved much of the criticism that came his way after his singularly lacklustre performance during the Brexit referendum. Reports circulated that Corbyn's team actively sabotaged the Remain campaign by refusing to unambiguously back EU membership.[7] That said, what Corbyn did not do during the campaign is join in with the chorus of voices demonising migrants, whipping up scare stories about an imminent invasion of people from Syria, Turkey or the so-called 'Jungle' refugee camp in Calais. Nor did he, in the wake of the vote to Leave, participate in the unedifying spectacle of politicians competing to demonstrate how clearly they 'got the message' about the need to cut immigration. Leading Labour figures such as Chuka Umunna and Rachel Reeves, long regarded as the heirs to the Blairite tradition – defined by a strong commitment to the European project – began to demand an end to European migration.[8] Reeves even called for the end of free movement on the Enoch Powell-esque grounds that her Leeds constituency was a 'tinder box' which would set alight with riots if immigration was not curbed.[9] This was despite the fact that free movement was a compulsory condition of membership of the Single Market, which meant that the economic costs of ending it were potentially immense. The triumph of sentiment over economic reason was being felt across the entire political spectrum, disorientating even the most 'pragmatic' and 'moderate' of politicians.

Despite coming under severe pressure from Theresa May's domineering new government, who had made a land grab for Labour Leave voters by making the reduction of immigration its top priority, as well as the press and the right of his own party, Corbyn refused to buckle on free movement. For some of his critics, the problem with this stance, as admirable as it was, was that it threatened to place Labour on the wrong side of the debate when an election arrived. Brexit, it seemed, had not only destroyed the rationale for austerity, but had settled the 'debate' on immigration. It was now virtually impossible to find any contemporary politician or commentator defending the right to free movement either as a principle, or even just on the pragmatic grounds that it was the only way to ensure membership of the Single Market. On this question, Corbyn stood alone, facing down the entirety of the British political and media class, a good chunk of his own party, and – aside from a section of his supporters and the few liberal Remainers willing to raise their heads above the parapet – the majority of the electorate.

And yet, when Labour's 2017 manifesto arrived, this heroic commitment to the continuation of free movement had disappeared. In coldly neutral language the manifesto asserted, as a *fait accompli*, that 'Freedom of movement will end when we leave the European Union'.[10] But there was nothing inevitable about this conclusion. All non-EU members of the Single Market retain free movement. As such, Labour's policy on immigration in the 2017 election was well to the right of that which was so disparaged by the left in 2015. Indeed, in that election only UKIP and the British National Party had advocated a complete cessation of free movement. Now, remarkably, it had become the shared objective of both major parties.

The effect of this was to entirely drain the potency of 'immigration debate' from the election in a way unimaginable even six months beforehand. There was nothing left to debate. All agreed that free movement would be coming to an end, whatever the economic cost. In this way, another obstacle was cleared from the electoral path that the Leave campaign's sublimation of 'the deficit' had unexpectedly opened up. It enabled Labour to make their pitch to their former voters who had switched to UKIP, without 'legitimate concerns' over immigration taking up all the oxygen.[11]

And it worked. Labour were estimated to have won around 20 per cent of the 2015 UKIP vote in 2017, enough to keep hold of a large number of Leave-voting Labour seats threatened by the Conservatives.[12] One study found that the late swing to Labour which sealed May's fate was driven not by the widely-touted (and comprehensively debunked) 'youthquake,' but by older voters who were more 'Eurosceptic, socially conservative and opposed to immigration' than

Labour's core vote.[13] Moreover, Labour managed to attract
these voters while retaining the support of large numbers of
liberal Remainers in the big cities who thought that Corbyn
represented the best chance to halt May's march to isolationism and protectionism. And yet the price of this electoral
masterstroke was paid by the millions of European migrants
living in the UK – some for decades – who suddenly faced
the prospect of their legally-secured rights to live, to work, to
study and to love in the UK being unceremoniously stripped
away. The security of their very existence had now become
the plaything of political forces over which they had no control, subject to the utopian demands of a 'national community' apparently convinced its prosperity depended upon the
speed at which the alien intruders could be removed.

Corbyn's motives for moving into this political space were
very different from those of his opponents. He has never
come close to the incendiary language of Rachel Reeves. For
Corbyn, the problem with free movement was not cultural
but economic. He began to argue that European immigration
had undermined British workers' wages, particularly through
the 'wholesale importation of underpaid workers from central Europe in order to destroy conditions'.[14] This was in
all likelihood a reference to the controversial yet little used
'Posted Workers Directive', rather than free movement itself,
but Corbyn skilfully conflated the two to insinuate that immigration had negatively affected wages. John McDonnell was
even clearer, telling Andrew Marr that free movement had
directly 'forced down wages.'[15] Quite apart from the questionable politics of dividing workers in this way, such rhetoric
continued in defiance of extensive evidence to the contrary.[16]

Beyond the leadership, with admirable exceptions including Shadow Home Secretary Diane Abbott, diverse quarters of
Corbynism came to back controls on or an end to freedom of
movement. The demand for controls on immigration emitted

from the largely Stalinist hard left and, perhaps more surprisingly, 'postcapitalist' proponent Paul Mason.[17] Apparently made in support of the pay and conditions of the national community of waged workers, in its different complexions the Corbynist case against freedom of movement reduces the right to move in search of labour to an immediate expression of the abstract forces of global capital. A worker's decision to move in search of work or a different life is seen not as an expression of real human action or desire, but solely as a Pavlovian response to capital's demand for factors of production. Their 'right' to do so is seen only as a legal justification of the capacity for capital to move resources around the globe.

What Corbynists miss is that the abstraction active here – the international provision of abstract rights or the abstract movement of capital across borders – contains within it a concrete core that expresses real material relations of struggle and subsistence. By characterising movements of labour as mere movements of capital resources, they steal all agency and powers of struggle from the workers who seek new lives across borders. Rights are both abstract but also concrete insofar as they were won through struggle and permit the search of concrete human beings for their reproduction as such. In a world where we live by labour, the freedom of movement of labour is the freedom to move full stop. By seeking to limit it, attacks on freedom of movement imply that these rights are reducible to a liberal or capitalist conspiracy to exploit workers or place them in competition with national communities.[18]

But from the perspective of capital, it is in fact preferable to exploit irregular migrant labour with no rights at all, or to establish a guest worker system in order to legally differentiate 'foreign workers' from their 'indigenous' counterparts, rather than having to face a workforce universally endowed with enforceable political, civil and workplace rights.

The right to free movement – while limited to those fortunate enough to be born within the Single Market area – should therefore be seen as necessary (though insufficient) step to a universal right to freedom, not an obstacle to be removed. But with the Brexit vote came a strange and unanticipated shift in how socialists considered this issue in the UK – and Corbyn was the crucial precondition that paved the metaphorical road to Damascus.

~~~

For the core drivers of Project Corbyn, the main problem with free movement was its status as one of the 'four freedoms' attached to the Single Market. For the Bennite tradition within which Corbyn and McDonnell have been immersed their entire careers, the rules of the Single Market – particularly around the 'state aid' that can be provided to national industry – amount to an illegitimate neoliberal imposition upon British sovereignty, blocking the road to state-sponsored British socialism. For the Bennite 'hard left' tradition, the post-1945 international order of pluralistic, transnational and rule-based liberalism epitomised by the European Union seems nothing more than an undemocratic, superficial cover for class, if not national, oppression.[19] Viewed as an appendage of the Single Market, free movement becomes a mere tool of the bosses, enabling them to move workers around Europe as pawns, undermining indigenous working conditions and presenting an obstacle to the nation state's ability to plan and control production, employment levels and wages. This belief in the EU's inherently oppressive character is why McDonnell was quick to urge a mourning Labour Party to stop 'taking the side of certain corporate elites' in the wake of the Leave vote and embrace the 'enormous opportunity' presented by Brexit.[20] It also explains why, in the days after Labour's startling performance in the election, when May's vision of Brexit had been comprehensively rejected by the electorate and

Labour's ability to shape the direction of political travel was at its height, McDonnell rejected the chance to force May to ameliorate her stance on the Single Market, Customs Union and free movement, instead reiterating Labour's commitment to the same position.

Despite the admirable steadfastness of Corbyn's initial support for free movement, as time went on, and the prospect of escaping the supposedly neoliberal strictures of the Single Market grew ever more enticing, support for free movement was sacrificed. Meanwhile, the right of the party made the opposite journey. Again, it was not the rights of immigrants which was of primary concern, but rather membership of the Single Market. Once their initial post-referendum disorientation had subsided, the Labour right realised that the economic consequences of leaving the Single Market were so dire that they trumped any fears over the cultural impact of immigration. They thus decided that, on reflection, they were willing to sacrifice their opposition to free movement in order to remain in the Single Market.

The question raised by this *volte face* is why the left were happy to go along with it. Some claimed that Corbyn's hand on immigration had been forced by the right of the party. Even if this was the case, this was not an excuse granted to Ed Miliband. But it manifestly was not. The election result gave Corbyn complete control over the direction of the party. He could have switched positions on free movement, but chose not to do so. Rather than protesting this clear rightward drift on immigration, many of Corbyn's supporters on the left went out of their way to justify it. As Michael Chessum puts it:

> *activists who have spent years declaring their*
> *solidarity with migrants and calling for a borderless*
> *world can now be found contemplating ways for*
> *the biggest expansion of border controls in recent*

British history – which is what the end of free
movement would mean – to seem progressive, or
like an opportunity.[21]

The main way in which Corbyn-style 'controls on immigration' has been justified is by a turn to the once-mocked
'Lexit' argument that remaining in the Single Market, whatever its economic benefits, would prevent the implementation
of Labour's manifesto.[22] At best, some quarters of Corbyn's
support argued that free movement should be separated
from its attachment to the Single Market and kept even after
withdrawal from the EU's institutions. But most did not.
The rights of migrants and the promise of British 'socialism'
were thus opposed to one another. Corbyn's 'jobs-first Brexit'
turned out to be a more palatable version of Gordon Brown's
much-derided call for 'British jobs for British workers'.[23]

We will consider the 'Lexit' argument in Chapter 4, putting it
in the context of Corbynism's Bennite legacy. But the key point
to be emphasised here is the willingness displayed by much
of Corbyn's support base to shift their own positions in order
to accommodate the latest policy development. The dizzying
twists and turns of the Corbynite commentariat in the months
following the election, as they desperately tried to adhere to the
correct line on immigration, the Single Market and the Customs Union – even if it meant condemning their own previous
position – is testament to the depths of loyalty Corbyn is able
to command from his supporters.[24] This tendency extends so
far as to, in the case of free movement, induce a willingness to
sacrifice a legal right on the say-so of the leadership, with no
recompense aside from the assumption that a Corbyn government would come to pass and establish a generous immigration
system. Here actual rights, sanctioned by law, are cast aside
in the name of Corbyn's moral integrity. The possibility that
supporting the removal of rights on the guarantee of Corbyn's

honourable intentions may, in the future, strengthen the hand of those far less noble – such as those responsible for the 'hostile environment' immigration policy and the subsequent Windrush scandal – is barely considered.

The refusal of Labour politicians on both the left and right of the party to articulate what should have been axiomatic in Britain's immediate post-referendum deliberations – leaving the Single Market was not on the referendum ballot paper; it will be economically devastating; free movement is not the cause of Britain's economic problems – not only gave May a free hand to interpret the result in the way she saw fit. It then resulted in a ridiculous situation where the only people making what should have been eminently noncontroversial points were Tony Blair, Alastair Campbell, George Osborne and a motley crew of pompous Twitter personalities granted a disproportionately high political platform by default.[25] This rather queasy combination has seen the sobriquet 'Remoaner' adopted by both the Corbyn left and the Brexiteer right, the term now synonymous with elitist, sneering 'globalists', those ambivalent at best to war and austerity, and woefully out of touch with both the 'real people' who have been 'left behind by globalisation' and the socialist wonderland that will be built after 'Lexit'. An uncompromising defence of free movement of people, or the recognition of the economic rationality of remaining in the Single Market, risks the shame of being branded with the contemporary left epithets of choice, 'liberal' or 'centrist'. Indeed, the logical conclusion of where Corbynist thinking on the topic has ended up is to make opposition to austerity and opposition to Brexit mutually exclusive – despite the fact that a hard Brexit will radically reduce the resources required to overcome austerity, not its end.

Given this background, how then to explain the apparent belief amongst the Remain-voting 2017 electorate that Corbyn and McDonnell represented a 'softer' path to Brexit than May's

Conservatives? As we have seen, neither Corbyn nor McDonnell have been reticent about their opposition to continued membership of the EU, in particular the Single Market. Shadow Secretary of State for Trade Rebecca Long-Bailey even admitted that Labour 'want[ed] to have our cake and eat it, as do most parties in Westminster' – retaining the economic 'benefits' of Single Market membership while 'having greater control over our laws, greater control over our borders.'[26] This impossible position was identical to that infamously proposed by Leave campaign and hard Brexit talisman Boris Johnson. And yet these explicit comments were seemingly ignored by the bulk of liberal-left Remain voters in the 2017 election, particularly those in urban areas, who turned to Corbyn in their millions as a defence against Theresa May's rabid nationalism.[27] Voters who would otherwise have never countenanced something as reckless and potentially catastrophic as the no-holds-barred hard Brexit promised by May threw caution to the wind for Corbyn. The latter's integrity alone was enough to conveniently elide, for many, the political reality, which was that Labour's own Brexit policy was just as 'hard' as that offered by the Tories.

Thus while other politicians are assumed – sometimes not without reason – to be perpetually lying, their public statements disregarded on the grounds that they must be hiding something, in Corbyn's case the opposite seems to be true. Actual evidence of his statements and his actions, both past and present, comes a poor second to whatever he is presumed to have meant, which for much of the left appears to happily cohere with what they already think. Aside from Brexit, this is perhaps the most important reason why evidence of his past and present associations with a rogue's gallery of Stalinists and antisemites, and his at least implicit support for anti-democratic forms of violent direct action, failed to ruffle the feathers not only of Labour members in the leadership contests, but also the wider spectrum of liberal-left voters in the election. On the assumption that many do not share these affinities, it seems they simply could not tally the stories told in the right-wing press with the genial, gentle man on their television screens. So bewitching is the power of Corbyn's image of unshakeable integrity that the historical details of his career, the content and context of his statements, his choice of political alliances, and the possible consequences of his actions, are relegated to irrelevancy. Corbyn's imagined persona is the means by which the internal contradictions of the piecemeal theoretical construction of Corbynism are temporarily contained and concealed – a concord altogether impossible without the political cover that his symbolic status provides.

How then, did Corbyn's politically-indispensable reputation of moral exceptionalism come about? The key to understanding this phenomenon lies not in the first instance with Corbyn himself, but in the fundamental shift in the public image of his mentor Tony Benn over the last three decades. This shift extended to the general perception of the Bennite wing of the Labour party (known, not originally in a pejorative sense, as the 'hard left') as a whole, and its changing relation to the rest of the party, particularly during the Blair era. Without the radical process of dehistoricisation and depoliticisation which transformed Benn from the 'most dangerous man in Britain', as he was labelled by the *Sun* in the 1980s, to cuddly 'national treasure', Corbyn would not have been able to win the trust of the broader liberal-left so easily, nor shake off the more dubious aspects of his past.[28] Therefore the story of Corbyn's moral mythology must begin with the great transformation of Tony Benn and the Bennite tradition.

FROM BENN TO BLAIR

In 1981, Benn challenged Denis Healey, doyen of the 'Old Labour' right, for the deputy leadership of the party. Once

a technocratic and modernising cabinet minister, Benn had
shifted tack in recent years, in part due to his frustration with
the civil service whilst in government. Benn and his supporters accused Healey and the previous Labour government of
betrayal – despite Benn being in the cabinet throughout –
blaming the party's 1979 defeat on Healey's decision three
years earlier to take a loan from the IMF, predicated on public
spending cuts, in response to a collapse in the value of the
pound. From the Bennite perspective, Labour had lost the
election because they had abandoned their leftist principles –
a familiar refrain. The answer to Britain's economic and
Labour's electoral woes, they claimed, could be found in
what came to be termed a 'siege economy,' in which British
industry would be saved from the pressures of the world
market and international finance through the raising of protectionist national barriers to imports, mass nationalisation
and state direction of production.[29] This domestic agenda,
which we will explore in more depth in Chapter 4, would be
accompanied by an isolationist foreign policy and a defence
strategy founded upon unilateral nuclear disarmament and
withdrawal from NATO. It would be achieved through the
'democratisation' of the Labour party's internal structures.
Rather than Labour policy being determined by a process of
negotiation between the leadership, ministers, MPs, members,
trade unions and affiliates, in Benn's plan members would be
given full control.

Benn's bid for deputy leadership was the culmination of a
long process in which his wing had gradually taken control of
large swathes of the party. By the early 1980s, they ran a number of city councils, controlled the majority of CLPs, secured
a substantial base of MPs within the PLP and counted on the
support of some union leaders – if not always their members. The growing strength of the left – which was only briefly
stymied by Benn's narrow defeat to Healey – led to tensions

within the party. As well as the SDP breakaway in 1981, it was ultimately responsible for the internal schism between the 'hard' and 'soft' Labour left. The latter felt that the magnitude of the defeat in 1983, in which Labour had run on a manifesto clearly shaped by the Bennite programme, demanded a shift to a more pragmatic, ameliorative approach, regardless of whether the policies were 'correct' in the abstract. The 'hard' left – including Corbyn, who remained a stoic, if rather inconspicuous, supporter of Benn's programme throughout his parliamentary career – would accept no such compromise. For the right of the party, meanwhile, the left's insistence on its electoral appeal, against all the evidence, was regarded as a collective delusion, the only real effect of which was to give the Conservatives the freedom to wreak havoc while an impotent Labour watched on.

Some 30 years later, the increasingly likely prospect that Corbyn, one of Benn's acolytes, would achieve what his mentor had not – winning the leadership of the Labour party – caused partisans of the soft left and Labour right to revisit these same, by now rather shopworn, arguments about the hard left's lack of 'electability'.[30] This represented an instinctive reaction on the part of those who genuinely feared that a unreconstructed Bennite leadership heralded another 1983-style electoral disaster, especially given what had just happened to Ed Miliband. But there was a fundamental difference in the context within which this familiar argument was now deployed. In the 1980s, the organisational strength of the left both within and without the party was not in doubt. The prospect of the Bennite faction emerging victorious from the internal party struggle was very real. Benn was recognised by all sides as the leading representative of a specific political faction, propagating a clearly identifiable worldview rooted in a particular analysis of capitalism, its problems and its solutions, with which one could rationally agree or disagree.

As such, the 'electability' issue, while important, was only
one aspect of a broader, and much more substantive, debate
which centred on fundamental, *practical* disagreements
over the specific content of a Bennite political programme –
particularly around economic protectionism, defence, internationalism and the internal structure of the party – as well as
the fiercely sectarian nature of the means proposed to implement it within the party. It was a battle that had to be fought
out in both intellectual and organisational terms on this
concrete political basis – constituency party by constituency
party, council by council. Eventually pragmatic and democratic left groups like the Labour Coordinating Committee
combined on-the-ground organising and theoretically savvy
soft-left intellectual renewal to best the hard left and pave the
way first for Kinnock and then for Blair.[31]

By the time of Blair's first landslide victory, this practical
battle within Labour was essentially over. Three successive
Labour governments meant the 'electability' argument had
been comprehensively won, while the 'hard left' had shrunk
to a rump. Many of Benn's supporters had left the party altogether. Those who remained, including Corbyn, seemed to give
up on domestic affairs altogether, focusing nearly all of their
attention on foreign policy, particularly through the vehicle
of the 'Stop the War Coalition' (StWC). What had once been
a substantive struggle over economic policy, democratic processes and competing visions of capitalist society was reduced
to a formalistic ritual, emptied of real content, in which the
remnants of the hard left bemoaned the new direction of the
party but offered little concrete opposition. It was reduced to
presenting its ideas in the form of an abstract moral critique,
in which New Labour was ceaselessly accused and unfailingly
convicted of betraying the supposed true values of an ill-defined
Labour interest. The left had always, in some sense, seen themselves as morally superior to the rest of the party – and Labour

as a whole certainly regarded itself as morally superior to the Conservatives. But now, precisely because it lacked any means to apply its ideas in practice, this overweening sense of moral superiority became the sole determinant of what it meant to be a 'socialist'. And nothing symbolised this process of depoliticisation and moralisation better than the transformation of the public image of Benn himself.

In his heyday, Benn had been regarded, quite rightly, as a threat to the status quo. Agree with his vision of a protectionist command economy or not, there was no denying that it would have entailed a fundamental shift in the nature of British politics. But by the late 1990s, when the practical political power of the left had dissolved to almost nothing, the concrete details of Benn's agenda had faded from memory. A defanged Bennism was stripped of its political content in the public mind. Ken Livingstone's Mayoral administration in London constituted some thread of continuity, with veterans of the broad 1980s Bennite left grouped around a Socialist Action cell – some of whom would later go on to staff Corbyn's leadership operation – placed in central positions within the city's governance.[32] But Benn himself was increasingly romanticised into a cuddly elder statesman figure, the benighted custodian of Labour's moral conscience, a man whose principles, while perhaps a little naïve, were now beyond criticism. As would later be the case with Corbyn, Benn's personal character – his quaint manner, pipe in mouth, mug of tea in hand – was of the utmost importance to this process of domestication. Few of those who were enamoured of his status as a 'national treasure' knew or cared about his political past. His new-found identity as a benevolent elderly mascot for all of those who instinctively felt themselves to be 'on the right side of history' meant that the details of any particular policy he supported mattered less than the mere fact he supported it. The specificity of his analysis was gradually reduced to his famous five questions for those who wield power: 'What power have you got?'; 'Where did you get it from?'; 'In whose interests do you use it?'; 'To whom are you accountable?'; and 'How do we get rid of you?'.[33] This intensely personalised conception of power, combined with his conviction that asking *cui bono* ('who benefits?') was all that was needed to explain any historical event, became the dominant feature of his popular reception as his firebrand image gently smouldered. The influence of Benn's latter-day pseudocritical perspective is clearly visible in the conspiracist underpinnings of Corbynism's own understanding of how politics, economy and international relations work under capitalism.

'TWO CAMPISM' AND THE ANTI-IMPERIALIST SCHEMA

The 2003 Iraq war was a pivotal moment in the romanticisation of the Bennite tendency. Tony Blair's decision to join George W Bush in the invasion of Saddam Hussein's Iraq was perhaps even more crucial to the later rise of Corbynism than the 2008 financial crash. Opposition to the war in Iraq stretched far beyond the 'hard left' itself, incorporating the vast majority of the liberal-left, for whom the proposed invasion was as morally clear-cut an issue as one could find. Indeed, opposition to the Iraq war swiftly became – and remains – the baseline of left-liberal politics, as evidenced since in the widespread inability to take humanitarian intervention in Syria on its own merits, without conflating it with the very different circumstances in Iraq.

The popular uptake of this isolationist position should not obscure how, in organisational and presentational terms, the protest movement against the war was undoubtedly a very successful 'hard left' affair, quickly taken over by the Stop the

War Coalition (StWC). The StWC was now home to much of the Bennite tendency – including Benn and Corbyn himself – alongside members of the Socialist Workers Party, various other revolutionary socialist groupuscules and conservative Islamists from the Muslim Association of Britain. Many of its leading figures and associates – Corbyn himself, Andrew Murray, McDonnell's economic advisor James Meadway – now hold positions at or near the top of Corbyn's Labour. Indeed, in the weeks after Corbyn's initial leadership victory his team was described by one staffer as 'Stop the War with bells on.'[34] The StWC was and is defined by a crude application of a 'two-campist' approach to questions of geopolitics. Understanding the nature of this 'two-campist' worldview is absolutely essential to grasping both Bennism and Corbynism. It shapes not only the foreign policy views we interrogate below, but it is also the key to grasping why domestic policies of economic protectionism are taken to be the precondition of socialism, as we will go on to consider in the second half of the book.

For the two-campists of Stop the War (StWC), the world is severed into two halves or 'camps', one irrefutably 'good' and the other irredeemably 'bad.' In this Manichean world, 'my enemy's enemy is my friend.' The 'West' – primarily the 'imperialists' of the USA, Israel, the UK, the EU – falls squarely in the enemy camp. Whoever styles themselves as the opponents of the 'West' are in turn considered 'friends,' comrades in the anti-imperialist struggle, regardless of the content of their wider political programme. For two-campists, the West is taken to be the sole origin of all that is bad in the world. Where the West alone acts, the rest can only respond. Agency exists only on the side of the evil-doers, not those who reflexively react; a perspective that implies the paternalistic, colonialist and culturally racist assumption that the capacity to act upon the course of history is denied all those outside the

'West'.[35] Indeed, the fact that an 'anti-imperialist' state might have its own objectives which are not directly related to 'the West' falls out of view altogether, even if – as in the case of Iranian interference in both Syria and Iraq – those objectives are themselves manifestly imperialist.[36]

This binary worldview has long been the price of entry into Corbyn's milieu. Those who share in it must seemingly forego the capacity to be shocked by any action, however indiscriminately violent or even genocidal, taken by those who by virtue of their ascribed 'anti-imperialist' identity are deemed to belong to what David Hirsh describes as the 'community of the good.'[37] Every deed, however heinous, can be immediately explained as an automatic response – unfortunate perhaps, but perfectly understandable – to an all-determining 'Western foreign policy.'[38]

The origins of the 'two-campist' worldview lie in the Leninist conceptualisation of 'imperialism' as the 'highest stage' of capitalism.[39] Leaving aside the question of whether it makes any sense to talk of 'stages' of capitalism, as opposed to the categories of commodity, labour and money which remain its essential characteristics, this theory nevertheless became the prism through which much of the left viewed the Cold War. Here it was relatively straightforward to view the world as being split into two categories, each dominated by a single superpower state – the capitalist and thus 'imperialist' United States of America, and the communist and therefore 'anti-imperialist' Soviet Union. The principled 'third-campist' tradition aside, for the substantial section of the international left which opted to take its cues from Moscow, the Soviet 'camp' was to be regarded as innately superior to the American one, notwithstanding its faults, because of its nominally 'Communist' character.[40] Regardless of how oppressive or imperialist the Soviet Union was in practice, it needed to be defended in principle. Loyalty to the position of the Soviet state in any conflict with 'the West' took precedence over any other consideration, including the level of democratic rights and freedoms within that state.

Indeed, the priority given to the geopolitical battle between the 'good' and 'bad' states leaves a two-campist perspective unable to recognise the formal distinction between a state and the people living under it, a distinction that is both necessary for a democratic polity but also an antagonism exposed as such when, as in Syria, a government turns on its citizens and the latter lay claim to the aspiration for a new state altogether. Two-campism captures no such distinction and no such antagonism between states and their peoples. An 'anti-imperialist' state leadership, of whatever political persuasion, and its people are treated as a single, indivisible unit. Two-campists cannot grant legitimacy to any internal struggle for democratic rights and freedoms against a regime deemed to be objectively 'anti-imperialist' – such a struggle must be judged as objectively 'imperialist', staged or influenced from without.[41] The existence of those struggles is therefore generally explained as being the result of 'Western' interference and manipulation.

Nor are differing political factions, tactical disagreements or class contradictions within the 'anti-imperialist' movements or states themselves recognised. All political distinctions are collapsed into the moral sanctity of the singular 'anti-imperialist' identity. This is why Corbyn can extol the reactionary Islamists of Hamas as 'an organisation that is dedicated towards the good of the Palestinian people and bringing about longterm peace and social justice and political justice in the whole region,' despite clear evidence of Hamas's violent repression of the Palestinians living under its rule in Gaza.[42] Such an one-dimensional worldview cannot acknowledge that those struggling for democratic freedoms against an oppressive state deemed 'anti-imperialist' may, at times, seek the solidarity and practical support of those living in the 'imperialist' states – including the provision of weapons, the military enforcement of 'no fly zones' to prevent dictatorial rulers destroying 'their' people, or direct intervention to prevent an ongoing genocide. This possibility is implicitly denied outright by two-campists, genuine international solidarity between peoples dangerously blurring the lines of distinction between 'good' and 'bad' states.

Corbyn's personal brand of two-campism draws more upon the 'third worldist' tradition of the 1960s and 70s 'New Left' than unreconstructed Stalinism. The latter is more the terrain of his advisors Seumas Milne and Andrew Murray.[43] Indeed, Corbyn often remarks that his political outlook was shaped by his two years working in Jamaica as a volunteer youth worker. For its part, the New Left emerged as a response both to the constraints of Stalinist dogma and the singular failure of the proletariat in the Western capitalist economies to develop a revolutionary consciousness. Hopes for revolution were now placed in the movements struggling for independence from the colonial powers, and those post-colonial states which had already achieved liberation. These nationalist movements were now regarded as the true subject of history, while workers in the western colonial states were deemed to be complicit in the oppression of the colonised. As Dave Rich summarises, 'where the Old Left dreamed of class solidarity across nations, the New Left argued that colonialism created an insurmountable framework of conflict between occupiers and occupied'.[44] The role of the left was to take the side of the latter in all circumstances. In this way, the old idea of working class internationalism was replaced by a strict binary of competing nationalisms, some deemed to be inherently progressive, others innately reactionary. The widespread adoption of this fixed schema of eternally 'imperialist' and 'anti-imperialist' nation-states – the rigidity of which risks draining the historical content from 'imperialism' as a concept altogether, particularly when the Russian annexation of Crimea, aggression in Eastern Europe, and involvement in Syria are classed as 'anti-imperialism' – has led to a situation in which anti-imperialism is no longer treated as 'one element in a constellation of democratic principles' but is 'turned into an absolute truth which prevails over all other democratic principles.'[45]

Rejecting the two-campist form of 'anti-imperialism' categorically does not mean denying or exculpating the US for its history of supporting repressive political movements and overthrowing leftist governments. It merely means refusing to oppose such manoeuvres through the uncritical support of equally repressive movements and regimes, purely on the grounds of their professed 'anti-Americanism.' As Marcel Stoetzler argues,

> *those who think that 'imperialism' is a valid*
> *category of analysis still must make any support*
> *dependent on what the social content of any*
> *particular anti-imperialist struggle is: in the*
> *name of which societal goals is the struggle being*
> *conducted?*[46]

STOP THE WAR: THE IRAQ EFFECT

The two strands of two-campism – Stalinist and third worldist – came together in the StWC, which both Corbyn and Murray have chaired. The organisation had its roots in the 'broad front' established by the Socialist Workers Party in opposition to NATO's 1999 intervention to prevent the genocide of Kosovan Albanians by Slobodan Milošević's Serbian forces. This campaign itself was an extension of the 'hard' and extra-parliamentary left's opposition to intervention in Bosnia during the wars that followed the break-up of Yugoslavia in the early 1990s. This wing of the left, with Benn, Corbyn and Seumas Milne playing prominent roles, rejected the view of most analysts that both the Bosnian and Kosovan conflicts

were primarily the result of Serb nationalist aggression laced
with genocidal intent. For this faction, the true cause of the
violence was 'Western' hostility to Yugoslavia, based on the
supposed fact that after the overthrow of Communism in
Eastern Europe, Yugoslavia 'remained the only nation in that
region that would not voluntarily discard what remained of
its socialism and install an unalloyed free market system.'[47]

As Marko Atilla Hoare characterises it, from this 'revisionist left' perspective, 'the US engineered Yugoslavia's destruction and then bombed Serbia in order to bring about the
privatization of its socialized economy.'[48] Milošević's quasi-
fascist belligerence was thus construed as an 'anti-imperialist'
defence of 'socialism'. The fact that Milošević had already
begun a privatisation programme with the help of Conservative Foreign Secretary Douglas Hurd is passed over in silence,
as is 'the West's' effective support for the Serbs throughout
much of the early 1990s via an arms embargo which prevented the Bosnian-Muslims from responding to Bosnian-Serb
aggression, and thus laying the path for the massacres that
followed.[49] The arms embargo was actively supported by the
hard left, including Tony Benn and Diane Abbott.[50]

Within such circles, much time and effort went into downplaying the gravity of Serbian and Bosnian-Serb war crimes,
up to and including the denial of genocide in Kosovo itself.[51]
Using his failsafe logic of *cui bono*, Tony Benn even suggested
that the bombing of a food market in Sarajevo in 1994, which
left 70 dead, could have been a so-called 'false flag' operation
performed by Bosnian-Muslim forces on their own people
in order to smear the Bosnian-Serbs.[52] In 2004 both Corbyn
and McDonnell signed an Early Day Motion 'congratulat[ing]
journalist] John Pilger on his expose of the fraudulent justifica-
tions for intervening in a 'genocide' that never really existed in
Kosovo'.[53] Milne went so far as to conspiratorially claim that
the post-Milošević Serbian administration had 'dug up corpses

to order' at the behest of Western imperial powers, intent on ensuring the conviction of Milošević at the Hague by whatever dubious means necessary.[54] As we shall explore in the final chapter, this kind of pseudocritical, historically revisionist approach to geopolitics is one of the main sites cultivating the potential for a highly dangerous red-brown 'crossover' (or '*querfront*,' as it is known in German leftist terminology) of the hard left and fascist right.[55]

StWC was officially established two weeks after the 9/11 attacks on the World Trade Centre, as a preemptive response to any American reaction. Just over a month after his effective defence of Milošević, Milne gave a glimpse of the direction StWC would come to take. In a reaction piece published two days after 9/11, entitled, somewhat extraordinarily considering what had just happened, 'They do not know why they are hated', he patronised New York 'rescue workers struggl[ing] to pull firefighters from the rubble' for failing to sufficiently appreciate the 'connection between what has been visited upon them and what their government has visited upon large parts of the world.'[56] To this day, the theory that terrorism represents a rational 'blowback' from Western aggression remains Stop the War's automatic explanation for every atrocity. In 2015, for instance, an article on the group's website, swiftly removed once exposed to scrutiny, described the siege of the Bataclan music venue in Paris by jihadist militants, in which 90 gig-goers were shot dead, as France 'reap[ing the] whirlwind of Western support for extremist violence in the Middle East.'[57] This kind of reflexive 'foreign policy determinism' mirrors the more innocuous economic and/or technological determinism which, as we shall see in Chapter 5, characterises orthodox Marxism and has been carried over into both the Bennite and postcapitalist wings of Corbynism.

Initially, Stop the War's myopic response to 9/11 and its opposition to the US invasion of Afghanistan, a campaign

waged in order to topple the Taliban rulers who had
harboured multi-millionaire terrorist Osama Bin Laden, did
not attract support amongst the public beyond those with pre-
existing links to the hard left or Islamist milieus. But Bush and
Blair's decision to pursue 'regime change' in Iraq dramatically
transformed the group's standing. For the broader liberal-left,
Iraq was one cause, at least, that seemed to neatly map onto
the 'two campist' binary. As a consequence, that binary began
to be retrofitted onto all preceding cases, regardless of their
historical specificity. The particular conditions of the Iraq war
were universalised, projected back in time and then used to
dehistoricise all questions of war and intervention against dictatorial and genocidal regimes. The question of international
responsibility for genocide and mass killing was reduced to
a simplistic good/bad morality tale. 'Peaceful' inaction now
became always-already the 'good' response, regardless of the
consequences on the ground. That inaction is itself a conse-
quential action was conveniently set aside.

The resulting dichotomy ironically replicated the equally
rigid and simplistic rhetoric of Bush and Blair on the other
side. Blair in particular generalised his experience in Sierra
Leone and Kosovo and applied the same logic to a very different situation in Iraq, with catastrophic consequences. But
Corbyn's much vaunted 'consistency' when it comes to questions of war and intervention acts in precisely the same way,
implying, were it practically applied, equally catastrophic
results. The refusal to countenance military intervention of
any kind in any circumstances often translates into effective
support for the most brutal of regimes on the grounds of
respecting national sovereignty.[58] This can be seen today in
the way that the question of Syria is seen entirely through
the prism of Iraq, with half a million dead somehow seen as
a triumph for the 'anti-war' movement. The easy option of
inaction is excused with the solipsistic injunction 'not in my

name,' as the chemical and explosive slaughter of civilians by Assad, Putin and ISIS continues.

Iraq therefore became the prism through which the entirety of Benn and Corbyn's brand of two-campism was viewed. Blotting out the sometimes unsavoury political consequences, only the glow of moral righteousness remained. What made the anti-war movement an ideal vehicle for the process of depoliticisation which was to become a crucial factor in Corbyn's leadership prospects was its entirely negative and abstract character. Stop the War was (and remains) a campaign utterly devoid of positive political content. No real interest was shown in the plight of those suffering under Saddam's rule (or that of Gaddafi, Assad or Abu Bakr Al-Baghdadi), and nor were any concrete progressive demands made on Saddam – such as the establishment of liberal freedoms, democratic elections and the like – in exchange for the protestors' opposition to his demise. Tony Benn certainly did not raise the issue of human rights in Iraq during his interview with Saddam shortly before the war, preferring instead to ask him for a message to 'the peace movement of the world that might help to advance the cause they have in mind.'[59] The inverted nationalist message seemed to be that as long as 'we' did not soil our hands, the matter was closed.[60]

The breadth of opposition to the war in Iraq – stretching from the revolutionary left and left-leaning liberals through to Islamic fundamentalists and right-wing isolationist 'paleoconservatives' – was a result of this abstract, dualistic and depoliticised character. The lack of positive demands enabled groups whose political and social perspectives had little in common to set aside their differences and come together to form a singular 'No.' Yet when concerns were raised within the anti-war movement about the reactionary character of some of the groups involved – particularly the more fundamentalist Islamic organisations – they were dismissed by leading member

Lindsey German: 'I'm in favour of defending gay rights,'
she declared. 'But I am not prepared to have it as a shibbo-
leth, [created by] people who ... regard the state of Israel as
somehow a viable presence.'[61] The carving out of this negative
space of empty moralism, in which reactionary alliances were
excused and democratic principles abandoned in the name of
a hollow 'peace' which merely signalled continued repression,
was a vital factor in the increasingly widespread acceptance of
Benn himself as the embodiment of an exceptional moral force
standing above the petty squabbles and squalid compromises
of everyday politics. This, in turn, led the way for a rehabilita-
tion of Bennism by means of Corbyn's similarly effective pitch
as an anti-political politician perched serenely above the fray.

Those anti-war leftists who saw fit to stay within these
bounds of abstract negation, refusing to venture further than
the odd call for a vague, politically meaningless 'peace,' were
able to bask in the warm glow of liberal approval for years
after the war itself. Those who were not content to remain in
the realm of banal platitude risked the loss of their newfound
status as the moral conscience of British politics. This distinction explains why a figure like George Galloway could not
capitalise politically on the benefits accrued from his leading role in the anti-war movement, outside of the communal
Islamist politics found in pockets of East London and Bradford. Galloway's irascible personality was certainly a factor,
contrasting unfavourably with Corbyn's reassuring Benn-
like gentleness. But the main reason Galloway could never
lead Labour to 40% in the polls is because, unlike Corbyn,
Galloway cannot help but follow the logic of his positions
through to concrete political conclusions.[62] He was open
about his explicit support for the campaign of terror inflicted
by the Iraqi 'insurgency' and indeed for Saddam himself, not
to mention an endless series of other authoritarian dictators

and theocratic regimes. With ugly results, Galloway refuses to depoliticise his politics by eschewing positive proposals.

That said, the logic of Corbyn's positions on foreign policy often points to the same conclusions as Galloway, the same *de facto* support for some of the most brutal regimes in the world. Indeed, Corbyn defended in Parliament a post-invasion StWC motion which supported the 'legitimacy of the struggle of Iraqis, *by whatever means they find necessary*' – means which at that point included jihadi suicide bomb attacks on queues of Iraqi civilians, the murder of Iraqi trade unionists, and the kidnapping and beheading of hostages.[63] But, in the main, whether through act or omission, Corbyn has invariably kept his rhetoric to the more politically-amenable territory of a generic concern for 'peace' or 'dialogue.'

The advantage that Corbyn has over his fellow travellers when it comes to appealing to a broad audience is thus the very thing that had led Milne to once deem him 'wholly unsuited' for the task of leadership: genial vagueness, rote platitudinousness, uselessness with specifics.[64] Where others around him ground their politics in specific claims and commitments that can be verified and contested, Corbyn is far harder to pin down. There is a certain naiveté – whether spontaneous or studied – to both Corbyn's manner of expression and its content. He generally prefers the quiet, simplistic homilies of 'common sense' and 'decency' rather than the fist-thumping polemics beloved by traditional leftist leaders. There is no doubt that Corbyn communicates his worldview with brilliant simplicity, particularly in one-on-one interviews. Indeed, the underestimation of his ability to do so was one reason for the abject failure of the challenges mounted against him by both his internal Labour rivals and the Conservative election campaign. The beauty of his natural tendency to pitch arguments at a level of childlike innocence is that their very meaninglessness makes them virtually impossible to contest. Who can possibly be against 'peace' or 'decency'? Corbyn is thus able to disguise the true consequences of his political positions, in a way that John McDonnell, for example, honouring the 'bombs and the bullets' of the IRA, can or will not.[65] Corbyn can sidestep every attempt to pin him down while retaining the veneer of moral infallibility that was crucial to his rise to power.

~~~

The next chapter will explore how the specific narrative of Corbyn's own exceptional integrity emerged from this background during his first leadership campaign. It shows how the tale of Corbyn's moral exceptionality was pieced together from a patchwork of apochrypha, anecdotes and photographs from his past, each abstracted from their historical context and transformed into moral fables whose relation to the truth became increasingly tenuous. The power generated by this mythical, nostalgic image of Corbyn as always-already 'on the right side of history' carried over into the General Election campaign itself.[66] As already noted, it led to the left giving him far more political room for manoeuvre than that granted to his predecessors. And it enabled him to deflect, with remarkable ease, every criticism of his long-standing associations with assorted authoritarian, antisemitic and theocratic groups and individuals. Evidence of Corbyn's dubious connections failed to move those on the liberal-left who might be thought reticent to back someone who regards Hezbollah or Hamas as 'friends'.[67] This was in no small part due to the way that Corbyn's history was rewritten by his supporters in order to sanitise and retrospectively vindicate every decision he had made.

The willingness of much of the liberal or 'soft' left to fall into step with Corbyn once the 'electability' question was settled in his favour, overlooking his past associations and implicitly lending their approval to this historical revisionism, raises some troubling questions. It suggests that the tendency to forgo the processes by which ideas and actions are rationally appraised according to their content and consequences, and to replace them by a form of prejudgment based solely on the presumed identity of those expressing them, is by no means reserved for the Manichean worldviews of the 'revisionist left' or the Brexiteer hard-right. It is now the dominant standpoint of contemporary politics *tout court*. This, we contend, holds disconcerting implications for the future of liberal and social-democratic political norms. Understanding the role of Corbyn's mythical reputation is crucial not only in order to account for his startling success. It is also vital for what it reveals about the theoretical basis of Corbynism as a distinct set of ideas, and its relation to the current political conjuncture as a whole.

3

ON THE RIGHT SIDE OF HISTORY: THE MORAL MYTHOLOGY OF CORBYNISM

As we saw in the last chapter, the abstract, politically vacant character of the anti-war movement allowed the hard left to claim the moral high ground during the 2000s. It was a perfect vehicle for Corbyn's own brand of homespun moralistic commonplaces. Equally important, however, was the seemingly terminal weakness of the hard left when it came to positive political action. Had the Bennite wing of the party retained power throughout the 1990s and 2000s, had their policies been tested in practice rather than merely idealised in theory, their platform would not have accrued the aura of unquestionable moral authority that was fundamental to Corbyn's success. Even the most successful governments end in failure. Choices would have been made, unexpected consequences suffered, plans unravelled, hopes disappointed. Nor would the right of the party have allowed the political content of Corbyn's Bennite platform – as opposed to merely its supposed lack of 'electability' – to go unchallenged.

But as it was, the fragility of the Bennite left after its final defeat, signalled by Benn's risible performance in his 1988 challenge against Neil Kinnock's leadership, was such that by the early noughties, the substance of the original dispute over his particular vision of 'socialism', a dispute which was not based primarily on morality but rather arose from fundamentally different political worldviews, was lost in a haze of nostalgia and post-Iraq sentimentalism. The sepia-tinged image of the gentle, unfailingly polite Tony Benn was the means through which the hard left's isolationism and protectionism shapeshifted into a set of charmingly idealistic principles whose only flaw was the unfortunate fact of their electoral unpopularity. And it was this image that Corbyn inherited when he stood for Labour leader.

It is highly doubtful that Corbyn would have even made it onto the ballot for the 2015 leadership election, Iraq or no Iraq, had he – and the 'hard left' in general – been viewed in terms of genuine political power, rather than as the unthreatening residue of a long-gone era. True, the PLP still contained a smattering of MPs who doggedly adhered to belief that Labour loses because it is not left enough. Corbyn among them, these elements coalesced around the parliamentary Socialist Campaign Group and general membership Labour Representation Committee. But for the vast majority of their parliamentary colleagues, these veterans of yesterday's battles were no longer to be feared but patronisingly patted on the head. There was a feeling that this heritage brand of old-school socialism should at least be granted the opportunity to 'broaden' a debate they had already and definitively lost, as centrist MPs put it when lending Corbyn the nominations necessary to get him on the ballot.[1]

The precedent for 'broadening the debate' in a leadership contest had been set in 2010, when frontrunner David Miliband donated a handful of spare PLP nominations to the left candidate Diane Abbott. But on that occasion Abbott barely received seven per cent of the vote. This time, of course, it would be different – primarily, although not wholly, due to the influx of 'registered supporters' drawn from the wider anti-austerity movement who flooded into the 'selectorate,' stumping up £3 specifically to vote for Corbyn. The introduction of the 'registered supporter' scheme had, ironically enough, been a reform touted by the right of the party as a means to dilute the influence of the trade unions.[2] It aimed to make the party more responsive to 'moderate' voters rather than the more radical activists. To say this idea backfired would be an understatement. But Corbyn did not win the leadership election solely on the back of the support of the £3 entryists. He also won nearly 50% of the vote from the longer-term membership, those same members who in 2010 had narrowly favoured David Miliband, the anointed heir to the now hated Tony Blair – trumped only by the trade union preference for his brother.

Why had Abbott done so poorly in 2010 and yet, a mere few years later, Corbyn destroyed the rest of the field? Abbott suffers the worst racist and misogynist abuse of any serving British MP, receiving a third of all abuse sent to politicians in the UK, so much so that her staff send a bundle to police each week.[3] The prejudices to which Abbott is subject as a successful black woman should not be discounted as a factor behind the poor performance of her leadership campaign. But the divergence between the left's performance in 2010 compared to 2015 within the longer-term membership was so large that it cannot be easily explained by this uncomfortable prospect, nor by dint of reference to a radically transformed selectorate alone. Nor can it be entirely put down to Corbyn's role in the anti-war movement and the spread of 'two campist' anti-Americanism across the liberal left we have charted in the previous chapter. In short, these were necessary, but insufficient, preconditions. They held a latent power that could only be unlocked in a particular configuration of political factors specific to post-crash Britain.

~~~

The final crucial precondition for Corbyn's victory arrived with the particularly moralistic way in which the broad liberal-left came to terms with both the 2008 financial crash and the Tory programme of public spending cuts that followed. As we have seen, both the austerity narrative and its anti-austerity antagonist had implicitly suggested that the solution to this sorry situation was the removal of those unproductive elements – whether 'scroungers,' 'immigrants,' or 'the banks' – who had undermined the vitality of the productive national community. What was needed was someone or something with the strength to enact this removal and restore the community back to health. The desire for a Corbyn-like figure existed long before his eventual arrival onto the scene.

The symbolic space he was to fill had been carved out in negative by the economic and political collapse of the preceding years, and the productivist narratives utilised to explain it. He was the beneficiary, not the instigator, of this shift. But it was because this broader movement was based on an essentially moral critique of both capitalism and politics that Corbyn's standing in what was now a thoroughly romanticised 'hard left,' guaranteed by his specific personal qualities, made him an unwittingly perfect candidate to take advantage of this development. In the post-Iraq, post-crash, post-austerity context of 2015, the contrast his supporters were able to draw between his authenticity—'straight talking, honest politics,' as he put it in his stump speech – and the craven conformity of his opponents was electoral dynamite.[4] Here was someone who gets it. He was undoubtedly helped by the paucity of the rest of the field – Andy Burnham's unconvincing claims to Northern 'authenticity', Yvette Cooper's robotic bromides, Liz Kendall's antagonism of a leftwards-listing selectorate. But underpinning it all was the depoliticised image of moral exceptionalism that Corbyn – and Corbyn alone, not Galloway, not Abbott, not McDonnell – had inherited from Tony Benn. It had to be him.

Once the MPs who had patronisingly 'donated' their nominations to Corbyn realised their mistake, it was too late.[5] The PLP's desperate and increasingly ludicrous attempts to dislodge Corbyn during his disastrous first twelve months in charge were fuelled by the genuine fear that their arrogance would see the contemptuous verdict of the British electorate come crashing down upon the Labour Party, in such a way that it might never recover. The problem they faced was that, thanks to the now-dominant romantic image of the hard left as the custodians of the party's 'real values', the only thing they had to fall back on was the 'electability' gambit. They had lost the means to critique the practical content of the hard left prospectus, precisely because their own arrogance had allowed it to attain an image of moral purity that somehow existed on a higher plane than that of mundane politics.

Among politicians, Tony Blair, ironically enough given his caricatured reputation as a politician who discarded principle for power, was one of only a few who made any serious attempt to criticise the substance of Corbyn's politics. Privileging analysis over electoral calculation, Blair went so far as to say that he 'wouldn't want to win on an old-fashioned leftist platform. Even if I thought it was the route to victory, I wouldn't take it'.[6] For the rest of the party, however, the problem seemed to lie with the electorate, not Corbynism. They would never go for it; if only they would. Such meagre utilitarian arguments were never likely to move those parts of the membership enchanted by Corbyn's purported integrity. After all, if 'electability', rather than policy, was the only problem with Corbyn's leadership, why make it worse by undermining him? The uncritical acceptance of the depoliticised, moralised image of Corbyn therefore meant that his critics fell into a trap of their own making, one from which they are still struggling and failing to escape. Indeed, most have now given up entirely.

THE MAKING OF A SAINT

More than anything else, Corbyn's campaign for the leadership was driven by the belief he had always been on 'the right side of history'.[7] In addition to Iraq, this narrative was constructed out of a series of historical photographs and events from Corbyn's political career which were interpreted in such a way as to demonstrate his extraordinary integrity and political prescience. While each story contained a kernel of truth, when repositioned in its proper context, reality rarely lived up to the legend. But the truth was not really the point. What was important was what those stories represented – the hope, the possibility, of a politics and a world free of contradiction, conflict and compromise. The symbolic space that had been carved out long before his decision to run for leader began to overdetermine reality. In this way, Corbyn's life was transformed into a series of moral fables, the meaning of which now existed on a symbolic plane high above petty squabbles over whether they actually took place or not.

One such fable was based on an expenses claim that Corbyn had filed in 2010, the year after the parliamentary expenses scandal – an emotionally powerful reference point, not least because it was there that the anti-political wave that helped carry Corbyn to prominence began to break. It was said Corbyn had filed the lowest expenses of any MP, claiming a mere £8.70 for an ink cartridge. His supporters were quick to use this to frame Corbyn as a man who represented a complete rupture from what had come before, an MP whose 'parsimoniousness', in his own words, cast an unforgiving light on the rapacious greed of the rest of the political class. The truth was somewhat less sententious. It turned out that Corbyn had not filed the expenses for the running of his office. Once he did so, his expense claim sat somewhere in the middle of the MPs table. A moment's thought would have made clear that if Corbyn actually had only spent £8.70, he would have not have been able to do his job. But that would risk dissolving the illusion. Corbyn as symbol took precedence over reality. The story took on a life of its own.[8]

Another story centred upon a photograph taken in 1984 of a young Corbyn being arrested outside South Africa House. Around his neck hangs a sign with the message 'Defend the Right to Demonstrate Against Apartheid / Join This Picket.' The picture went viral, gaining iconic status amongst his supporters, who endlessly pointed to it as evidence of Corbyn's willingness to swim against the political tide. Here was irrefutable proof of Corbyn's lifelong commitment to causes once deemed unfashionable, but now regarded as inarguable. But once again, the truth was somewhat different. Corbyn's support for the anti-apartheid movement is not in dispute. But he was by no means a lone voice. By the mid-80s, virtually the entire labour movement had adopted a stringent anti-apartheid stance. And Corbyn was by no means the most active or influential participant next to other Labour figures like Peter Hain, a minister in successive New Labour governments who was recognised by the post-apartheid South African state honours system for his record of non-violent direct action in the campaign against apartheid.[9]

Moreover, a closer reading of the sign around Corbyn's neck indicates that he was not actually arrested for protesting against apartheid, but rather for protesting *for the right to protest against it in a particular way*. The demonstration Corbyn had attended was against a court ruling banning a 24-hour rolling picket outside the South African Embassy. The ruling was being challenged in the courts by the main

Anti-Apartheid Movement (AAM). The AAM had official links with the African National Congress (ANC), itself heavily influenced by the unreconstructed Stalinists of the South African Communist Party, and tended to discourage street protests against apartheid in the UK.[10] Corbyn's arrest took place at a splinter protest organised by the City of London Anti-Apartheid Group (CLAAG). Corbyn and CLAAG's intransigence regarding the picket, and the wider challenge to the AAM's leadership of the anti-apartheid movement it presented, drew the wrath of a young Seumas Milne, who argued in the *Guardian* that the CLAAG had 'flouted' the authority of the AAM.[11] The CLAAG was duly expelled from the AAM the year after Corbyn's arrest.

Once the image of Corbyn is placed in its proper context, the story that emerges is not then that of 'a lone man, prescient in his opposition to the evil apartheid regime', but rather of a participant in an internecine power struggle between different strands of the hard and revolutionary left.[12] This does not mean that Corbyn's actions were without moment – such a challenge to the rigid structures of residual Stalinism may be one of the few occasions he has been willing to critically appraise the internal politics of an anti-imperialist movement. But this story is a far cry from that of the heroic figure single-handedly fighting apartheid in the face of universal opposition. For his supporters, it seems, the proper context of the photograph is neither here nor there. What matters is the iconography, the mythology, the absolute break with a tainted history that they want the image to represent.

A similar pattern was visible in the third key myth which powered Corbyn's leadership victory. This was based on a parliamentary vote that took place during the contest itself. In July 2015, barely six weeks after Cameron's shock election victory on a pro-austerity ticket, the Conservatives introduced a 'welfare reform and work' bill. This set out £12bn of cuts from the welfare spend, including real terms reductions to many in-work benefits. In the mythologised version of this story, the three other Labour leadership candidates, and 181 of their cowardly 'Blairite' colleagues, refused to vote against this brutal act of Tory austerity and instead abstained. Only Corbyn dared to stand up against both the Conservatives and the 'Red Tories' within his own ranks. Before the abstention on the welfare bill, Corbyn's campaign had been gently gathering pace. After he became the only candidate to vote against the bill at the second reading, things really started to move.

Once again, there is an element of truth to this tale. Labour had just heavily lost an election dominated by the austerity-populist 'scrounger' narrative. George Osborne intended to exacerbate Labour's travails by simultaneously cutting benefits and raising the minimum wage, hoping that Labour opposition to the former would cement their image as the party of scroungers, in contrast to the Conservatives' new-found status as what the Tory MP Robert Halfon called the 'worker's party'.[13] Interim leader Harriet Harman was wary of casting Labour even further into the electoral wilderness. In her mind, not opposing the bill – one that Labour would not be able to stop in any case, due to the new Tory majority – would act as a means of neutralising the issue for the new leader, and prevent Labour from being caught on the wrong side of Cameron and Osborne's populist divide.[14]

Unsurprisingly, for most Labour supporters this looked like moral collapse. Harman's decision thrust the party into a state of all-out war. Eventually the shadow cabinet agreed a compromise position. Labour would propose a series of amendments which, if passed, would effectively kill the bill. If not, they would abstain in the second reading, try to alter the bill in committee, and if it was still not satisfactory, vote against the bill in the third and final reading. This they then did. Corbyn, never one to worry unduly about party loyalty or collective responsibility – at that point at least – abstained on Labour's amendments, and then voted against the bill on the second reading.

Corbyn's supporters have made hay with this story ever since. And yet, as so often with Corbyn mythology, there is something of a double standard at work. Labour's 2017 election manifesto, as we have seen, was weighed down with spending commitments. But there was one strange omission. The manifesto does not mention the benefit cap. Nor does it refer to the benefits freeze, let alone promise to reverse it. The very issue that was instrumentalised to such great effect during Corbyn's leadership campaign, ruthlessly utilised to demonstrate that Corbyn was not merely politically but *morally* superior to the rest of the field, disappeared entirely when it came to the electoral crunch.[15]

Did Corbyn himself decide to cynically 'abstain' on the issue, draining the power from the Tories' 'scroungers' party' rhetoric by effectively capitulating on welfare, much as accepting the end of free movement 'de-weaponised' immigration? A more generous reading is that Corbyn's team simply forgot to include it, an impression given by Corbyn himself. When questioned about the lack of welfare policy, he said that benefits would, of course, be uprated in line with inflation. And yet, just hours later, he was contradicted by his Shadow Foreign Secretary Emily Thornberry, who said that 'I don't think we can reverse it entirely. We shouldn't be promising things we can't afford.'[16] The lack of a welfare policy has also been retrospectively justified on the grounds that other changes in the manifesto – such as a rise in the minimum wage and the building of council housing – would reduce the benefit bill and make the cap irrelevant. A fair argument, no doubt – and the precise one made, ironically enough, by the most reviled of Corbyn's rivals for the Labour leadership, the 'arch-Blairite' Liz Kendall. When questioned about her support for the benefit cap, Kendall replied that she wanted Labour to

> *face head-on the issues of welfare reform. I don't want to see £30 billion of taxpayers' money spent on tax credits subsidising low pay employers. We've got to have a living wage society. I don't want to see £27 billion going on housing benefit. I want to see that money going on investment in building new homes.*[17]

At the time the expression of such sentiments stood for all Corbyn had come to contest. Now, they are the *de facto* position of the party itself – a compromise only Corbyn has the political capital to pull off.

'ALL FORMS OF RACISM'

One of the most serious challenges to the rampant dehistoricisation and mythologisation of Corbyn's political past are the accusations that, as the *Daily Mail* put it, the Labour leader is an 'apologist for terror.'[18] It is fair to say that, up to now, this allegation has had scant purchase among the liberal left. Perhaps this is because of the dissonance between the actions such accusations scrutinise and Corbyn's genial demeanour and reputation for being 'on the right side of history.'[19]

Nonetheless, there are two aspects behind the accusation of 'terror apologism' that, beyond right-wing spin, say something about Corbyn, where he comes from and the character of the political movement constructed around him. Firstly, the attacks focus on the relationships Corbyn had struck up with various groups and individuals in the name of a variety of 'anti-imperialist' struggles, particularly but not only with regard to his role in Stop the War and career-long 'anti-Zionist' support for the Palestinian cause. Secondly, they centre on his association with Sinn Fein and the IRA during the 1980s and 1990s.

With regard to the question of Israel and Palestine, Corbyn has never explicitly denied Jewish people the right of self-determination, nor denounced Israel's right to exist – although he has caveated his support for a two-state solution on the grounds that 'at the moment,' it is 'all that's on offer'.[20] Either way, he has certainly spent much time in the company of those whose 'anti-Zionism' regularly spills over into the demonisation of Israel and the delegitimisation of the very concept of a Jewish state, if not outright antisemitism and Holocaust denial.[21] As a Corbyn victory in the 2015 leadership election began to look likely, this history led the *Jewish Chronicle* to ask him a series of questions about his links to the more dubious end of the anti-Zionist movement that shed light on exactly what was at stake in the by now familiar refrains about Corbyn's unsavoury associations.[22]

The paper asked: why had he donated money to a charity run by a Holocaust-denier, Paul Eisen; why had he defended a church minister, Steven Sizer, who had alleged that 9/11 was an Israeli plot, on the grounds that Sizer was only criticised because he had 'dared to speak out over Zionism,'; why had he described as 'friends' the Iranian-backed Lebanese terror group Hezbollah – responsible, amongst much else, for the 1994 suicide bombing of a Jewish community centre in Buenos Aires which killed 84 people; why had he argued that Hamas, the authoritarian rulers of the Gaza strip whose founding charter calls for the destruction of Israel and the murder of all Jews, were 'dedicated towards the good of the Palestinian people and bringing about long term peace and social justice and political justice in the whole region'; why had he failed to condemn the antisemitic banners carried during the annual Iranian-run Al Quds march, co-sponsored by Stop the War; why had he described the Palestinian leader Raed Salah as an 'honoured citizen,' inviting him for 'tea on the [House of Commons] terrace' after Salah had been convicted for 'blood libel' – accusing Jews of baking bread with children's blood, a medieval antisemitic conspiracy theory. Corbyn's answers were that he could not remember donating money, didn't realise Eisen was a Holocaust denier, nor Sizer antisemitic, and that he was only being 'diplomatic' when referring to Hezbollah and Hamas as 'friends', and to Salah as an 'honoured citizen.'

For many of Corbyn's supporters, however, the accusations of – at best – Corbyn's inability to recognise when criticism of Israel spilled over into antisemitism, conspiracy thinking and even Holocaust denial were nothing but a politically-motivated 'smear' aimed at destroying Corbyn's good name. Each time allegations were made, either against Corbyn himself or Labour party members expressing similar views, they were dismissed as cynical plots to bring Corbyn down. Unite leader Len McCluskey described the allegations as 'mood music...created by people who were trying to undermine Jeremy Corbyn.'[23] Diane Abbott argued that it was 'a smear to say that the Labour party had a problem with antisemitism,' while Corbyn-hardliner Chris Williamson MP described the complaints as a 'really dirty, low-down trick' in which antisemitism had been '[weaponised] for political ends.'[24] Corbyn himself described one article on the topic by *The Guardian's* Jonathan Freedland as 'utterly disgusting, subliminal nastiness.'[25] Ironically, Freedland's article had outlined precisely the analysis of left-wing antisemitism that Corbyn himself was to belatedly adopt – at least rhetorically – when the crisis reached boiling point two years later.[26]

For his supporters, Corbyn's reputation as a life-long campaigner against 'all forms of racism,' as Corbyn routinely put it, meant that it was inconceivable he could have been antisemitic, wittingly or unwittingly. Just as 'anti-imperialist' states and leaders were objectively progressive, regardless of their commitment to democratic values or social equality, so too does the logic work the other way around. Given that Corbyn is objectively 'anti-racist', as proven by the anti-apartheid picture, he cannot, therefore, *in principle*, be susceptible himself to entertaining racism, even accidentally. Any allegations that say otherwise can only be politically-motivated 'smears'. Such a defence extends to all those deemed to belong to the 'community of the good.' Owen Jones leapt to the defence of Labour and Momentum activist Jackie Walker after she was suspended by the party for claiming that Jews 'were the chief financiers of the [transatlantic] sugar and slave trade,' an antisemitic conspiracy theory originating with the Nation of Islam.[27] Jones called for people to 'protest against the outrageous suspension of Jackie Walker from the Labour Party on spurious grounds of anti-Semitism,' and justified his support on the grounds that he had 'known Jackie's partner Graham Bash for many years: he's a socialist Jewish activist with decades of political involvement. The idea he or she are anti-Semitic is just beyond ludicrous.'[28] For Jones the fact that he regarded Walker as a member of the 'community of the good' meant that there was no need to critically examine her statement to see whether it was antisemitic or not. As a longstanding 'socialist activist,' it was objectively impossible for her to have been antisemitic, and that was the end of the matter. Corbyn seemingly agreed, as he appeared on a platform with Walker a few months after her statement and while she was still suspended by the party.[29]

This kind of response amounts to what David Hirsh describes as a 'politics of position' – a politics concerned more 'with the 'objective' position of a person or a group, in a fixed and essentialist schema, than with what that person or group says or does.'[30] Here a prescribed and prejudged identity trumps the process of rational debate, critique or the building of solidarity across 'categories.' It is precisely this form of ahistorical, identity-driven anti-politics which marks the populist space shared by Brexit and Corbynism. And it proved to be a highly effective first line of defence during the 2017 campaign when it came to fending off allegations of antisemitism and at least proximity to, if not support for, various groups engaging in indiscriminate violence against civilians.

Indeed, the power of Corbyn's image is such that even on those rare occasions when he admits fault, many of his supporters refuse to accept even his own self-criticism. Thus when the concerns about antisemitism finally came to a head after revelations of Corbyn's active involvement in an anti-Zionist Facebook group which had regularly posted antisemitic and Holocaust denying materials were swiftly followed by the reemergence of a story about his support for an antisemitic graffiti artist – Corbyn's acknowledgement that 'anti-semitic attitudes' had 'surfaced more often' within Labour 'in recent years' was rejected by a sizeable chunk of his own base.[31] Instead they doubled down on the previous line that accusations of antisemitism were politically-motivated 'smears,' aimed at both discrediting Corbyn and deflecting criticism of Israel.[32] Corbyn's symbolic representation thus takes precedence even over the words from his own mouth. This illustrates how Corbynism has relative autonomy from Corbyn, but all the same cannot exist or survive without his image at the centre, holding things together. It also demonstrates how, once unleashed, the sentimental energies that power an identitarian 'politics of position' can rapidly spiral out of the control of those trying to channel them to their own ends, with unpredictable consequences.

BOTH SIDES

Corbyn's support for a united Ireland was just as legitimate as his support for Palestinian statehood. But, on Ireland, it was once again the particular way he expressed this support that was at stake. The media claim was that Corbyn had unequivocally sided with Sinn Fein and the Provisional IRA while it was actively engaged in a bombing campaign both in Northern Ireland and on the British mainland. Examples were in plentiful supply. It was reported that Corbyn had been on the editorial board of the magazine *Labour Briefing* when it published an editorial which effectively condoned the IRA's bombing of the Conservative Party conference hotel at Brighton in 1984, on the grounds that 'the British only sit up and take notice when they are bombed into it.'[33] Two weeks later Corbyn invited Gerry Adams, the head of Sinn Fein, and two former IRA prisoners to Parliament.

The next year Corbyn voted against the Anglo-Irish Agreement, the precursor to the Good Friday Agreement, following the Sinn Fein line that, regardless of the opportunity for peace, it made the prospect of a united Ireland less likely. And in 1996, a year in which the Provisional IRA bombed both Manchester and the London Docklands, Corbyn was condemned 'unreservedly' by Mo Mowlam – Secretary of State for Northern Ireland during the crucial moments of the Good Friday process – for again inviting Gerry Adams to Parliament.[34] Corbyn did, in the event, vote in favour of the Good Friday Agreement, once again following the Sinn Fein line. John McDonnell did too, though he initially opposed the negotiations which led to the Agreement, rejecting the idea of a power-sharing assembly up until the point that the IRA changed tack and accepted the deal.[35]

Corbyn's response to these accusations was that he was merely attempting to engage in 'dialogue' with Sinn Fein and the IRA as a means to engender peace. Corbyn's critics asserted that the fact this 'dialogue' took place while the bombing campaign was ongoing, rather than being premised on its cessation, as well as his complete lack of engagement with the SDLP and the non-violent wing of the Republican movement – let alone the Unionists – suggest that his commitment was not so much to peace, nor even republicanism in the broadest sense, but rather an IRA victory. Either way, this episode is only one example of Corbyn's reliance on 'dialogue' as his go-to get-out-clause from grappling with the complexity of world affairs.

~~~

To explore further the consequences of this concern with 'dialogue', we might reflect on more recent events. The solution to the Syrian crisis, Corbyn has repeatedly suggested, is the continuation of a peace talks process long discredited by Russia's violently assertive stance in shoring up Bashar Al-Assad and the unthinkable human consequences of a 'political' resolution that kept any part of Assad's fascist regime in place.[36] Corbyn's protestations of the 'legality' of targeted air strikes enforcing the international prohibition of chemical weapons rests on the assumption that the UN, a body whose efficacy is hamstrung by the continual use of Russia's veto to obstruct humanitarian action, should be the arbiter of what is right or wrong.[37] Interestingly, left 'legalism' when it comes to foreign policy may be juxtaposed with a countervailing left tendency to otherwise dispute the legitimacy of 'bourgeois' law. As Michael Walzer asserts, this belief in legal 'reasonableness' often militates against a more radical position of 'mutual assistance'.[38] It sometimes seems that the legalistic and apparently pacifistic belief in pursuing peace through diplomatic channels, without the implicit or explicit guarantee of military intervention to back it up, is a convenient alibi for a policy that in reality enables international law to be routinely ignored.

Rather than grappling with the contradiction inherent in trying to enforce international law through a body partly composed of the very forces breaking it, as well as the problem that the only 'legal' voice an oppressed people has within the UN is invariably that of the regime oppressing them, Corbyn and the StWC faction simply ignore the issue altogether. Assad is therefore empowered to wage a war against the Syrian population aided and abetted by the same imperialist power responsible for rendering legal order ineffective at the UN level – Putin's Russia. Despite Russia's persistent use of the veto to protect the Assad regime from intervention to protect civilians, Corbyn continually centres his criticism on the use of the veto by 'both sides' – a slick argumentative tic that all but implicates the United States as the cause of Syria's misery, contrary to all evidence.[39]

If a statement of blunt good faith, the call for a solution sanctioned through the UN effectively demands Russian agreement and involvement in a solution to a problem for which Russia itself must take a large part of blame. But a more circumspect reading would suggest that Corbyn knows full well no such agreement is possible, and the call allows a claim of a concern that something should be done whilst *de facto* calling for nothing to be done at all.

This reflexive rhetorical cloak of 'dialogue' performs a similar role when it comes to Corbyn's preoccupation with the conflict between Israel and Palestine. As with his 'dialogue' with Sinn Fein and the IRA during their bombing campaign, Corbyn defends his friendly relations with Hamas on the grounds that a peace process means 'you have to talk to people with whom you may profoundly disagree.'[40] This is a legitimate position, but it appears the groups with whom Corbyn 'profoundly disagrees' when it comes to the Middle East are not Palestinian but rather Israeli - and, for one reason or another, Corbyn routinely rejects invitations to meet Israeli politicians and ambassadors. He failed to attend the Labour Friends of Israel party conference event in 2017, rejected the chance to meet Israeli Prime Minister Benjamin Netanyahu – surely the very epitome of a person with whom Corbyn profoundly disagrees – at a dinner to mark the centenary of the Balfour Declaration, and even turned down an invitation from the Israeli Labour Party to visit the Yad Vashem Holocaust museum in Jerusalem.[41]

Corbyn is perfectly entitled to refuse to meet the representatives of any state or party, of course – not least, in the case of Netanyahu, when they are responsible for the kind of state violence being meted out against mostly unarmed protestors at the time this book was being written. But it is the unevenness with which the rule is applied that stands out. Corbyn, for instance, met with Assad in 2009 at a time where the Syrian regime's repressive apparatus was already well in evidence, and having colluded with the US rendition and 'torture by proxy' of terror suspects to which Corbyn has been implacably – and admirably – opposed.[42]

Corbyn's commitment to 'dialogue' thus speaks from two sides of the same mouth: promising peace whilst at once offering cover for the continuation of armed conflict by whichever 'anti-imperialist' force fits the frame – even where, as in the case of Russia's involvement with Syria, or its annexation of Crimea, the frame of imperialism might be employed more productively with reference to that 'anti-imperialist' force itself. The pacifism is genuine insofar as he does not seem to see the violence of some states or groups as significant in itself, however terroristic or genocidal, but only that for which one side of the 'campist' divide is responsible. The demand for 'dialogue' allows Corbyn the walk this line, and with him, his supporters. This masquerade of a concern with avoiding conflict is too often effectively cover for a policy that extends it.

As evidenced in Corbyn's consistent attempt to assert that chemical weapons abuses in Syria are the consequence of actions by 'many sides' of the conflict, blaming 'both sides' frequently tips the scales towards the aggressor – protecting those with primary responsibility for violence by blurring the lines and sharing the blame, something Corbyn seems happy to do so long as the violence comes from those states who stand on the 'right' side of the 'two-campist' divide. Thus when chemical weapons are used by Assad in Syria, Corbyn refuses to attribute responsibility until an 'independent investigation' 'find[s] out who did it,' in this way casting doubt on the clear evidence of the regime's culpability.[43] Yet when a previous joint UN Organisation for the Prohibition of Chemical Weapons investigation confirmed that the Assad regime was responsible for a 2017 chemical attack in Khan Sheikhoun, Corbyn did not even respond, let alone change his position in response to the report's conclusions – despite having called for an investigation in the immediate aftermath of the attack.[44] Similarly, there was no comment forthcoming with regard to the Assad regime's savage destruction of the Palestinian refugee camp in Yarmouk, nor the 3700 Palestinians reported to have been killed in Syria since the beginning of the civil war - far more, it must be said, than had been killed by Israel in the same period.[45] By contrast, when it comes to violence from those on the 'imperialist' side of the ledger, particularly Israel, Corbyn has no problem immediately (and often quite correctly) condemning it by name, without waiting for an 'independent investigation.'[46]

The idea that the real divide between oppressors and oppressed could run *through* states and their populations and not only *between* them is never considered in this two-campist schema. Hence, the sovereignty of Syria and the Assad regime are to be respected above and beyond the violent war it wages against the people who by dint of birth belong to the citizenry of that state. The sovereignty of the state is seen as synonymous with that of the people who live within it, regardless of how antagonistic, undemocratic or even genocidal the relationship between the two. The state is to be secured and saved, in spite of its citizenry. This runs against the grain of any truly internationalist understanding of a universal and cosmopolitan global humanity, united across borders by a common set of rights and solidarities and, crucially, a 'shared capacity for suffering'.[47] It is this pessimistic form of universalism which lies at the root of Judith Shklar's concept of the 'liberalism of fear.' Shklar's defence of liberalism, and in particular the separation of state and society, or public and private spheres, is built upon scepticism towards utopian political projects which purport to act in the name of a *summum bonum*, the highest good. Instead she argues that freedom rests on the recognition of a *summum malum*, the greatest evil: 'that evil is cruelty and the fear it inspires, and the very fear of fear itself. To that extent the liberalism of fear makes a universal and especially a cosmopolitan claim.'[48]

Instead of this expansive understanding of human community, built upon the negative baseline of the universal fear of cruelty, we see in Corbynism a defence of the sanctity of the nation-state shared with the abstractly anti-imperialist and 'anti-war' trad-left which forms its principal political constituency. Here the world is seen as one comprising impenetrable national borders any force claiming an international or global legitimacy cannot reasonably contravene, even in an attempt to avert the greatest of evils. Whereas Corbynism has been critiqued, specifically by Blue Labour, for not taking the nation seriously and basing its politics on a borderless global world, in fact, the opposite is true.[49] Corbynism, like Blue Labour, focuses too on the nation-state as the irreducible agent of political action.

For when it comes to foreign policy, Corbynism's key principle is that the sovereignty of a state cannot be infringed, regardless of whether groups within the country have called for assistance or multilateral consent granted.[50] By refusing to acknowledge legitimate claims for international assistance by the people crushed under tyrants like Assad, Corbyn's stated commitment to 'dialogue' between states as the central geopolitical actors therefore masks the fact that he actually goes out of his way to *avoid* the political processes which might provide some resolution to the conflicts he condemns. Not only does he lack any practical experience of such processes – which might go some way to explaining his obliviousness as to why the multiple previous rounds of talks on Syria have failed – but the apparently uncontroversial moral platitudes he offers are not tantamount to politics, but rather serve to foreclose the latter. When translated into practical terms, this anti-political approach to 'dialogue' does little to further any peace process. Indeed it often does nothing but block it.

~~~

The reactionary implications of Corbyn's rhetorical demands for 'dialogue' have not prevented the cultivation of a public image of a peacemaker and pacifist hero. Here, as in so much else, moral perfection steps in for practical politics. For Corbyn's most fervent supporters, the practical process through which a fragile peace was actually achieved in Northern Ireland – culminating in the 1998 Good Friday Agreement, the Blair government's greatest triumph – is of no real importance. The only question of interest is the extent to which Corbyn can be credited with it. Thus social media posts responded to the 'smears' about Corbyn's unconditional support for Sinn Fein and the IRA by insisting that such support was not merely the equivalent of government negotiations for a ceasefire, but actually laid the framework for the Good Friday Agreement itself – something that Corbyn himself insinuated in various interviews.[51]

Others, such as the rabidly pro-Corbyn 'alternative' news outlet *Skwawkbox*, went so far as to claim that Mo Mowlam had personally requested that Corbyn act as her 'secret envoy' in the negotiations.[52] So secret was Corbyn's position that it was not mentioned by a single participant of the Good Friday process in any book or interview. As Seamus Mallon, one of the key SDLP figures involved in the peace process, put it: 'I never heard anyone mention Corbyn at all. He very clearly took the side of the IRA and that was incompatible, in my opinion, with working for peace.'[53] *Skwawkbox*'s account therefore had to rely on a single anonymous Facebook post. Nevertheless, it did not stop the site pushing the fantasy that Corbyn had not only paved the way for the Good Friday Agreement but that 'without him there would have been no deal' at all. This objectively preposterous line then circulated widely on social media.

Just as in the anti-apartheid case, the actual historical detail of Corbyn's behaviour with regard to Northern Ireland – the particular context in which he was acting, the specific positions he held and contested, and the political consequences of his decisions – was completely erased in favour of an image of protest or peace based on nothing but the unfounded assertion of his exceptional moral integrity. This has the somewhat perverse effect of depoliticising what were intrinsically political movements, draining both the anti-apartheid struggle and the Northern Ireland peace process of their specific content – the very means by which they succeeded. In doing so the messiness of politics is smoothed over, eliding the risks and the calculated compromises necessary to achieve something concrete in a contradictory world where justice is not inevitable. The emptiness of the generic notion of 'protest' represented by Corbyn's anti-apartheid photograph matches that of the abstract, ahistorical 'peace' he is purported to have ceaselessly pursued – a 'peace' that somehow exists outside the world of politics, rather than as something which is necessarily built through it.

In this one-dimensional application of the appeal for 'peace', the victory of the 'good' is attributed not to the long, painstaking, difficult work that comprises the reality of political struggle, negotiation and mediation between competing claims, but is rather guaranteed by the inevitable progress of a linear 'history' devoid of any actual historical content. In a sense, abstract morality is placed in opposition to concrete politics – with politics regarded here as the problem, not the solution. Such a 'moralizing attitude towards the realities of power' once again betrays Corbyn's populist tendencies.[54] As Maxine Molyneux and Thomas Osborne argue, 'politics, so far as populists are concerned, has to translate the people's will in as pristine and *unmediated* a form as possible. Indeed, what populists have in common is really a moral idea – that political opinion can be expressed, so far as possible, without the mediation of institutions.'[55] From this perspective, attempts to translate competing demands into a political solution through a *genuine* dialogue between conflicting parties, as opposed to Corbyn's ventriloquism on behalf of the always-already 'good' side, can only end in compromise – and thus the 'betrayal of the moral integrity' of the pure will of the good.[56]

It is testament to the extent to which this hyper-moralised form of anti-politics has become common currency amongst the left that Corbyn's supporters were able to portray the real political achievements of people like Peter Hain and Mo Mowlam as the fruits of Corbyn's own supposed moral exceptionalism, and present what amounts to a form of inverted nationalism as a genuine effort to secure universal human rights. What is truly remarkable – and deeply worrying – about this historically revisionist and anti-internationalist sentimentalism was that it worked. The idea that Corbyn was somehow instrumental in both ending apartheid and the Northern Ireland peace process has now become an unchallengeable truth within vast swathes of the Labour membership.

Moreover, the image of Corbyn as a prescient man of peace, willing to risk everything in pursuit of 'dialogue' was crucial to his ability to fend off legitimate criticism of his actual actions and associations during the General Election. The ease with which this rewriting of history has been accepted by both Labour members and much of the wider electorate raises the question of the limits to this political and historical manipulation. What is the policy or position that will not be emptied of historical content and retroactively justified in the name of Corbyn's presumed infallibility?

Some of the implications of this could be seen, once again, in the response to Syria: one unexpected result of the generalisation of the Stop the War worldview has been the emergence of a previously unthinkable anti-Muslim bigotry amongst the 'anti-imperialist' left.[57] The eagerness to defend Corbyn's effectively pro-regime position has led to the widespread characterisation of the Syrian resistance as consisting entirely of Islamist extremists. The word 'jihadist' now falls from the lips of Labour figures with an ease lacking in the wake of, say, the Bataclan or *Charlie Hebdo* attacks.[58] The conviction of being among the community of the morally good provides those previously reticent about such language political cover for calling out the so-called 'headchoppers,' while simultaneously denying the very existence of Syrian democratic leftists altogether. As Leila Al-Shami puts it, denouncing the 'anti-imperialism of idiots' who now replicate the once-despised rhetoric of the 'War on Terror': 'Syrians are not seen as possessing the sophistication to hold a diverse range of views. Civil society activists (including many amazing women), citizen journalists, humanitarian workers are irrelevant. The entire opposition is reduced to its most authoritarian elements or seen as mere conduits for foreign interests.'[59]

Those who once railed against the 'war on terror' now find themselves seduced by its binary logic, albeit now with Putin and Assad, rather than Bush and Blair, beating the bad guys. This indicates just how far the politics of position can go in justifying even the most incongruous policies. Throughout this book, we examine how this politics of position has given cover for numerous other seemingly jarring contradictions in the Corbynist worldview. Once unleashed, the politics of position is not something that can be controlled, even by those who initially reap the political rewards. The resistance to contradictory evidence or critique, the insistence that history must be forced into an unalterable, pregiven template, and the belief that politics is nothing but struggle between two essentially, even ontologically, opposed camps of good and bad, eventually outruns any attempt to ride it for particular purposes. The triumph of this form of politics across the spectrum poses serious problems for the 'democratic norms' which sustain liberal rights and freedoms, rights and freedoms.[60] For all their flaws, they remain the basis for any future emancipatory political project to construct global forms of solidarity which take as their basis a common and universal humanity regardless of states, their borders and their so-called sovereignty.

~~~

For a section of Corbyn's support, the intellectually disenchanted left that went into his leadership with their eyes wide open about his limitations, the possibility of a Corbynism without Corbyn has always been the eventual endgame.[61] But what the past two chapters have demonstrated is that there can be no Corbynism without Corbyn, or, at least, not without rendering the project incapable of containing its internal contradictions. Corbyn is not only a vehicle for a set of ideas quite apart from his own, but their alibi – giving cover for political positions even the adherents of which would otherwise recoil from, but which guarantee in the short term the construction of a relatively successful electoral coalition.

This chapter and its predecessor have demonstrated that the power of Corbyn's reputation as a moral exemplar is such that the socialist and liberal-left now finds itself uncritically

supporting a number of political positions which, only a
few years before, it would have regarded as reactionary. On
immigration, Brexit, welfare cuts and a commitment to internationalism and support for emancipatory movements worldwide, the left has set aside previously-held principles – even
sacrificing free movement as a legal right – on the grounds
that Corbyn's integrity will act as collateral for future gains.
This has been achieved via a process of historical revisionism in which the past forty years of political history are now
read solely through the prism of Corbyn's supposed moral
exceptionalism and political prescience. The insistence that
Corbyn has always been on the 'right side of history' betrays
a schematic and essentialist understanding of society, politics
and of history itself. Here the innately 'good' – whether individuals, groups or states – are locked in permanent struggle
with the irredeemably 'bad.' This leads to a radically dehistoricised and depoliticised perspective, which disregards the
very processes through which liberal rights and freedoms and
the gains of social democracy have been first won and then
sustained through political struggle.

Our contention is that the reason why it is so important
for his supporters that Corbyn retains his reputation as a moral
paragon lies in the theoretical premises of Corbynism, which
result in a particularly personalised understanding of capitalist society. By examining those premises, we suggest in the
next chapter that Corbynism's foreign policy positions and its
grasp of capitalism are inextricably linked. In order to show
this, we need to go back further, to the roots of the Corbyn
perspective – back to, once again, Tony Benn and the Bennite
political worldview.

4

TAKING BACK CONTROL: CORBYNISM IN ONE COUNTRY

Following the success of the 2017 election, many of those who had voted for Labour in the hope of a 'soft' Brexit – or perhaps no Brexit at all – seemingly expected the party would cast aside the constructive ambiguity of its manifesto and commit to staying in the Single Market and Customs Union, if not the default Remain position that was the democratically-decided party policy.[1] Corbyn was 'playing a long game' on Brexit, we were told.[2] After all, every one of Corbyn's much-vaunted manifesto pledges relied on an increased tax-take and growth strategy – growth which virtually every economist agreed was predicated upon remaining in the Single Market, and thus retaining free movement. As Mariana Mazzucato, a former advisor to John McDonnell and an advocate for the 'entrepreneurial state', put it, supporting Brexit 'defies reason (political and economic).'[3] Surely an about-turn was in the offing, particularly given Corbyn's newfound post-election authority.

We are still waiting. Moves have been made towards a proposal of the establishment of 'a' customs union – predicated on the somewhat ambitious demand that Britain be given an effective veto on free trade deals negotiated by the rest of the EU.[4]

Time will tell whether this is the first move in the fabled 'long game.' Given that Corbyn and McDonnell repeatedly passed up the post-election opportunity to force May into remaining in the Single Market, it seems unlikely. Remainer hopes seemed to be finally dashed when Corbyn ruled out backing a Norway-style 'soft Brexit,' in which Britain would remain within the Single Market as a member of the European Economic Area.[5]

There may yet be movement enough to make this all moot, although Corbyn extolling the weaker pound brought by Brexit as a boon to business suggests not.[6] Regardless, we do not intend to make predictions about the latest policy twist and turn here. Instead this chapter will explore the theoretical basis for the reticence shown towards EU membership by the political tradition from which Corbyn derives, tracing it back to the particular analysis of capitalism, and British capitalism in particular, developed by Corbyn's mentor and forerunner, Tony Benn. Only by understanding this prehistory is it possible to understand why, should Labour eventually end up accepting Single Market membership – the position supported by the vast majority of Labour members and voters – it will be experienced as a defeat for those in Corbyn's inner sanctum.[7]

Bennism and Corbynism are not identical phenomena. They emerged in radically different social conditions, and, as detailed in the Introduction, the internal political makeup of the Corbyn movement is more heterogeneous than its predecessor. That said, there are a number of clear lines of influence from the old to the new. The first is of course Corbyn's close personal relationship with Benn himself. Corbyn was effectively Benn's protégé from the moment he entered Parliament in 1983.[8] The second is Corbyn's reputation as a man of otherworldly integrity, which, as we have seen, he inherited from the latter-day, and thoroughly domesticated, version of Benn the 'national treasure'. But in this chapter we will argue that the personal relationship between the two men is only the most visible manifestation of a set of shared theoretical principles and political aims, ultimately founded upon a common analysis of what capitalism is, how it works, what is wrong with it and what needs to be done to fix it.

In what follows we will take a closer look at the origins of Bennism, the claims it made about capitalist society, the role it attributed to national sovereignty as the first line of defence for British workers in a global economy, and its vision of socialism. We will then demonstrate how this analysis of the relation between capital and labour – a prime example of the kind of 'truncated' critique of capitalism that is our target in this book – is carried over into Corbynism, comparing the theoretical premises of Benn's 'Alternative Economic Strategy' with those of Corbyn's 'Alternative Models of Ownership' report. In so doing, we draw out some unexpected parallels between the understanding of capitalism and the nation-state prevalent within Corbynism and that proposed by the Blue Labour faction of the party. It is here, in this nationalist political space, that we can situate the shift that has taken place within Corbyn's core support when it comes to Brexit. From being a much-derided minority position during the referendum campaign, the idea of 'taking back control' by means of 'Lexit' is increasingly dominant amongst the intellectual coalition behind Corbyn, regarded as a vital plank of the wider programme of national renewal Corbynism has come to represent. Delving deeper into the theoretical underpinnings that make these positions possible, we locate the protectionist economic policies which increasingly characterise the Corbynist worldview in the context of a so-called 'substantialist' theory of labour and value rooted in a certain understanding of how capitalism works.

Our intention, therefore, in this chapter is not simply to bemoan either the conception of capitalism that underlies

Bennism and Corbynism, or the political programme built on the back of it, as not being 'radical' enough. Nor do we reject every policy proposal out of hand – indeed, the expansion of trade union rights, prioritising workers' wages and working conditions when it comes to awarding government contracts, and the encouragement of workers' cooperatives are good and necessary objectives. Our claim is somewhat different: it is that the policies put forward by Corbynism are not commensurate to the problems they purport to solve. This mismatch between diagnosis and prognosis stems from a reliance upon what we argue is a flawed, naturalistic and highly personalised model of capitalism, which in turn leads to a failure to recognise capitalism in its determination as a historically specific set of globally constituted social relations. It is this misrecognition which ultimately lies behind the erroneous, and potentially highly dangerous, equation of economic nationalism with socialism in both the Bennite and Corbynist worldviews.

The chapter will expand on this argument by outlining an alternative theory of capitalism, which in contrast to the positivist sociological interpretation Corbynism takes forward from its Bennite origins, is instead based on the recognition of its historically specific form of 'socially mediated labour' on a global scale. This focus on the globally and socially mediated character of capitalist society poses serious questions for theories which posit a direct relationship between labour and value within a local or national frame of reference. Suggesting that labour creates value in time and space simultaneously implies that the same kind of production can somehow be divorced from its constitution in a certain set of social relations and social forms historically specific to capitalism, and set free. Remove the capitalist and the banker, let the workers 'take back control' of production and the state, and you have socialism – a system where, as Corbyn puts it, 'we produce what we need for people who need it, rather than the greed of people who don't need it.'[9]

These appeals to human need are complicated when the 'natural' status of production and labour is called into doubt, and questions posed over the exact manner in which productive labour is so central to both capitalist and socialist society. To simply hold that productive labour is that which produces goods which can then either be sold for profit or used to fulfil social needs is to fundamentally misrecognise the particular way that needs are fulfilled in capitalist society, and the reasons why they have to be fulfilled in that way. To understand this, we argue, an understanding of social mediation is required that radically denaturalises what is, historically speaking, an extremely strange state of affairs.

This exposes the practical implications of seemingly obscure theoretical interpretations of the relationship between labour and value. For one, it leads to the misconception that national sovereignty is in some way a barrier to the development of capitalism, and the generation of support behind a programme of economic protectionism. The fundamental flaws in such a conclusion become clear once capitalism is understood as a global system of socially mediated labour, which holds abstract power over all who live within it, rich or poor, capitalist or worker. As such, we suggest that the protectionist economic policies Corbynism proposes as a solution to the problems produced by capitalist society are not only doomed to failure, but may actively contribute to the process of global political-economic fragmentation and breakdown currently threatening the liberal cosmopolitanism of the post-1945 international order, a trajectory with deeply reactionary potential.

IT'S OBVIOUS, ISN'T IT?

When asked what first drew him to socialism, Corbyn did not have an answer. 'There was no sudden conversion to socialism,'

he told the *Sunday People*. 'It's an obvious way of living. You
care for each other, you care for everybody, and everybody
cares for everybody else. It's obvious, isn't it?'[10] For Corbyn, socialism is completely self-evident, natural, something
instinctive that emerges from the core of one's being. It is not
something that needs to be thought about, rationally debated
or constructed. But whether Corbyn himself regards this attitude as 'obvious' or not, his reliance on a natural understanding of social relations is a clear, if inadvertent, indication of
his theoretical bent, and that of the political tradition within
which he has spent his life. It is precisely the assumption of
natural or self-evident social forms which unites Bennism
and Corbynism.

The notion of 'nature' operative here implies a series of
bifurcations or oppositions – between 'nature' and 'artificiality', 'need' and 'profit', 'real production' and 'parasitical finance', 'rationality' and 'irrationality', 'concrete' and
'abstract.' In each case, capital – or rather, the individuals
or groups taken to concretely personify its abstract rule – is
depicted as being on the side of the latter category. Capitalism is thus regarded as an artificial, irrational deforma-
tion of productive society, in which greed and the desire for
profit – expressed through the anarchy of the market and
the abstract workings of a deterritorialised financial sector – prevents the direct fulfilment of needs. Socialism takes
up the opposite set of categories: based on a direct relation
between labour, value and the fulfilment of needs, it represents a controlled and rationally planned process of production grounded in a concrete, unified and natural society. As
the Ken Loach-directed '#WeDemand' Labour election video put it, socialism is a form of productive society no longer
'subject to grand profiteering, but planned, transparent, exe-
cuted in efficient fashion under democratic control.'[11] In each
case the two branches of the bifurcation are seen as being

completely separate from one another, existing in radically distinct spheres. The relation between the two can therefore only be an external one, wholly contingent, imposed by force or ideological trickery. It is the positing of this external relationship that distinguishes both Bennism and Corbynism from other, more critical analyses of capitalism and its alternatives.

The theories of capitalism and socialism which underlie the Corbynist vision, and to some extent that of Bennism too, have been dominant within the labour movement for much of its history. Their origins can be traced back to Marx himself, and in particular the way that his 'labour theory of value' has been popularly interpreted and used a means of political inspiration. According to this orthodox account, the value of an object produced in a workplace is measured by the amount of labour that has gone into it. The longer an object takes to make – or else the greater intensity or skill expended in its creation – the more valuable it is. This direct relationship between labour and value is assumed to hold across all kinds of societies, in all kinds of historical circumstances. It is an expression of the natural way humanity interacts with its environment.

The particular problem with capitalism as a mode of production, according to this analysis, is that the people who do all the labour, the workers who create the value objectified in the product, do not receive the full amount of that value in exchange for the work they have performed. Rather, the owner of the workplace claims the entirety of that value for themselves, and then distributes a small portion of it to the workers in the form of a wage. The owner is able to do this because they own the means of production as their private property. Their right to this property is protected by a state itself controlled by the capitalist class. In its classical liberal form, this 'bourgeois' state ensures that private property rights are upheld, through violence if necessary, but does not intervene in the realm of production. Politics and economics are in this way deliberately kept apart, allowing capitalists to have a free hand not only when it comes to organising the labour process but also over the decision of what to produce, and whether to invest in production at all.

In such a situation, those who 'produce the real wealth' do not have control of either their productive activity or the wealth it produces. The formal equality and impersonal rules of the bourgeois state are therefore seen as something of a fraud, merely a means to disguise the real political power of the capitalists over the economy, and the continuing exploitation of workers. For socialists of the Benn–Corbyn mould, in such a system production is not aimed at satisfying the needs of the workers or society as a whole, but rather the private greed of the capitalists. The global expansion of a system shaped by the selfish desires of profit-chasing capitalists has led to the emergence of an international financial and banking sector, again controlled by capitalists, which enables money to be moved from one country to another in search of higher profits. This makes it even harder for workers to claim the value they create.

The alternative to this unjust system is, it is suggested, a socialist mode of production. The aims of this notion of socialism are still best summed up by the old Clause IV of the Labour Party constitution, controversially changed by Tony Blair in 1994: 'To secure for the workers by hand or by brain the full fruits of their industry and the most equitable distribution thereof that may be possible upon the basis of the common ownership of the means of production, distribution and exchange, and the best obtainable system of popular administration and control of each industry or service.' In such a society, the Corbynite–Bennite tradition suggests, workers would take control of both the means of production and the state, and in this way receive the full amount of the value their labour had created. No longer would unproductive capitalists, global financial institutions or vested interests have the power to cream off profits from the productive class. Nor would they be free to withhold investment from the 'real' economy or allow locally-produced wealth to 'slide away' from the local community. The distribution of goods would not be left to the 'anarchy' of the market, under the fraudulent auspices of formal equality. Nor would the choice of objects to be produced be any longer determined by the requirements of the profit-seekers. Politics and economics would be reunited in the form of a socialist workers' state, with both production and distribution democratically planned according to the immediate desires of the workers themselves.

From this perspective, the key differences between a capitalist and socialist society lie in the relative share of goods (and value) distributed to the workers, the means by which those goods are produced and distributed, and what those goods actually are. These factors are ultimately determined by the distribution of power within the economy between workers, capitalists and international finance, each of which are regarded as discrete entities, interacting but not essentially connected to one another. In a sense, workers and production itself are construed as somehow existing outside of capitalism. Their administration under capitalist social relations is therefore the consequence of either deliberate ideological mystification or unadulterated state violence – 'consent' or 'coercion', in the Gramscian framework.[12] The central promise of the Bennite and Corbynist vision of socialism is that by building up local and national state barriers to the global flow of capital, workers will be able to gain the power required to 'take back control' of their productive activity, the results of that activity, and of the society that is built upon it. As we shall see, this echo of the Leave campaign's infamous slogan is by no means coincidental.

ALTERNATIVES

Bennism as a distinct mode of political analysis emerged as a response to the first stirrings of the worldwide breakdown of Keynesian capitalism that would culminate in the crisis-ridden 1970s. The Bennites argued that in addition to this general crisis, there was a specifically British crisis, which was not inherently linked to the first.[13] This latter *national* crisis was due to the failure of the British capitalist class to invest in industrial production at home. Instead they had focused their attentions on the supposedly unproductive banking, finance and property sectors, using the pound's status as a global reserve currency to speculate on the world market. Benn regarded the 'unproductive' global financial sector and the 'productive' domestic industrial economy to be externally related competitors in a zero-sum game.[14] Britain's problem was that its economy was radically unbalanced in favour of international finance and away from national industry. The decision of the British bourgeoisie to invest their money in financial speculation rather than expanded production was regarded as a moral failing on their part. They had failed to live up to their assigned historical role. Their intransigence and inefficient management had led to a lack of productive capacity, a loss of markets to foreign competitors and rising unemployment, and it was this that lay at the heart of the specifically British crisis.

Benn's solution was laid out in his 'Alternative Economic Strategy' (AES), which he proposed to the Labour Cabinet during the 1976 sterling crisis, as an alternative to approaching the IMF for a loan.[15] Rejected at the time, much of it found its way into Labour's 1983 manifesto. The fundamental aim of the AES was the withdrawal of the British economy from the clutches of global finance and the vacillations of the British bourgeoisie. A Bennite government would retreat behind the borders of the nation-state in order to rebuild the 'real' productive economy, expand industrial capacity and competitiveness, and redirect production towards the needs of society rather than the profits of the banking or financial sector. In order to achieve this, the strategy proposed the imposition of controls on imports, exports, and the movement of capital in and out of the country; a wages and prices policy; public ownership of British banks and financial institutions; the nationalisation of at least the top 25 companies, if not 250; the introduction of compulsory planning agreements in which the state would co-determine the content and level of production of both nationalised and private organisations; leaving the European Economic Community (forerunner of the EU) and its Common Market; and an extension of democratic procedures within the workplace, in order to establish 'workers' control' of production. This latter move would enable workers to replace production aimed solely at profit with 'socially useful' production aimed at satisfying democratically determined social needs.

The outcome of this programme would be a state with complete control over the national economy, able to direct its development in any way it saw fit, free from the pressures imposed by the global market. As such, production could be placed in the service of the needs of the British people, rather than being enslaved to the profit-seeking of the banks and financial institutions. To critics who accused him of wanting to establish an insular 'siege economy,' Benn argued that Britain was already under siege from the global financial sector. The difference between the two 'sieges' was that in one the Labour government had joined forces with 'the bankers,' with 'the British people, the trade unions, outside the citadel storming you,' while in Benn's version 'it will be the other way round,' with the government, the British people and the trade unions combining to defend themselves against the intrusions of the banks.[16] In Benn's telling, this latter model, in which national production was planned by the state in consultation with self-managing workers, amounted to a radical socialist alternative to capitalism.

The ideas and analysis found in the AES remain of fundamental importance to the Corbyn movement. That said, the core tenets of Benn's AES were not those expressed in the 2017 Labour manifesto. The latter had little to say about capital controls or workers' control of production. However, if the policies outlined in the manifesto marked the limit of Corbyn and McDonnell's ambitions, their insistence on the need and desirability of leaving the Single Market, a key part of Benn's strategy, would not make sense. Corbyn and McDonnell argue that it is necessary to leave the Single Market so as to escape the restrictions on 'state aid' and procurement that prevent member states from supporting national industries beyond a mutually agreed level. As Corbyn put it in March 2018, when it comes to Brexit, a Labour government would

> *seek to negotiate protections, clarifications or exemptions where necessary in relation to privatisation and public service competition directives, state aid and procurement rules, and the posted workers directive. We cannot be held back inside or outside the EU from taking the steps we need to support cutting edge industries and local business, stop the tide of privatisation and outsourcing or from preventing employers being able to import cheap agency labour to undercut existing pay and conditions.*[17]

He contrasted his approach with Theresa May's supposed desire 'to tie the UK permanently to EU rules, which are used to drive privatisation and block support for British industry,' arguing that he would not 'sign up to a Single Market deal without agreement that our final relationship with the EU would be fully compatible with our radical plans to change Britain's economy.'

As many commentators have pointed out, there was very little in the 2017 manifesto which could not have been implemented under the EU's current state aid rules.[18] Corbyn's firmness on this point therefore implies that, once in power, he intends to go much further than the manifesto – although he is yet to explicitly propose any specific policies requiring greater state aid than currently permitted.

We suggest that the 'Alternative Models of Ownership' (AMO) policy document, produced at the behest of John McDonnell and Rebecca Long-Bailey in 2017, represents the clearest exposition of what a Corbyn economic programme would look like in practice. Even here, there is only the vaguest reference to policies which could *possibly* fall outside the rules of the Single Market. Nevertheless, the economic analysis in this document has a definite Bennite ring to it. Indeed, it is best viewed as an extension or reformulation of the AES itself.[19]

Like Benn, the AMO argues that the 'fundamental structural flaws' of the British economy are 'a lack of long-term investment and declining rates of productivity,' which are attributed to the 'predominance of private property ownership,' by which is meant the private ownership of productive firms.[20] This is exacerbated by the 'commonplace implicit assumption in UK society that there is a natural separation between the political and economic realms, with democratic structures and processes only applying to the former.'[21] In reality, this suggests, there is no such separation – or rather, the *appearance* of such a separation, of the non-political character of the economy, is somewhat paradoxically evidence of its *non-existence*. The presumed separation of politics and economics is accordingly merely an ideological trick played by a 'narrow elite' on the rest of society, as a means of disguising the true nature of their political power over the economy.[22] This power is, this tale implies, precisely that expressed by the decision to favour global financial speculation over national industry, and production for profit over social need – that which stimulated the Bennite critique in the first place.

A Corbyn government, the document suggests, should challenge this false appearance of a separation between politics and economics by using state power to invest in national production, and facilitate the growth of worker-owned cooperatives, which would be both more efficient and productive than private firms. Indeed, the report claims that the predominance of private ownership explains the UK economy's low level of productivity (although it paradoxically acknowledges that up until 2005 UK productivity matched that of other G7 economies, without any corresponding change in ownership models).[23] The example of the Mondragon workers cooperative in the Basque region is cited as an alternative approach to ownership.[24] Mondragon was set up by a Catholic priest in the wake of the Spanish Civil War. It was envisioned as 'a social and political project to overcome class struggle,' held to be to blame for the war.[25] Here class struggle is regarded as a technical problem, one which can be resolved through the redistribution of control over production. This is effectively how Benn and Corbyn view class struggle too. Rather than seeing class struggle as inherent to capitalist production, it is regarded as something imposed on production from the outside, which can then be ameliorated through what Benn called a fundamental 'change in the relationships between capital and labour under the self-discipline of democratic control.'[26]

In addition to encouraging the growth of 'self-disciplined' cooperative production, the Alternative Models of Ownership report argues that a Corbyn government should use procurement policy to favour 'local supply chains' and national firms, so as to stop nationally-produced wealth 'leaking' or 'sliding away from localities.'[27] This latter policy is currently being implemented by Preston council, often presented as a small-scale prefiguration of what a Corbyn national economy would look like. The council and other local so-called 'anchor institutions' – universities, housing associations, the police, colleges – pledge to give procurement contracts to local businesses wherever possible. Local companies are assisted in applying for contracts, while residents are encouraged to set up new workers' cooperatives to fill the council's procurement gaps. Advocates of the scheme argue that the policy should be scaled up to a national level. Joe Guinan, a US-based researcher and trenchant supporter of 'Lexit', who has advised Preston on the procurement policy, suggests that under a Corbyn government the NHS 'could be the mother of all anchoring institutions.'[28] The ultimate 'anchoring institution', of course, is the nation-state itself, and here the clear similarity between Corbyn's favoured 'Preston model' at the municipal level and Bennite protectionism at the level of nation comes into view. In both cases, the primary task of the state is to ensure that locally-produced wealth does not leave a given community, while production is controlled and directed so as to fulfil the needs of the state. In so doing, the thinking around the AMO and Lexit conforms with a much wider history of how value has been interpreted, with roots in a similar set of debates about protectionism and free trade played out centuries ago. This requires a brief detour through value theory.

VALUE AND SOCIAL MEDIATION

From the perspective advanced here it can be seen that the Corbynist position rests on what Philip Mirowski calls a 'conservation' or 'substantialist' theory of value.[29] Uniting classical

political economy with the kind of orthodox Marxism we dis-
tanced ourselves from at the outset of the book, substantialism
holds value to be the property of a given thing in a given space
or time. It is this physical understanding of the character of
value in a capitalist economy that we contest, in favour of a
theory – outlined in more detail below – that apprehends value
as the expression of a socially mediated relationship *between*
things and not inherent *within* things themselves. This is by
no means merely an academic or 'idealist' distinction. The
way that capitalist society is understood to work in theory
feeds into the political programmes put forward to change,
defend or overthrow it in practice. Populist ideologies reject
the notion of mediation – whether institutional or dialogical –
in favour of the direct and immediate expression of the will of
'the people' or the 'community of the good.' Our suggestion
here is that this fetish for immediacy is replicated in theories
of capitalism that posit an unmediated relation between an act
of labour and the value of a particular object. The two sides of
this double rejection of social mediation, value conservation
and populist politics, thus come together in leftist appeals for
'socialism in one country' – which, as Moishe Postone asserts,
'is really nationalism in one country.'[30]

The Corbynist application of the substantialist idea to a
politics of trade that seeks to contain this conserved value
within the location to which it properly belongs harks right
back to the very foundations of such a value theory in 'balance of trade' mercantilism.[31] The latter was based on the
belief that a trading system of equivalent exchange must
always mean, in the words of Francis Bacon, that 'whatever
is somewhere gotten is somewhere lost'. This was tied up in
the competitive imperialisms of the age of conquest, justifying inter-country rivalry on the basis that 'trade is a zero-sum
game'. Value is here taken to be something conserved, and to
the extent the exchange in which it features is conducted with

the national currency, containable within the borders of the state from which it arose.

For this substantialist strand of value theory, if money is the index of value, the state is its unit of analysis. Hence the positive trade balance – a contemporary saw of the Bannonite wing of the Trump movement and Brexiteer backwoodsmen – comes to represent the relative conservation and augmentation of the value substance. We see the same kinds of claims arise in the Corbynist literature on protectionist economic alternatives. The support in some quarters for new 'sovereign' fiat forms of money, inspired by so-called 'Modern Monetary Theory,' rests on the claim that they allow nation-states to step outside the international monetary system and gain more control over the currency as the means of conserving the value produced within their borders.[32] This suggests that the problem with money is not its status as the form of appearance of value as a social mediation of people and things, but rather the ownership of the literal currency that constitutes it as a store of value as a conserved substance. But there is no 'sovereign' way to opt out of the universal social relation that money represents.

Of course, the 'conservation principle' on which all such substantialist theories of value rest also sustains further links with the nationalist protectionism which, echoing balance of trade mercantilism, rears its head once again today. As we have already noted, and will explore further in subsequent chapters, the intellectual imaginary of contemporary populisms of both right and left pose 'productive' sections of the economy against the 'unproductive'. This position, Mirowski points out, is 'isomorphic to the statement of a conservation principle in the theory of value'.[33] Instead of being incidental to nationalist protectionism, the posing of the productive against the unproductive is part of a conservationist value theory that is rooted in the conceptualisation of value as a zero-sum game fought for between nations.

Interestingly, it is actually at the neoclassical foundations
of neoliberal economics – the villain of the piece for the line of
Corbynist thinking covered in this book – that we finally see
value theory establish a mainstream alternative to the national-protectionist political economy of the conservation principle. It does so not only by thinking it 'a fallacy to indict any
economic activity as simultaneously necessary-but-intermedi-
ate and yet unproductive', but also by recognising that trade
is central to value not through its *limitation* between national
borders but through its *extension* in the name of maximisation
of opportunities for utility, and thus a widening of the 'field'
of value established between transactions.[34] It is still today
out of fidelity to such a principle that the so-called 'neoliberal'
bogeymen of the Lexit left recognise the risks of economic isolation better than some Marxists. Marx, for his part, alight-
ed later in life on a value theory that both anticipated most
neoclassical work on the topic and bettered it, insofar as his
understanding of value as a 'field' relationship between things
was grounded in an account of the class antagonism as the
constitutive precondition of commodity society. In this sense,
we might see Marx, quite controversially by all accounts, 'as
a proto-Austrian rather than a post-Ricardian' – a distinction
the contemporary left might do well to consider.[35]

~~~

Rather than value being something locatable in things or
places at a given time, value is really a relationship existing
between things, constituted across time and space. This means
it is reducible neither to a specific act of physical or 'concrete'
labour or a specific national frame of reference, but rather to
the totality of labour in society as a whole, which in a world
market is to say on a scale that is not national but global.
Hence labour– as an activity rooted in time and space, within
certain local and national frames of reference– relates to value

only in and through its social *mediation*. Arguments to render unto the national community of productive labour what it is rightly due, therefore, completely miss the specific social and historical character of the practical reality on which they base their theoretical and political claims. Capitalism functions around a system of abstract economic compulsions a simple return to concrete order cannot comprehend nor confront.

In order to understand the specific role of labour in capitalist society, we need to compare it (albeit rather schematically) with the role of labour in feudal society.[36] Here, peasants produced what they needed to survive from their own land – they grew crops, raised cattle, made their own clothes, built their own homes. They therefore had direct access to their means of subsistence, and immediately used or consumed the products of their own labour. Their social relationships with one another were not determined by production or commodities, but politically and personally. A peasant retained access to his land via his political relationship with a lord, while the lord's position was secured by his personal relationship to the monarch. Likewise, lords appropriated a portion of the peasants' produce by virtue of their political position of authority.

In capitalism, by contrast, workers have been separated from the land and can no longer produce their means of subsistence directly themselves. Instead they use their labour to produce a particular type of object, one which is not meant for their own use, but rather used as a means of getting hold of the other things they need to survive. These things have been produced by other people, each of whom is separated from their own means of subsistence too, and thus also produces their object not for their own use but entirely for the sake of getting hold of the things they need. The relationship between an individual and their means of subsistence in a society characterised by such a division of labour is thus *indirect* and socially *mediated*. Equally, the relationship between an individual act of labour and the object it produces is also indirect – the object is not for the immediate use of the person who produced it. It is merely a means to another end, which is attaining the objects that they actually do need to survive, which have been produced by other people. This means that the connection between people living in such a society is itself mediated, by means of the monetary exchange of commodities, as *social labour*, the totality of labour performed by society. And it is upon this socially mediated, indirect form of labour that each individual's very survival depends.[37]

In liberal forms of capitalism, built upon an impersonal legal and political structure of formal equality, this process of mediation is generally not determined politically. Everyone has more-or-less the same right to sell the products of their labour, and buy the products of others, on an open market, and in so doing attaining access to their means of subsistence. But this structure of formal equality is contradicted by an unequal distribution of ownership of land and the means of production, a legacy of the process by which peasants were separated from direct access to the land during the transition to capitalism. Such landless peasants often ended up becoming wage labourers – selling their labour power (their capacity to work) on the market to someone else for a wage, rather than making their own product. It was one of Marx's key insights in *Capital* that the unequal distribution of the means of production sanctioned by private property rights, and the uniquely productive capacities of human labour, meant that it was possible for capitalists to pay workers the full value of their labour power – the costs involved in ensuring they were fed, clothed and rested for work the next day – and still make a profit. As we have seen, it is precisely this perceived injustice – in which the worker is deprived of the full value of their labour under the cover of political and legal equality – which lies behind the orthodox Marxian critique of capitalism, and by extension that of Bennism and Corbynism.

~~~

But this is only half the story. As noted above, the success of any attempt to access the means of subsistence through indirect labour is determined by the relationship of the private act of labour to social production as a whole. In liberal capitalist societies, this mediation takes the form of commodity exchange on the market. If a particular object produced by a private act of labour is not wanted by society – if is regarded as too expensive, if the market is already saturated with similar products, or if it is no longer desired – it cannot be sold. Understood like this, the direct or 'substantialist' relationship between labour and value posited by orthodox Marxism, and adopted by Bennism and Corbynism, is false. The value of the labour that went into making an object only appears as such – usually in the form of money – once it has been socially validated as part of the total social labour of society as a whole through its sale. If it is not validated, it is effectively unproductive labour, regardless of the fact it produced a physical object. It is a literal waste of time. Therefore labour does not produce value in a direct, concrete sense. Value is not a thing, which is somehow injected into an object during the labour process. It exists only through a particular social relation between objects, which comes into being at the moment of their successful mediation.[38] And whether this takes place is a contingency on which both the reproduction of the capitalist relies, and thus also the reproduction of the worker dependent on the sale of their labour power to live.

It is the abstract economic compulsion to ensure that expended labour is validated as value that forces producers to move from one branch of production to another in search of guaranteed social validation. To succeed in this process they are forced to compete with the others to either cheapen the costs of labour or reduce the amount of labour time required to make that particular product, undercutting their rivals by creating more for less. The reduction of labour time is achieved by the introduction of new labour-saving technologies which speed up the process the production, or by reducing its costs. If the other producers of the same product do not follow suit, their products will be too expensive to sell – their price will have to be reduced to match that of their speedier rival, meaning they are not fully recompensed for their labour time or the costs of their raw materials. Unless they keep pace with what Marx terms 'socially necessary labour time,' they will soon go out of business, and therefore be locked out of social existence.[39]

The problem here is that labour is the one 'factor of production' which produces more in the labour process than it costs to reproduce. Labour is thus integral to the necessary expansion of value on which survival in capitalist society depends – even as the competition to ensure the social validation of labour as productive of value encourages the development of technology which lessens the amount of labour required in the production process. Rather than the outcome proposed in contemporary utopian or dystopian visions of automated worklessness, this requirement that labour take the form of value even as more and more wealth is produced without the direct intervention of physical labour is one of the founding contradictions of capitalist social relations. This contradictory dynamic between physical labour and its necessary social form lies at the root of the historical pattern of capitalist development. It is not a new problem. So it does not, by itself, lead inexorably to a terminal crisis of capitalism – and certainly not to communism – but rather sets the ever-shifting framework within which strategies to ensure the continued social validation of labour take place.

It is the seriousness of the consequences of failure to ensure that labour is socially validated as value, in a situation where everyone is separated from direct access to their means of subsistence, which makes competition within capitalism so cut-throat. This applies, differently and unequally, for both capitalist and worker, alone and together in a bond of mutual but coerced interdependence. Unlike in feudalism there is no political backup to failure which ensures access to food and shelter – aside from the welfare state for workers. But this state is also dependent on the successful social validation of labour for the taxes used to supply the 'social wage.' Ensuring continued profitability of that state's national capital, and thus the continued income of the state itself, is not a choice for the state personnel. It is a compulsion. Without it, the state itself would collapse. The social background of politicians and state officers may well influence the particular strategy they undertake to ensure continued profitability – this is one of the central arguments in Ralph Miliband's theory of the state in capitalist society, which we explore in the next chapter. Nor is there is any doubt some strategies have more equitable results than others. But without a foundational transformation of the system of socially mediated labour itself, all strategies must eventually convene on the continued validation of value.

The problem for everyone living under this system is that the movement of the measure of validation is not possible to consciously control. Because the status of any individual act of labour depends on the entire system of production, which is joined together as one through the status of labour as the universal form of social mediation, no single individual, group or institution can alter its trajectory. Indeed, from the perspective of an individual, the capricious movement of this abstract yet all-powerful standard of measure appears as a law of nature, something completely out of reach of human activity but to which that activity must adapt if one is to survive.

It is the unpredictable and uncontrollable movements of this measure of validation (known in Marxian terminology as the 'law of value') and the desperation to ensure products match up to it – in a situation of life or death – which lends capitalism its incessant drive for ever greater production and capital accumulation, as well as its crisis-ridden character. But it is also what underpins the existence of the financial sector, which enables the movement of money from one sector to another, and, as capitalism expands around the globe, from one country to another, in search of profit. Seen in this way, international finance is not a parasitic excrescence restricting the development of the 'real' national economy – it is rather that economy's precondition.

The shift to financialised capitalism in the wake of the crisis of Keynesianism cannot be explained merely by means of ideology, greed or even class warfare, but has to recognised as an attempt to overcome the limits of the previous model of profitability (or strategies to ensure the social validation of labour). The constant need to produce more goods and make more money in capitalism is not the result of the personal greed of any individual (which is not to say that greed plays no part in capitalist society). Nor is it in itself indicative of a moral failing – although of course there are better and worse ways to go about the mandatory pursuit of profit, which is why liberal frameworks of rights are so important. Rather it is an unavoidable consequence of a society in which access to the means of subsistence is mediated by social labour. Similarly, and contrary to many left analyses in the wake of 2008, crises in capitalism cannot be attributed to the conscious acts of individuals (which, again, is not to say that the acts of individuals cannot exacerbate a crisis situation). They occur as a result of the inherent instability of a system which is driven by non-stop competition under conditions which are out of any single actor's control.

It is therefore the mediating role of labour which produces the social relation that is capital. The capital relation is not something imposed from the outside but runs through the whole of society itself. The harder people work to ensure their objects match the standards of socially necessary labour time and thus unlock access to the means of subsistence, the more taxing those standards become, and the more ruinous the consequences of failing to do so. We are all in this way under the sway of a power which we produce through our own activity. The power of capital is produced by the form of capitalist labour itself. Labour and capital are two sides of the same coin. They are not two separate 'worlds' brought together through force or trickery. Nor does capital 'capture' a pre-existing form of value. Value is always-already a form of capital. Class struggle is the constant battle to secure access to the means of subsistence. It is non-stop, and affects everyone in different ways.[40] Some people undoubtedly have a much better deal in this situation, and it is the historical task of social democracy to remedy that radical disparity. But even the richest person in capitalist society lives under the sway of the law of value and the struggle to survive, just as the poorest depends on the continuation of a system that dominates and degrades them. There is no escape, and this demands a politics uncomforted by the notion that one is achievable without wider change.

'HOLD THIS COUNTRY BACK'

This detour through the history of value theory and the concept of social mediation shows the extent to which the contemporary left political economy of nation and locality presuppose a substantialist 'conservation' understanding of value that carries with it the burden of its origins in a protectionist politics of trade not fit for comprehending, let alone confronting, the character of global capitalism. In line with such an understanding, the AMO suggests that policies to ensure wealth stays within the borders – local, municipal or national – and that confer upon it its value are hindered by membership of the Single Market.[41] As Joe Guinan and Thomas Hanna put it elsewhere, Corbyn's Labour should therefore reject 'the icy-smooth frictionlessness of the single market' in favour of

> *the rooted participatory democratic local economy.*
> *Instead of the extractive multinational corporation,*
> *the worker- or community-owned firm. Instead*
> *of asset-stripping privatisation, plural forms of*
> *democratised public enterprise. Instead of austerity*
> *and private credit creation by rentier finance,*
> *the huge potential power of public banks and*
> *post-scarcity sovereign fiat money.*[42]

The establishment of this protective local and national economic structure of worker-run firms, the AMO document concludes, would 'overturn the hierarchies of power in our economy, placing those who create the real wealth in charge.' It would 'end decades of under-investment and wasted potential by tearing down the vested interests that hold this country back.'[43]

'Hold this country back': surprisingly nationalistic words coming from the left, perhaps. But Guinan and Hanna's strand of Corbynism, like various forces arraigned to its right, senses opportunity in Brexit to reinstate the sovereignty of the nation-state against global capital and international finance.[44] A common thread here uniting Corbynism with Blue Labour, its most coherent intellectual opposition within the Labour mainstream, is the foundational influence of critiques of contemporary capitalism inspired by Karl Polanyi. Polanyi's work opposes the 'artificiality' of 'market society' to the 'natural and human substance' of communities based on intuitive

reciprocity and redistribution.[45] He has been a key influence
on Blue Labour thinkers such as Maurice Glasman, as well
as those in the Corbyn coalition pushing most strongly for
Lexit.[46] Polanyi's thesis has been recently updated by Wolfgang Streeck, widely 'admired' within Corbyn's inner circle.[47]
Indeed, the feeling appears mutual, with Streeck and comrades from the German *Die Linke* party recently announcing
the development of a new 'social national' political project,
striking a halfway house between the social movement structure of Momentum and the Polanyian return to the nation
posited in Blue Labour and elements of Corbynism.[48] Streeck
is also a supporting signatory to the founding statement of
The Full Brexit, a recently-launched group advocating for a
hard Lexit, bringing together as bedfellows representatives of
Blue Labour, the Corbynist and Leninist left, as well as those
associated with the media-savvy Revolutionary Communist
Party cell behind *Living Marxism, Spiked* and other controversialist outlets.[49] These diverse voices all sign in the name
of national sovereignty against transnationalising social and
political forces.

Streeck's analysis makes a sharp distinction between a
national folk identity and the so-called 'market people' identified as working in finance and the international corridors of
power, a portrayal that, as Adam Tooze suggests, sits uncom-
fortably close to ascriptions of a mysterious border-hopping
rootlessness to cosmopolitan elites.[50] Corbynism is itself not
immune from these resonances, as we shall see in the final
chapter. Streeck sees the power of international and global
bodies and organisations, the EU included, as catalysing a
democratic crisis of nation-states. He thus sees nation-states
as the most viable vehicle for resistance to capital today. On
the Blue Labour side, this is reflected in Glasman's recent
statement that '[i]t is now no longer forbidden to think about
a *national* economic system. It is our duty to develop this

position and commit to the renewal of the complementary institutions that characterise our national economy.'[51]

The Blue Labour critique of Corbynism as hopelessly globalist in inclination is thus disingenuous in its suggestion that Corbynism does not also desire the same Streeckian return to the nation-state against capital as its critics.[52] It is a surprising area of overlap between Corbynism and its principle intellectual opposition in the Labour Party that this perspective is imported into the mainstream of Corbynist policymaking by the same source – Streeck himself. Just as Blue Labour sees the national community at threat from global process of commodification and flows of people and capital, over which the so-called primary community must be granted a greater measure of control. Corbynism too suspects the power of foreign or non-local capital to procure and profit from the flow of commodities within the UK. This much is evidenced in two Momentum video campaigns engaging in jingoistic parodies of Dutch, German and French people to suggest they benefit from ownership of 'our' railways to enjoy better rail services themselves.[53] But it goes far beyond it, as the theoretical and empirical basis supporting increasingly forceful appeals to 'Lexit' gains in cogency and uptake.[54]

In posing the nation against global and international capital, Corbynism, in common with other pro-Brexit strains in British politics, mistakes sovereignty for a *thing*, to be passed back and forth, salvaged or lost.[55] They fail to recognise that sovereignty is merely a particular social relation of power, inextricably tied up with the wider organisation of class society. This results in a dehistoricised understanding of how power functions. Sovereignty is ripped from its social context and turned into an abstraction, which is then presented as the cure for all social ills. This '*souverainisme*' is insatiable and impracticable.[56] The abstract, pristine sovereignty sought is impossible in a global society where standards, rules and regulations must by necessity follow the flow of commodities. Because both Corbynism, in common with Blue Labour – and indeed the Brexiteer nativist right – sees the world as constituted essentially of nations, its partisans are blinded to the extent to which what makes the world go around is the search for profit, and all dreams that propose to deny this are useless. The sovereignty they seek is pooled and shared between nations not only because the challenges they face and solutions they require are global in character, whether this be restraints on capital, migration, climate change, jihadist terror, Russian destabilisation or cyber warfare, but because we live in a world structured and socially reproduced as and by capital, a social relation which exists as a world market, from which single states cannot abdicate, no matter how hard they try.

~~~

What are the real economic consequences of this foreshortened reckoning with the contradictions of sovereignty in a world shaped by capital? Once viewed from the perspective of the world market – or a world system of socially-mediated labour, dictated by a law of value which is, by its very nature, out of the control of any individual, group or government – the flaws in the idea that the nation state can exempt its 'local' community from the pressures of the world market become horribly plain. Under capitalist relations of production there is no escape from the demands of the law of value, regardless of the cooperative or democratised organisation of the production process. Social needs cannot be forcibly separated from profitability, however attuned to 'socialist rationality' any particular politician or state official is. And the level of profitability and productivity necessary to comply with the law of value is necessarily determined socially – on a global level. The idea that wealth 'leaks' away from local economies through global finance completely misses the fact that the form of wealth is *always* a global affair – local wealth only appears as such through its validation as social, or global, wealth. The state can step in and attempt to direct this process, but it cannot escape or resolve it. The problem merely shifts its expression.

This is no minor theoretical quibble, but has practical ramifications. In the first instance, a scaled-up protectionist policy of 'local procurement' backed up by tariffs or by banning bids from 'non-local' companies would inevitably raise prices, as cheaper foreign (or non-local) goods are rejected in favour of those 'made in Britain.' This would require increased state subsidies of national industry (or 'state aid') to compensate for higher production costs and to ensure that exports did not collapse – assuming that exports had not already been stymied by rival 'local procurement' schemes. In short, Corbyn's favoured 'state aid,' the prize which apparently necessitates leaving the Single Market, is an attempt to unilaterally overcome by political means the centripetal force of profit. While such a voluntaristic policy might work for a short time, within the bounds of a certain branch of production, the problem it targets is not solved but merely displaced. And by not replacing but displacing capitalist dynamics, the contradictions of the latter are not escaped but exacerbated. The negative effects will be felt elsewhere in the economy.

Not everyone is a true believer in this agenda. Interestingly, commentators from another wing of the wider Bennite tendency out of which such demands for control come – in this case among them Socialist Action affiliates associated with Ken Livingstone's mayoral operation and his longstanding policy mouthpiece the Socialist Economic Bulletin – have carved a lonely place on the broader Corbynist left in making some robust criticisms of national protectionism. For example, Livingstone's former economic advisor John Ross suggests that under protectionism money that might have been spent on other parts of the economy would be funnelled into subsidising more expensive 'local' goods, leading to a drop in profits in those branches of production which do not find favour from the state, and a potential rise in unemployment.[57] Moreover, protected from competition, and from 'participation in the international division of labour, the international socialisation of production,' national or local industry may become less productive, with no independent incentive to innovate or cheapen the costs of production.[58] This could lead to a drop in investment, as companies seek to invest in more productive industries elsewhere. This process can only be prevented via capital controls, increasing the economy's isolation, or, what is more likely, a state-led increase in productivity, which, governed by workers' control or not, necessitates an increased rate of exploitation, intensified working conditions and/or technologically induced unemployment.

For his part, Tony Benn's proposed solution to this problem was one that sounds very familiar to post-Brexit ears: that the British state, once free of the constraints of the EEC, would be able to 'negotiate the best trading arrangement we could get with the common market to meet our national interests.'[59] This 'national interest' would in the last instance be defined by the state. Benn was thus quite clear that workers control of production would take place within a framework determined by 'the needs of the nation' as interpreted by the state.[60] National production, managed directly by workers or not, would therefore be beholden, via planning agreements, to the levels of cost, quality and productivity stipulated in trade deals drawn up by the state.

For Benn this settlement constituted a fundamental move away from the 'discipline of the market' – in short that production would no longer be subject to the law of value. Instead production would be run by the principle of workers' 'self-discipline.' But without fundamental changes to the

underlying social relations of capitalist production, 'workers' self-discipline' merely means that market discipline is
enforced by the workers upon themselves. The establishment
of such 'self-discipline' cannot escape the imperatives imposed
by a global system of socially mediated labour. Either production matches the demands of the law of value; or the state
subsidises the difference; or the 'trading arrangement' is of
an imperial character, meaning that the UK is able to force
its partners to purchase its goods at a higher price than they
could find elsewhere. In neither of these cases is the 'discipline
of the market' or the law of value overcome – it is merely
mediated in a different way.

In practice it seems clear that far from workers being free
to produce what and how they choose, in order to directly
fulfil social needs, production must remain within the constraints set by the state (or local government) in order to fulfil
its side of the bargain with its trading partners. If workers
refuse to adhere to the 'needs of the nation,' the state must
ensure that they do. Thus workers' control of production, in
and of itself – and for all its undoubted merits – does nothing
to eradicate the central contradiction of capitalist labour, but
merely temporarily shifts it onto another plane. Nor does it
provide any answer to the crisis of profitability to which 'neoliberalism' was one temporary response, a crisis which raised
its head once more in 2008. As Eric Hobsbawm notes, Bennism has no means to explain exactly *how* economic democracy or 'democratic socialism' solves the 'log-jam' of British
capitalism, the 'specific problems which monetarism [or neo-
liberalism] and corporatism purport to solve.'[61] An expansion
of workers cooperatives, however welcome, would not have
prevented either the crisis of Keynesianism, nor that of neoliberalism. It does not overcome the foundational contradiction of capitalist society. The idea that it would have done is
precisely a consequence of the misrecognition of capital as

merely a mode of concrete power of one social group over another, as opposed to a universal form of social domination.

Attempts to control the flow of financial capital through the nationalisation of the banking and financial sectors – a suggestion put forward by Corbyn's head of policy Andrew Fisher in his 2014 book *The Failed Experiment* – risk being equally counterproductive.[62] In a global economy, in which production relies on tightly integrated, transnational supply chains lubricated by the movement of finance, the idea that a single nation state can stymie those flows or channel them to their own advantage is, as Jamie Merchant argues, to

> *re-impose narrowly local solutions on worldwide problems...This amounts to simply wishing away the forces of global financialised production. Because these forces form a transnational whole that is larger than the sum of its parts, demands to nationalise or collectivise the commanding heights of finance would not bring forth the egalitarian world they aim at. Rather, they would more likely accelerate current trends toward world economic breakdown and geopolitical belligerence.[63]*

Such a trajectory will only be intensified by a decision to leave the world's biggest trading bloc, the Single Market. Replacing a larger 'frictionless' market with a smaller 'rooted' one, hedged off by protectionist barriers and buttressed by state aid, will reduce the overall productivity and profitability of labour in the long-run, and thus, on the very terms of the Corbynite–Bennite search for a society based on production for human need, the ability of that labour to fulfil the needs of society. Like it or not, today production is a necessarily transnational affair. Splitting up pan-European just-in-time supply chains and shared regulatory frameworks in the name of a 'national economy' is to sacrifice thousands of jobs and livelihoods on the altar of a fetishised sovereignty matching anything to be found on the hard right.

The idea of the NHS as the 'mother of all anchoring institutions,' proposed by Joe Guinan, is particularly problematic in this light, raising the possibility of healthcare being rationed due to being forced to 'buy British' rather than cheaper alternatives.[64] Moreover its nationalist overtones are ripe for exploitation by the populist right, in much the same way as the rhetoric of 'our NHS' was utilised by the Leave campaign for nativist purposes. Indeed, at times, the localist policies proposed in the AMO document sound remarkably similar to those of former May advisor Nick Timothy's 'Erdington Conservatism,' discussed in Chapter 1. Worse, they chime neatly with the Trumpian moves to reorganise capital on national-protectionist lines as a solution to the rumbling crisis of the neoliberal free trade settlement, that was itself the solution to the collapse of Keynesianism.

Such protectionist measures will inevitably generate a response from rival national-economies, usually through the form of raised import tariffs. Taken to extremes – if every locality and nation implemented the same protectionist programme – these policies would universally lower living standards, lower wages, and decrease the funding available for public services. Furthermore, they contain all the ingredients for a full-on 1930s-style trade war, effectively turning localities into giant state-run capitalist enterprises competing on a world stage determined by direct, unmediated force.

It is precisely to avoid such an antagonistic 'race to the bottom' between national economies that state aid regulation is a fundamental part of the Single Market and multilateral trade deals in general. This is not only to prevent the 'dumping' of goods (such as state-funded Chinese steel) produced below the rate of socially necessary labour time thanks to state-subsidies – thus forcing the rest of the market to cut costs, win similar subsidy or risk bankruptcy.[65] Mutually agreed limits to state aid are also a means to prevent states competing to offer preferential conditions or tax breaks to multinational companies in the hope that they might set up offices or production sites in that country.[66] Therefore reports that the EU are insistent that any post-Brexit trade deal with the UK must be subject to a 'level playing field mechanism' is not evidence of the former's irredeemably 'neoliberal' character, as some Corbyn supporters have claimed.[67] Nor is it an attempt 'by European leaders to prevent an elected socialist government enacting socialist policies for which it has a democratic mandate,' and thus 'a straightforward attack on British democracy,' as Owen Jones breathlessly argued.[68] It is merely a defensive measure to ensure that Brexit does not lead to Europe fragmenting into competitive national capitals engaging in a trade war, with mutually destructive results.[69]

There is nothing 'socialist' about sparking such a war – or intensifying one already under way – through the myopic insistence that British enterprises be unilaterally allowed to undercut their competitors via state subsidies, with any attempt to counteract that subsidy via the raising of tariffs painted as 'neoliberal.' As James Stafford and Florence Sutcliffe-Braithwaite put it, if the Corbynist–Lexiteer vision entails the pursuit of policies 'genuinely incompatible with the European treaties (for instance, permanent capital controls or the unilateral adoption of trade quotas),' its supporters need to explain why their 'broader objectives can only be achieved through what would amount to a declaration of economic warfare against Britain's closest neighbours and most reliable allies.'[70]

The irony of such a scenario being willed into being by a movement which places a tremendous store by its 'anti-imperialist' credentials, often above and beyond any other democratic principle, is that it risks replicating in contemporary form the antagonistic and expansionist political-economic backdrop of nineteenth century imperialism. Even if the potentially catastrophic consequences of such a development are left aside, and even if the controversial claim made by Costas Lapavitsas that World Trade Organisation rules are less 'neoliberal' than those of the Single Market is accepted, the idea that a UK standing alone would be able to come out on equal terms in such a war is sheer fantasy.[71] Evidence of what is in store was already on display both in Trump's decision to impose tariffs on European steel and aluminium, and the immediate response from the EU, which placed retaliatory tariffs on a range of US goods.[72] The idea that the UK would somehow be able to escape such a similar fate through the negotiation of Trump-esque zero-sum 'deals' can only exist through the wilful ignorance of both the general trajectory of the global political economy, and the realpolitik of power relations within a fragmented and increasingly antagonistic multipolar world. Squeezed between powerful regional blocs trading protectionist blows, far from 'taking back control,' the Lexiteer delusion would see workers in the UK beholden to the personal whims of authoritarian nationalist rulers across the globe.

~~~

In this chapter we have suggested that the fundamental problem with the Bennite prospectus – a problem that is replicated in Corbynism's Alternative Models of Ownership prospectus – is that the globally mediated character of the social form of labour in capitalism is not recognised at all. Instead, as we have noted, a direct relationship between workers and wealth is posited. From this perspective, a localist or national policy of protectionism which rejects 'globalisation,' epitomised in the Lexit schema by the EU, in order that the nation-state might stop wealth 'sliding away from localities', as the AMO puts it, makes perfect sense. However, once it is recognised

that the value of a commodity is not something that is created directly by workers but is a result of the mediation of
social labour as a whole – which today is a necessarily *global*
form of mediation – the illusionary, and in many ways politically dangerous, nature of protectionist solutions becomes
clear. The same can be said for their similarly mediation-free
political foundations in populisms that establish a direct and
unmediated relationship between state and society, power
and subject.

None of what we say here means that increased state aid
(within EU rules), a national investment bank, ensuring that
small businesses are able to easily apply for government
contracts, or the expansion of workers' cooperatives are not
policies worth pursuing. These are indeed some of the policies that recommend Labour's domestic agenda – but still
carry with them the ideological contours of the wider Corbynist project. Their potential success hinges on full recognition of the real and inescapable contradictions inherent in
capitalist relations of production as a global system, rather
than the pretence that all that is required to remove them
is the emergence of some socialist form of national sovereignty which will allow workers to 'take back control.' The
inevitable failure of such a model in an irreversibly global
society just sets up yet another narrative of betrayal, one
greatly intensified by the faith in Corbyn's personal integrity
and the self-regard of the broader movement as being the
'community of the good.' This is in common with all such
demands for the taking back of control in a world where we
are *all* out of control.

Short of autarky, the purity of national sovereignty is
impossible in a world where legal frameworks and standards
of measurement follow the path of trade, establishing equivalent grounds for commodity exchange. Capitalism's drive to
commensurate everything under the rule of value, and the

fateful objectification of our human activity in alien forms that dominate us from without, puts paid to any dream of control by means of sovereignty preserved among peoples of nations. The only means by which the forces of capital might be overcome or, at best, constrained is the pooling of sovereignty across and irrespective of borders. Global challenges cross borders, and our 'sovereignty' is only made stronger for the capacity to face them together with other states. The desire for control through national sovereignty, on the other hand, is a demand that can never be met because it is impossible. Capital will win out. Political commitments that promise to satiate that which is insatiable thus only uncork forces they will be hard pressed to rebottle.

The real trouble will thus come when the inability of a protectionist state to protect its national community from the inexorable workings of the capitalist law of value becomes clear. A narrative that is founded on the inevitability of betrayal and personal moral failure, one which understands the problems of capitalist society to be caused by the external intervention of alien elements in a natural, moral community of the productive, rather than the systemic pressures caused by a specific form of social organisation, is easily channelled by the hard-right.[73] This is particularly risky if the institutional structures of liberal capitalism – the impersonal laws and rights which ameliorate, however unsatisfactorily, the inherent conflicts and contradictions of a system of 'social labour' – are conflated with that self-same system of socially mediated labour, and thus recklessly cast aside in the name of 'taking back' an elusive and impossible 'control.'

When viewed through the prism of the historically-specific and inherently contradictory set of social relations that constitute capitalist society, it can be more clearly seen that contemporary capitalism is a tightly-integrated global system from which no single nation can escape. Our contention is that neither of these conditions is recognised in the Corbyn world-view. A theory which fails to adequately grasp its object can lead to actions with very different consequences from those intended. As such, the solutions which Corbynism proposes to the myriad problems of contemporary capitalist society, each of them centred upon the nation-state as the primary political actor and a turn away from internationalism, are not adequate to the task at hand. Neither can they be said to be definitively left-wing, if by left-wing we mean a set of policies aiming at emancipation from the status quo, rather than its affirmation. The implementation of what is, in truth, a politically ambiguous, and in many ways recklessly deluded, policy programme of nationalist protectionism, epitomised by the aspiration for a 'jobs-first Brexit' seemingly to be powered by kickstarting an economic war with Britain's closest trading partners, thus risks exacerbating, rather than challenging, the current trajectory towards world economic breakdown and belligerent nativist geopolitics. In the process it sets loose unpredictable political and social currents which may not be easily contained by a leftist project once up and running.

In its increasing swing behind a 'Lexit' position, theoretically justified through the Bennite critique of the Single Market as an outside imposition upon the national community of the production, Corbynism throws economic caution to the wind in pursuit of a sentimental politics that places the sovereignty and identity of a primordial and pre-political social force above the world of economic objectivity and commodified social relations. Any radical imperative inherent in this politics is undermined by the risk on one side of economic calamity, and on the other the termination of this agenda, specifically as it relates to Brexit, in a 'stab in the back' myth of national betrayal. No amount of energetic canvassing or witty memes can bridge such an abyss. It requires the political courage to be truly honest with the electorate about the consequences of withdrawal from the Single Market and the true costs of protectionism, traits which for all Corbyn's purported authenticity have been in short supply. But this has less to do with a weakness on Corbyn's part and more to do with the blunt fact that the same nationalist presumptions about the capacity for national or popular sovereignty against global capital that drive right-wing Brexit are present in their left-wing form in the very intellectual foundations of Corbynism. The accommodation to Lexit is neither positioning nor prevarication, but rather a logical consequence of the left's programme for national renewal which takes as much from Bennism as it does from any contemporary source. That is, with the exception of populism – which we will explore in the next chapter.

5

'THINGS CAN AND THEY WILL CHANGE': CLASS, POSTCAPITALISM AND LEFT POPULISM

Corbynism has frequently been proclaimed, by both its advocates and its critics, as the return to a Labour Party focused on the politics of class, and specifically the interests of the working class.[1] But in this chapter we will see that Corbynism gained part of its political power from the percolation of an analysis closer in spirit to a politics of 'the people', which misrecognises, and thus ends up obscuring, the true reality of class society. We survey how the unsteady coalition of Corbynism negotiates class in two ways. As we have seen, the old Bennite left, for its part, propagates a politically expedient but analytically flawed understanding of workers as the creators of all wealth, sure to inherit the future. Corbyn's leadership campaigns – peppered with platitudes about the barriers placed on workers' creativity by a parasitic 'elite' – exemplify this. Meanwhile, the fresher postcapitalist left seek new political subjects constituted beyond the traditional 'working class,' and based in the latter's abolition by means of new technological conditions pertaining to an automated end of work. Both strands of Corbynism unite over a common view of the relationship between classes and the system that has both conspiracist characteristics – in the sense that conditions are seen to conspire against social change – and teleological – in that the chosen social actor is forecast to achieve social change once the inevitable overcoming of these conditions occurs.

The first, more traditional interpretation of class appears in particularly clear form in the work of Ralph Miliband, a major theoretical influence on both Bennism and Corbynism. In this chapter, we suggest that for all its undoubted strengths, Miliband's analysis of the role of the state in capitalist society, as well as his historical work on the Labour Party, is founded upon a highly personalised theory of capitalism that fails to come to terms with the abstract forms of social domination that distinguish capitalist societies. Miliband's argument that the capitalist character of the state can ultimately be traced back to the personal background and social connections of state officials and politicians sheds new light on the crucial importance Corbyn's personal reputation holds for the movement as a whole.

Both the traditional and postcapitalist theories of class and history have their roots in selective readings of Marx. But they are suffused in Corbynism by something that moves them past this Marxian basis: a politically ambivalent 'left' populism whose contemporary origins are to be found in the post-Occupy trajectory of a politics based on the rhetorical division between the '99%' and the '1%,' the 'people' and the 'elite.' In his appeal to 'the people,' Corbyn is a man of his time. For the idea of the people is now as pervasive on the left as the idea of class once was. Its omnipresence owes to a surge in left populism in the wake of the 2008 crisis, the roots of which could be seen first in the Occupy movement, and then, in a more mature political form, the struggles against austerity in southern Europe. With Corbynism the UK caught in short-form what swept Europe post-crisis. It shows how, pinning their hopes upon a succession of popular subjects, of late the left has wended a strange trajectory. Post-crisis, horizontalism sought to 'change the world without taking power'.[2] Then things started getting serious. Shrugging off disdain for the state, winning elections and wielding power became the aim.

This is reflected in the new vogue for big thinking on the UK left. There has been a rediscovery of the concept of popu-list hegemony and how to build it.[3] Dreams abound of seizing state power to implement postcapitalism or so-called 'Fully Automated Luxury Communism'. The radical left accom-modation of statist solutions would have been unthinkable as tents sprung up outside St Pauls in 2011. In some ways, it shows the adulthood of the Occupy generation, and a wel-come and possibly transformative spirit of compromise with the world as it is. In others, it is not entirely without illusions, as these compromises lapse into complicity with that world. A reflex against Occupy's failure, the new verticalism still bears its foreshortened class critique. Against the 'elite', the 'people' stands in as the alibi for a state politics that lacks a social basis.

There is a teleology at play in how Corbynists under-stand the relationship between people, technology and social change that drives a lot of its optimistic appraisal of the possibility for political transformation. Drawn in equal parts from traditional readings of Marx and the opposi-tion of 'natural' and 'artificial' society found in the work of Karl Polanyi, for diverse strands of Corbynism social-ism is regarded as the culmination of the inexorable devel-opment of the 'forces of production', developing under the surface of society and making the political and legal structures of capitalism obsolete. In the latter, socialism is understood as a return to an original or natural state of collective life. In the second part of the chapter we show how these two perspectives are combined in different ways by both the Bennite and postcapitalist renditions of Corbynism.

Towards the end of the chapter, we take a look at how this perspective dovetails with contemporary theories of populism, whose origins we trace back to the hyper-antagonistic definition of 'the political' developed by the Nazi jurist Carl Schmitt. We see how Schmitt's division of the world into 'friends' and 'enemies' chimes with both traditional, uncritical interpretations of class and the Manichean moralism which infuses so much of the Corbyn worldview. We argue that this powerful combination explains why the Corbyn movement draws its greatest energies from the experience of coming under attack from those it can define as 'enemies' – and also suggest that this defensive, occasionally paranoid form of politics has the potential to lead in reactionary and, in volatile times, highly dangerous directions.

~~~

The critical Marxism advanced in our reading of Corbynism differs from more orthodox and traditional strands that stress the working class as the subject of history, with socialism achieved by the removal of a capitalist class preventing workers receiving a fairer distribution of the fruits of their labour. Class in the critical Marxian sense does not mean a particular group of people distinguished by certain cultural or occupational traits. Nor is it a simple opposition of groups or 'teams' representing 'socialism' and those personifying capitalism. As the Hungarian Marxist GM Tamas puts it, class is not 'a framework for a whole life or a Lebenswelt.' It is rather an inherently contradictory social relation between formally equal people whose access to the things they need to survive is mediated by money. This historically-specific form of social organisation forces the majority to sell the only thing they own – their capacity to work – for a wage. As such, class is not a 'human group with common interests and common moral and cultural values such as, say, solidarity and contrariness, but a structural feature of society.' A class is not, then, 'an actor' in a political or social sense.[4]

Classes are therefore not social groups. Rather, class is the form of social relations through which social groups exist. Class thus affects people in a complex variety of ways. There is no 'pure' proletarian or 'pure' capitalist. Seen like this, the persistence of class as a social relation does not depend upon the continued existence of a traditional working class culture nor a particular form of industrial or material labour. As Richard Gunn argues, a theory of class as a social relation avoids the 'embarrassment' suffered by sociological conceptions of class when faced with the realisation

> that not all individuals in bourgeois society can be fitted, tidily, into the groups which it labels 'capitalists' and 'proletarians'. This embarrassment is produced by the conception of classes as groups or places, and to escape this embarrassment, sociological Marxism has recourse to categories like 'the middle classes', the 'middle strata', etc.: such categories are residual or catch-all groups and, in short, theoretical figments generated by an impoverished conceptual scheme. The Marxist conception of class, on the contrary, faces no such difficulties: it regards the class-relation (say, the capital-labour relation) as structuring the lives of different individuals in different ways.[5]

One of the effects of a society structured by class, if left unchecked, is the creation of vast disparities of wealth between rich and poor. But this is not, in itself, a unique Marxian insight – the recognition of the negative side of 'commercial society' was a central part of the classical political economy tradition from Adam Ferguson to Adam Smith. A distinct Marxian theory of class thus goes further than the measurement of relative wealth. As Tamas puts it, class in a Marxian sense

> is that feature of capitalist society which divides it along the lines of people's respective positions in relation to reification/alienation, i.e., their degree of autonomy vis-à-vis subordination to commodities and value.[6]

But it is not the rich themselves who are personally responsible for the social organisation as a whole, even though, as we will see in Chapter 6, this is what the conspiratorial mindset of Corbynism sometimes suggests. The kind of class analysis we employ here – drawn from the work of theorists like Tamas and Moishe Postone – works at a higher level of abstraction than positivist sociological conceptualisations of inequality and elite power. Class in this sense is the social relation which *produces* capitalist society. As such, class struggle is not a breakdown in the functioning of an otherwise perfect system of wealth production, but is rather a permanent feature of that system. As Werner Bonefeld argues, the class antagonism, whereby one class must sell their labour power to live in the absence of any independent or collective access to the means of subsistence, and another class must buy it in order to valorise their capital and thus the conditions for the life of the former, can be seen to *constitute* the contradictory unity of capitalist society, rather than infringe it.

In a society constituted by the class antagonism, 'the people' is a placeholder for something that exists only as pure potential. But the people's non-existence does not diminish its political effect on the faithful. It rallies supporters around a rhetorical perch on which to rest their laurels. This is best seen in the logic of the 99%, which grants to the 1% the status of a perfect alibi for political failure, fixing reality against the popular will. As we will see, conspiracy theories such as that posited in the 99%–1% framing provide a convenient excuse to avoid the complex thinking and activity necessary to comprehend and change a world where power has no central point and there is no 'side' to take in the movement of class struggle.

On the other hand, an added sense of comfort rewards those sharing Corbyn's conviction that things can, and they will, change' owing to the sheer force of numbers commanded by the 99%.[7] The 1% might command the power, but all it takes is for the rest to come around the right away of seeing the world and all will be well. From this perspective, class as a constitutive social relation – the fact that in capitalism our subjective activity is and can only be realised in and through objectifications that come in turn to dominate us – disappears from sight altogether. This may be politically empowering, but it is potentially strategically disastrous. It unrealistically uproots itself from conditions as they are, orbiting this world from an external standpoint rooted entirely in how it is wished to be. As we shall see, by treating society as an essentially positive and non-contradictory force identical with the 'movement' and in turn the people, held back only by the machinations of what Corbyn describes as a 'rigged system' imposed from outside, any truly critical intent is stolen from the political moment.

The depiction of society as a direct power struggle between a unified, non-contradictory and natural community of a productive 'people' counterposed to an illegitimate, unnatural and non-productive elite (or underclass), is the *sine qua non* of populism. Moreover, this easily comes to assume a nationalist dimension. According to Ernesto Laclau and Chantal Mouffe, populism is about articulating difference along lines of equivalence – so that one grievance is shared by many.[8] But these attempts struggle against the plain fact that the peaceful construction of a unified people, even one constructed around an 'empty signifier,' is impossible in a society criss-crossed with class relations. Left and right alike attempt the temporary resolution of this antagonism at the higher level of the national people. Suspicion of transnational power can lapse into a *souverainiste* imaginary that, as we have seen with Bennism and its reconceptualisation in the 'Alternative Models of Ownership' document, envisages socialism as the protection of a nationally-defined people by a nation-state.[9] The blossoming of support for 'Lexit' demonstrates the worst of this tendency – projecting a personalised critique of capitalism onto a 'bosses' Europe'. This suggests the removal of a clique is all it takes to restore balance. Whether left of right, populism always finds someone to blame for an ailing nation.[10]

CLASS AND VALUE THEORY

The 'classic' understanding of class amongst much of the left, both within Corbynism and without, effectively rests upon a form of 'two-campism' which mimics that we have already seen with regard to abstract 'anti-imperialism.' Indeed, it is the latter's theoretical basis, the sociological depiction of class extrapolated and writ large on the world stage. At its heart lies the direct relationship between labour and value that we argued underpinned the Bennite understanding of capitalism, where one 'camp' – the 'working class' – produces the wealth of society, and another – the 'capitalist class' – steals it. This sociological notion of class relations made intuitive sense during the era of the 'worker's movement', based primarily on industrial labour, and peaking in the early twentieth century. It seemed self-evident that the working class physically created the 'value' contained in the objects they made, while the capitalist class merely appropriated it afterwards. It only required a small analytical step for this 'working class' to be personified as the representation, or prefiguration, of socialism itself, developing within the constraints of capitalism, and needing only to be rid of its 'fetters' (private property relations, held in place by a dictatorial capitalist class) in order to be brought into being.

This story was given a shot of irrepressible optimism, as we will see in later sections, by the pattern of historical development which lies at the root of orthodox Marxism, taken over from Hegel, whereby the growth of the forces of production would eventually make capitalist property relations untenable, and the communist society that had been developing under the surface of the old would finally come into being. In the classical figure of the working class, the forces of rationality and morality are combined. From the 'standpoint of the proletariat' it is not only *right* that the working class should take full ownership of what they have produced, it is self-evidently *rational* to move beyond the restrictive anarchy of capitalist social relations too.

Whilst appearing largely unversed in its theoretical intricacies, Corbyn has spent his entire adult life locked into step with a left political context in which such aspirations are common currency. It is thus unsurprising to see a form of the orthodox 'embodied' theory of value, whereby things carry value as a substance somehow inserted by the concrete effort of workers, reflected in Corbyn's rhetoric around 'wealth creation'.[11] Speaking in May 2016, Corbyn stated that

> *wealth creation is a good thing. Of course we all*
> *want greater prosperity. But let's have a serious*
> *debate about how wealth is created and how*
> *it is shared. It is a cooperative process between*

> *workers, public investment in services and yes,*
> *very often innovative and creative individuals and*
> *businesses... Wealth creation is a shared process- the*
> *proceeds must be shared too.'[12]*

The wealth Corbyn talks about here – the prosperity to be shared – is that which in capitalism takes the form of value, embodied in money. Wealth in the form of value, in this account, is seen as a neutral and transhistorical category produced by human effort, rather than a peculiar, historically specific and socially mediated category which exists only under capitalist social relations. Any mystery pertains not to the circumstances whereby we live through this category 'value' in the first place, but rather how it is differently appropriated and distributed among classes categorised along the lines of revenue delineated in classical political economy – the state with its taxes, the entrepreneur with her profits, the worker with her wage. This conceptualisation was notably savaged in Marx's critique of the fetishism of the 'Trinity Formula' found in the political economy of Adam Smith.[13] In an incomplete critique of value in capitalist society, the premise of that value is accepted but it is then taken to be the people's rightful property, and therefore in itself a positive thing. Problems only arise when one participant in the value creation process takes more than their fair share.

Here wealth as value is seen as something to which class is only incidental, rather than constitutive. The technical process of production itself, the concrete act of labour which supposedly produces value in a direct and immediate fashion, is regarded as being prior to the struggle over its distribution. Production is, in class terms, neutral and non-contradictory. The central role of production and its necessary appearance as value in capitalist society is not regarded as strange, as something to be questioned, nor the production process itself as riven with contradictions. Rather contradiction appears only *after* the moment of production, as a result of the unjustified and unnecessary intervention of the capitalist and the banker into that system of production and circulation. It is this depiction of social conflict as being the result of external interference in a productive process which would otherwise cater for the needs of all that lies behind Corbyn's intuitive faith in the 'obviousness' or naturalness of socialism covered in the last chapter. Such a perspective naturalises the process of capitalist 'concrete labour', regarding it as 'production as such,' and treats the abstract forms of capitalist society – money, finance, exchange – as artificial interlopers into an essentially natural system. By doing so it leaves the question of the specific social role of production in capitalism, and the specific nature of the commodified forms in which it results, completely untouched.

The difference between socialism and capitalism from this perspective therefore rests on the relative levels of control of workers or capitalists over a form of production that remains essentially unchanged. As we shall see shortly, the contention that capitalism and socialism are distinguished by the social background or personal ideology of those in charge of its structures, in particular the state, lies at the heart of Ralph Miliband's work, a key theoretical influence on both Benn and the Corbyn movement today.

However, Marx's mature work is based upon the rejection of this positivist conception of production, with labour only the creation of the specific thing that potentially carries value, and not the value itself.[14] Value was no longer regarded as some kind of physical fabrication, but something posited by the process in which products are brought into an abstract relationship of exchange with one another. The question Marx set out to answer was not therefore 'what is the best distribution of the value created by labour?' but why labour appears in the form of this strange thing 'value' in the first place. A critique of capitalism limited to the argument that workers are illegitimately deprived of the fruits of their labour by a capitalist class to whom they are only externally related, with socialism understood as a society in which they will receive the full amount of the wealth they produce, is not able to properly grasp the basis of capitalist social relations – the social form of labour, and of wealth itself.

As we set out in previous chapters, this form of wealth is predicated upon a universal separation from the means of subsistence, a situation which produces a system which forces people to access what they need to survive by means of socially mediated labour. For most people, this mediation takes the form of a competition for waged work in private enterprises, although it could equally take the form of state- or worker-run production and distribution. In the process workers create 'capital' as a seemingly separate power, standing over themselves, forcing production to match up to the measure of productivity set by the law of value. But 'capital' is not really a thing, with its own existence. It is merely a mode of existence of labour, a social relation founded upon the separation from the means of subsistence.

Workers and their employers – whether private capitalists or the state – certainly do come into conflict over the way resources are distributed into wages or profit, a conflict whose parameters run from all-out insurrection to the building of trade unions and parliamentary parties. Liberal forms of capitalist society channel these subjective struggles through legal and political recourses and processes through which piecemeal or emancipatory changes can be achieved. In actually-existing 'communist' states, on the other hand, strikes and trade unions are generally banned, or integrated into the state itself, because it is presumed that state ownership of the means of production has successfully 'resolved' class struggle. This purported 'resolution' of class struggle is also a feature of other totalitarian political imaginaries. A diluted version of this illusion is present in the idea that worker-controlled enterprises eliminate exploitation and thus present 'an alternative structure to capitalist firms,' as the Alternative Models of Ownership document puts it.[15] Although potentially providing the basis for better or worse mediations of the same underlying contradictions and conditions of reproduction, neither state ownership nor workers' control of production changes the fact that as long as society persists through relations of mediated labour, both the state and workers remain reliant on economic 'growth,' capitalists or no capitalists – a growth which is only possible through the continuation of that self-same crisis-ridden system of mediated labour.

In capitalist society workers are perpetually divided against themselves. They need a 'bigger pie' over which to fight just as much as any capitalist, despite that pie being the product of their own exploitation. Hence Marx's recognition that to be a productive worker is 'not a piece of luck, but a *misfortune'*.[16] The more the worker produces, the greater the capital which dominates their life through the abstract force of value. The contradiction upon which capitalism is founded runs through the 'working class' itself. This is the *objective* meaning of the 'class struggle' which underpins capitalist society. It is the constant struggle for survival, to access the means of subsistence. It pits worker against worker as much as it opposes worker against employer. Unlike subjective class struggle – conscious battles over wages or working conditions – this struggle for survival takes place continuously, regardless of the levels of consciousness of workers, or whether the state or the workers themselves own the means of production. By working, by subsisting, humans create 'a reality that increasingly enslaves them'.[17]

Socialism cannot mean, then, the 'victory' of the working class in a struggle between 'two camps,' while leaving
untouched the system of social labour and value which constitutes 'class struggle' as an objective, structural feature of capitalist society. This would merely constitute a different form
of distribution of value. The manifold failures of the Soviet
system of production, along with the crisis of profitability that
was the death knell of the post-war Keynesian consensus, demonstrate the practical limits of this kind of 'truncated' critique.
It is unable to account for the continuation, without end, of
crisis and social conflict over resources in societies which claim
to have overcome class struggle. This often leads to authoritarian political solutions as a means to close the gap between
the narrative of a glorious 'workers' state' and the miserable
reality, foreclosing the legal and political means to win gains
from and through that struggle. For Marx, by contrast, human
emancipation entails the destruction of 'class society' altogether, not the 'working class' taking control of it. And given the
global character of capitalism, this can only take place on a
truly international basis, not by turning away from transnational cooperation or opposing one nation-state to another.

All of this notwithstanding, the 'two campist' rendition of
class retains a powerful hold over contemporary leftist movements. Indeed, it is the conflation of sociological theories of class
with the 'friend'/'enemy' distinction of populism's political frontier that characterises the rising left across the globe. The depiction of capitalism as a straightforward power struggle between
capitalists and workers over the control of a form of production
itself regarded as neutral or natural – and of socialism as the
settling of that struggle in favour of the workers – has a long
(and in many ways quite effective) history within the workers'
movement. One of its clearest renditions appears in the work
of Ralph Miliband, who, as noted above, was and remains a
central theoretical touchstone for the Bennite–Corbyn tradition.

PARLIAMENTARY SOCIALISM AND THE STATE

Miliband's central concern was the role of the state in the perpetuation of capitalist control of production.[18] He disputed the thesis that the impersonal structures of the state are separated from the particular interests of society, with at least the potential to arbitrate between them – the founding claim of pluralist formal democracy. Instead, following Marx and Engels in *The Communist Manifesto*, he argued that the state's 'main purpose is to defend the predominance in society of a particular class': that class 'which controls the means of production and which is able, by virtue of the economic power thus conferred upon it, to use the state as its instrument for the domination of society.'[19]

For Miliband there is, therefore, a more-or-less direct relationship between the distribution of economic power over production and political control of the state. But this is not necessarily because capitalists become politicians themselves, although that is common enough. Rather, the capitalist character of the state arises from the 'general outlook, ideological dispositions and political bias' of the individuals in charge of its various apparatuses – the fact that in sociological terms they are drawn from groups ideologically and politically close or beholden to the capitalist class itself.[20] The process of formal democracy and the parliamentary system, based on a supposed plurality of political interests competing for the votes of a politically equal electorate, is not quite a sham. But the biases and 'dispositions' of the state personnel, combined with the fact that large parts of the economy are privately owned, provides a 'decisive and permanent advantage' to the capitalist class.[21] Whoever wins elections, the personal loyalty and ideological perspective of those running the state – not just in Westminster but across all state institutions – was to and of the capitalist class. As such, for all the pretensions of

the liberal bourgeois state to a separate structure of impersonal rules applied equally to all, it was in truth merely the
tool of the ruling class, to be used how it saw fit.

Miliband's sociological theory of the state mirrors the
uncritical, naturalistic approach to production and labour
outlined above. In the latter, as we have seen, the form of production itself is not called into question, merely the distribution of power within it. Production is regarded as capitalist
production when controlled by capitalists, and socialist when
controlled by the workers. Likewise, the question of the *form*
of the state, the particular relationship between economics
and politics in a capitalist society, itself drops out of a theory
which regards a state as capitalist to the extent that its offices
are filled by those identified as 'capitalist,' or those whose
'ideological disposition' is towards capitalism – and socialist
to the extent it is controlled by socialists. For Miliband, and
for Benn and Corbyn too, the state's relationship to capitalism is essentially voluntarist. The state and capitalism exist
in separate spheres – hence Miliband's book is entitled 'the
state in capitalist society,' rather than 'the capitalist state.'
The state ultimately supports capitalist forms of production
out of choice, out of the individual motivations of the people in charge of it. This choice may not be cynical. Those in
charge of the state may truly believe that the interests of their
citizenry are tied up with the success of capitalist production.
For Miliband, this belief was a monumental – and avoidable
– intellectual error.

That the capitalist character of the state (and production)
remained after a Conservative election victory needed little explanation – the Tories unambiguously represented the
interests of the capitalist class. The real problem, for Miliband, was with Labour. Despite claiming to represent the
workers, once in power successive Labour governments had
lacked the nerve to challenge the explicit capitalist bias of

the state personnel – not just those in Westminster, but in all state institutions, from the courts to the police to the Bank of England. Rather than taking hold of the state, radically reforming its personnel and, like the capitalists, wielding it as an economic instrument in the interests of the workers, Labour in government had, the story went, wound up cravenly surrendering to capitalist demands. Labour politicians had willingly, even eagerly, fell in line with the dominant capitalist culture of the state institutions. The result was the collapse of any pretensions Labour may have had of being a socialist party.

Miliband's account of this history of failure was laid out in *Parliamentary Socialism*, and various essays which followed. He accused past and current Labour leaders, MPs and trade unionists of intellectual and moral failure. The feebleness of Labour governments' attempts to establish socialism was to be explained by their 'dogmatic' commitment, not to socialist ideals but the 'parliamentary system.'[22] Labour politicians were unable to see through the façade of formal democracy, and not therefore recognise the capitalist unity of state and society. Nor could they grasp the capitalist character of the state personnel, and thus remained mystified by the false appearance of a distinction between politics and economics.

By refusing to countenance political action outside of the parliamentary system, and in particular rejecting the possibility of politicising the production process itself, Labour governments were wedded to a strategy of 'Labourism.' Labourism aims to advance 'concrete demands of immediate advantage to the working class and organised labour' – higher wages, better working conditions, housing, healthcare, transport, benefits and the like.[23] Labourism aimed only at ameliorating the problems of capitalist society rather than transforming it into a socialist one. The horizons of Labour governments had 'been narrowly bound by the capitalist environment in which they found themselves, and whose framework they readily took as given; and it is within its framework and the 'rationality' it imposed that they sought reform.'[24]

'Capitalist rationality' is understood here as way of seeing the world that one can choose to accept or not. Production and the state can be described as capitalist to the extent they come under the sway of that rationality. The transformation from a capitalist to a socialist society primarily depends on the rejection of 'capitalist rationality' and the application of a separate socialist rationality. This alternative socialist rationality must, by implication, make up one aspect of a self-constituting and wholly separate moral and cultural identity of 'the world of labour'.[25] This 'world of labour' consists of a 'dense network of institutions – parties, trade unions, cooperatives, a labour and socialist press, associations and groups of every kind,' standing in opposition to the 'world of capital.'[26] Miliband's subjective conception of class as two separate 'worlds' coming into conflict is therefore the complete opposite of the structural definition given by Tamas at the start of this chapter. Indeed, the depiction of class as a political and social subject blocks the recognition of the objective and continuous character of class altogether.

Miliband regarded the acceptance of the capitalist framework to be an intellectual and personal failing of this popular subject on the behalf of Labour's parliamentary representatives- both an ideological error and a form of conscious betrayal. Thanks to the intellectual failings and personal cowardice of their leading members, Labour governments had routinely 'act[ed] in ways which were bound to alienate masses of actual or potential Labour supporters in the working class.' These supporters 'wanted, and voted for, programmes of economic and social betterment, but...the betterment they got from Labour Governments was easily overshadowed by the negative side of the record.' And that negative side, whether it came courtesy of Harold Wilson, Jim Callaghan or, later, Tony Blair, was the direct result of their personal 'failures, derelictions and betrayals.'

The main task for the left was therefore to find politicians with the intellectual foresight and moral fortitude to refuse the temptation of falling in with capitalist or 'establishment' interests, and the building of a social movement which would stop their hand or replace them should they threaten to do so. These heroic figures would rip the ideological veil from formal representative democracy, change the social character of the state personnel, politicise production and reject so-called 'capitalist rationality.' Politics and economics would be brought together through a new unity of a socialist state apparatus and the working class, able to freely control productive society in the interests of 'the many, not the few', as Corbyn now puts it.[27]

The force of Miliband's analysis is not in doubt, and it is not without merit. The social background of those in power and in state offices has indeed tended towards privileged groups. Even Tony Blair complained about the conservative bent of the civil service, an opinion which may well be one of the few he shared with Tony Benn.[28] State officials and politicians have indeed tended to have a direct or indirect interest in the continuation of the capitalist system as a means for the reproduction of the economic conditions on which their own reproduction rests. But this dependence they share in common with *everyone* in capitalist society, regardless of the specific contradictory, antagonistic or downright oppressive way one relates to these conditions of subsistence. If capitalist society collapses, the state goes down with it. The political form of the state and the economic form of the 'economy' are mutually constitutive. The relation between the two is not one of voluntary choice but essential interdependence.

What the absence of such considerations seems to highlight is that, taken as a whole, Miliband's depiction of capitalism is seriously flawed. Indeed, it is quite clear from his arguments about both the Labour Party and the state that Miliband – and by extension, we suggest, Benn and Corbyn – has no real theory of capitalism as a historically specific set of social relations at all, and as such cannot obtain a properly critical perspective. This is because, as Nicos Poulantzas famously argued, Miliband reduces class, the state and the connection between the two to 'inter-personal relations of 'individuals' composing social groups and 'individuals' composing the State apparatus,' with no recognition of the objective character of capitalist social relations existing beyond the control of any particular individual or group.[29] The intertwining of the social reproduction of human life itself and the expanded reproduction of capital seems nowhere to be grasped. Thus, for example, Miliband argues that the

> combined period of eleven years of Labour
> Governments from 1964 until 1979, with a
> Conservative interruption of only four years,
> [saw]...no major improvement in the British
> condition to which Labour could point.'[30]

All well and good – but nowhere does he refer to the myriad structural crises of capitalism as a global system throughout that period, crises which we now know constituted the complete breakdown of the Keynesian mode of mass industrial production in 'developed' societies. In this, British capitalism and politics is treated entirely in abstraction from capitalism as a world-market – an analytical mistake that has its political corollary in the left-nationalist fantasies of 'Lexit'. Miliband does not enquire into how those crises, nor Britain's relative position in that world system, might have affected or restrained the decisions of those in power.

Instead he effectively explains the existence of those crises and their consequences as a direct result of those decisions.

This is a strange position to take for a follower of Marx, for whom capitalism has to be understood, at least in part, as 'a social process that goes on behind the backs of the producers' and political leaders.[31] Miliband's thesis is entirely voluntaristic. It rests on a totalising and essentialised vision of politics which, precisely because of that false totalisation – because it mistakes a part for the whole – has no means to grasp the peculiar nature of, and structural constraints upon, politics in a capitalist society. Paradoxically, such a position actually ends up *eradicating* politics by reducing it to the discovery and articulation of a pre-political form of subjective class 'rationality' or 'wills' whose origins lie in separate ontologised 'worlds' of labour and capital. Thus, as Simon Clarke notes, for all his attempts to avoid the pitfalls of orthodox Marxism, Miliband ended up 'reintroducing an economistic reductionism via the subjectivity of the class actors whose interests prevailed in the class struggle.'[32]

In the Bennite version of this analysis, the crises of British capitalism under Labour merely proved that, on the one hand, the post-war programme of nationalisation had not gone far enough. The capitalist class and international finance still retained too much power, which they had used to drain the British economy of its vitality. On the other, where industries had been brought into the public sector, their organisation had been too bureaucratic and top-down, and thus remained in the control of a political leadership still in hock to capitalist interests. The lack of industrial democracy – in the form of 'workers' control' – had meant that nationalisation had not redistributed power in such a way to produce a 'change in the relationships between capital and labour.'[33] Thus both the crisis of capitalism and the failure of socialism to emerge from the basis of the industry that had been nationalised (and thus in some way politicised) was attributed to the remnants of mediating factors that continued to corrupt attempts to restore the direct relationship between workers and their products – a direct relationship which Benn assumed would be the result of workers' control of production. This search for an unmediated set of social relations, as we see all around us today in rising nationalisms, fascisms and populisms, is a futile and dangerous one.

Indeed, there is an unexpected symmetry here between the form of analysis shared by Miliband, Benn and Corbyn, and that at the centre of the 'austerity populism' narrative promulgated by Cameron and Osborne. In the former, the crises of Keynesian capitalism are viewed as entirely avoidable and blamed on the 'betrayals' or cowardice of the Labour leadership and capitalist class. Labour governments failed to go far enough in politicising the economy or democratising society. In the latter, the 2008 crisis was to be explained by the 'overspending' on public services and welfare payments sanctioned by Gordon Brown during his decade as Chancellor. In both cases, highly individualised and voluntaristic explanations are offered for what, we suggest, must instead be understood as systemic crises of capitalism, with the roots of the latter being found in the former. As such, neither form of explanation is able to grasp the depth of capitalist crisis, nor comprehend the ineradicable contradiction that constitutes the relationship between politics and economics, and capital and labour, in a capitalist society on a global scale.

This relationship cannot be reduced to the level of state intervention in the economy, or the amount of workers' control over the productive process. Moreover, from a perspective which recognises capitalism as a global system mediated by social labour, it cannot be said that the democratic structures of liberal representative democracy – for all their undoubted flaws – are the main obstacle to the achievement

of socialism, if by that is meant a qualitatively different form
of society. Nor is the replacement of every state official with
an infallible 'true socialist' any answer, on its own, to the real
contradictions presented by the capitalist form of labour. For
regardless of whether labour is forced or freely sold, mediated by impersonal law and protected by democratic rights,
or directly organised by the state or workers themselves, it
retains its status as the mediating factor between an individual and their means of subsistence – a mediation the success
of which depends on adherence to the dictates of the law of
value. As such, the contradictory and crisis-ridden character
of capitalist social relations remains, regardless of the particular distribution of means of production or the ownership
of capital.

THE FORCES AND RELATIONS OF PRODUCTION

Soon after Corbyn was elected Labour leader, he gave an
interview to Andrew Marr, during which Marr asked him
whether he considered himself a Marxist. Corbyn answered
genially that he had not read as much as Marx as he would
like, but that the one aspect of his work that had struck him as
fascinating was 'Marx's transition of history and the analysis
of how you go from feudalism to capitalism and move onto a
different stage.'[34] As with his offhand comment about socialism being an 'obvious' or natural state of affairs, Corbyn's
words here revealed more about his worldview, and that of
the leftist culture in which he has spent his life, than he might
realise. The theory of historical development to which he refers
is that of the orthodox Marxian tradition, in which history is
seen as being driven by the growth of technological productive capacity, and struggles over the produce of that capacity.
The promise inherent in this theory of history – which comes

in various forms, some more deterministic than others – is that this singular transhistorical dynamic will eventually culminate in the transformation of capitalism into communism. Regardless of whether it is explicitly acknowledged or not, the orthodox Marxian depiction of historical development has, over the years, become the unspoken tenet of faith which has held together the British socialist movement throughout its darkest days. As such it is not surprising that it is the part of Marx's work that most interests Corbyn.

As with the orthodox reading of the 'labour theory of value', the roots of this theory of history can be found in the interpretation of select elements of Marx's work within twentieth-century Marxism, and in particular the theory of historical development laid out in the 1859 *Preface to the Critique of Political Economy*.[35] In this text, the development from one mode of production to another (say, feudalism to capitalism) is explained by changes in the economic base of society. This economic base is split into two categories, the 'forces of production' (in short, the technological capacity of production) and the 'relations of production' (the way that productive capacity is socially organised). The 'forces of production' are regarded as continually developing under the surface of society, bringing with them a rising class whose historical task is to propel this productive development forwards. The task of the bourgeoisie, for example, was to bring capitalism into being.

As the economic base develops, it throws up a political and legal superstructure (including, most importantly, the state) which is used by the dominant class to sustain their position in society. However, as the productive capacity of that society continues to develop, it brings with it a new 'rising' class responsible for their expansion. At a certain point, the relations of production of the old society, as well as the previously dominant class itself, become a 'fetter' on the development of these productive forces. Property, politics and production gradually come into contradiction, accompanied by a struggle between the respective rising and falling classes. This continues until there is a radical transformation of the outmoded form of property, political forms and the class hierarchy, so they no longer restrict but enable the full development of the productive forces.

This account helps us to see the link between the teleological reading of history and the 'campist' or orthodox understanding of class outlined above. Each rising or falling class is attributed historical responsibility for a different mode of production. While they may come into conflict during a period of transition from one mode to another (so the bourgeoisie struggles with feudal lords in the shift from feudalism to capitalism, and the proletariat in turn battles against the bourgeoise in order to bring communism into being) classes are essentially discrete entities, whose fate rests on the development of particular modes of production but who are not internally connected to each other. This is a very different understanding of class from that of class as a social relation. In the latter, classes only appear in their relation to one another in the process of the production of value. They do not exist as standalone social, cultural or political entities, who are then brought into conflict over the proceeds of production.

The orthodox account has been subject to considerable dispute within Marxian scholarship. Marx's 1859 *Preface*, the classic statement of the 'fetters' theory of capitalist development, is of questionable status in Marx's oeuvre, condensing work which Marx 'declared to be left to the gnawing criticism of the mice', later carefully repackaged in politically convenient form as *The German Ideology*.[36] Marx's latterday work, particularly *Capital*, owes very little, if anything, to the theory of history that appears sporadically elsewhere. Nevertheless, owing to the promotion of the fragmented manuscripts that comprise the *German Ideology* as canonical works of Marx, the notion of the 'fetter' has performed a lot of heavy lifting in Marxist politics and theory over the conflicted course of the twentieth century.

In response, a whole tradition of critical Marxism developed to counteract its ideological influence, inaugurated with Walter Benjamin. Benjamin bemoans the assumption on the part of socialist and social democratic movements in 1920s and 1930s Europe that all that was needed was to 'move with the current' and let the forces of production grant labour an earth to inherit.[37] History contains no guarantee that capitalism will be followed by communism, as opposed to fascism or theocracy. Things can get worse, as well as better. The 'New Reading of Marx' we draw upon in this book is an outcome, by way of Adorno, of this reckoning. Nevertheless, the influence of the orthodox account remains visible in the optimism that pervades the contemporary left, even in the most unlikely scenarios.

The absolute faith that capitalism will inevitably be followed by a better world is given new life in Corbyn's classless populism in which 'the many' will inevitably overcome 'the few', as well as the various theories of technologically induced 'postcapitalism' which constitute the most theoretically sophisticated wing of Corbynism. This post-work, basic income-funded, automation-enabled vision of the future has fed into Corbynism from the further reaches of postmodern Marxism via left columnists and other promoters.[38] It has had uptake from Corbyn and McDonnell themselves in their policy pronouncements. Alongside appeals to the possibility of a universal basic income, we have seen issued calls for a new digital agenda to free latent technological forces and drive British capitalism forwards by means of the development of 'socialism with an iPad'.[39] Corbyn, meanwhile, has made clear-voiced statements that suggest he has taken on board at least some of the new thinking arising from within his massed intellectual ranks. At the 2017 UK Labour Party conference, Corbyn extolled the 'new settlement between work and leisure' afforded by automation.[40] And, speaking to the Cooperative Party conference, he hailed, not without merit, the potential for 'an Uber run co-operatively by their drivers.' This was based on the presupposition that '[d]igital platforms are opening up huge opportunities for horizontal, more democratic, forms of organisation to flourish.' However, Corbyn continued: '[t]he biggest obstacle to this is not technological but ourselves'. In this, Corbyn gave a presentation of the dynamic between society and technology that rested on a very similar understanding as the relationship between the forces and relations of production at the centre of postcapitalist and accelerationist thinking.[41]

This account relies heavily on the traditional readings of Marx's theory of history outlined above. For example, Paul Mason – a leading proponent of the 'postcapitalist' prospectus – explicitly made Marx's controversial 1859 *Preface* the cornerstone of his influential book *Postcapitalism: A Guide to our Future*.[42] For Mason, while the 2008 crash signified the 'failure' of 'the neoliberal model' – essentially the relations of production – under the surface the productive forces have been inexorably developing, laying the foundations for a 'postcapitalist' economy based on the free distribution of immaterial goods, 'sharing' and the reduction of the working week.[43] In such an economy, the anarchy of capitalist production, in which individual firms care only about their profits and not the well-being of society as a whole, will be replaced by a rational system of distribution which will not only allow technology to reach its full potential but allocate resources in an equitable way, to the good of all. This will be achieved by the unfettering of the forces of production from the relations that inhibit their unfolding. The contradiction between the forces and relations of production, and between the economic base and superstructure will, in this way, finally be overcome.

Similarly, in the closely related 'accelerationist' schema, productive development is the bearer of a normative status infringed by the political strictures of the state and bourgeois

private property.[44] The development of technology and productive capacity is regarded as the driving force of history
and the measure of moral progress and rationality. The state
is understood either as a facilitator of productive development, or a parasitic body constructed in order to feed off the
productivity of an endlessly creative and non-contradictory
society. The accelerationist perspective implies, in Bennite
fashion, that while the interests of the capitalist class may
once – in the days when the bourgeoisie were a 'rising' class –
have led them to use their control of the state to support the
development of productive technology, in a contemporary
situation where the potential productive capacity of society
has outgrown both market exchange and human labour, the
state acts merely as a means for capitalists to slow it down
and channel it to their own limited ends.

The task of accelerationism is therefore to take control of
the state so as to use its apparatus to 'accelerate' the arrival
of a fully automated rational society of self-mastery, using it
to distribute a basic income directly to individuals, and ensuring that technology is allowed to develop to its full extent.
Once this is done, at last the true form of universal reason and
primordial human creativity, existing somehow prior to and
outside of history, and of which the rational and transhistorical development of technology and productive capacity is the
expression, is freed from its supposedly irrational fetters and
elevated to a position of dominance. In this way the partial,
contradictory and hopelessly outdated forms of bourgeois
property right are wiped out in the name of a harmonious
techno-social order, free from exploitation and oppression
centring on the work relation– whilst missing everything else
that makes this what it is. A preoccupation with a reduction
in working hours and the replacement of the wage with a
basic income indicates the extent to which this intellectual
viewpoint takes labour as such to be the problem of capitalism,
failing to recognise the social relations which give capitalist

labour its particular character – the radical state of dispossession whereby we cannot access the world of things except as commodities acquired through the means of money – and the historically specific socially mediated forms assumed by labour and its products in exchange. Rather, for the postcapitalists all the action happens after these conditions are established, and before direct labour loses its immediacy in the exchange of its products on the market. Having to *go* to work is the problem, and not the situation whereby we have to do it because we have no other means to reproduce ourselves, nor the form that work must take in order that it be socially valid and thus provide access to the means of subsistence.[45]

~~~

A key difference between the postcapitalist perspective and that of orthodox Marxism (and that of Bennism) appears in the question of the political subject who will be entrusted with the historic task of freeing the society to come from its neoliberal fetters.[46] For the orthodox Marxist and traditional workers movement, as we have seen, the answer lay in the industrial proletariat. But the contemporary left owes more to an increasingly influential strand of radical Italian leftism, *operaismo*, or workerism, that whilst apparently breaking with official orthodox Marxism, actually repeats its class theory in different form. The Italian leftist tradition in which Mason and the postcapitalist left follow, in its initial *operaist* incarnation, started out seeing working-class revolt driving capitalist change. In line with the 'Copernican Reversal' of key thinker Mario Tronti, this turned capitalist development on its head by suggesting that what Mason calls 'beautiful troublemakers' drove workplace innovation and not capital itself.[47] By the twenty-first century, however, and the mutation of *operaismo* into *postoperaismo* – or 'post-workerism' – the working class made way for a 'self-valorising' 'multitude' characterised by the rise of so-called 'immaterial labour', whose creative, cognitive and communicative desires are expressed in their postmodern work practices and determine the course and structure of world order.[48] So globalisation, for instance, is a reaction to the border-hopping boundlessness of uncontainable masses. Today, this appears in Mason's idea of the 'networked individual' as the revolutionary agent *du jour*, charged with the historic task of shepherding the world towards postcapitalism.[49] The 'Copernican Reversal' is still in evidence but with a different non-class actor in the driving seat- a multitude compromising all classes and none.

Thus the two wings of Corbynism simultaneously butter up the 'working class' as a positive social force possessed of the capacity to create all value, and, in its postcapitalist variant, claim that it no longer matters because things have changed and new actors take the reins. On the first count, this misrecognises the compulsion to sell one's labour in order to live as a position of political power rather than an original and continued dispossession of any other means to live. On the second, class is similarly seen as centring on the particular occupational forms that labour takes, rather than the persistence of the condition of dispossession which underlies it. It thus mistakes the eradication of particular forms of labour – in the multitude's case, replaced by the hegemony of immaterial labour – for the end of class as a social relation altogether, the social relation which produces the need to labour in the first place. Significantly, this is precisely the same error made by post-Marxian theorists of 'left populism' like Laclau and Mouffe, for whom a new popular subject must take over the reins from a working class who no longer exist.[50] In each case – traditional and postcapitalist Corbynism – the form of analysis remains the same – the arrival of either 'socialism' or 'postcapitalism' requires only the removal of the constraints imposed by those intent on capturing for themselves the productive capacity of workers or the creativity of the 'general intellect'.[51]

The same reticence old-left Corbynism shows in acknowledging the antagonistic relations that constitute a society built on 'wealth creation', reappears here. The underlying forces of production – the networked multitude's unstoppable ability to create wealth, spurring on the productive advances of capitalism – present the path to postcapitalism. The imminent age of the 'free machine' will restructure property relations, with scarcity replaced by surplus.[52] The notion of the multitude – or even the Corbyn movement itself – as a 'counter-power', standing outside and against capital, forcing it to bend to its demands, consoles us that the world is our creation. Eliding the fallen character of the human condition in a world reshaped completely by capital, this works on the presumption that people are in themselves good irrespective of context. And because we are uncomplicatedly good people, it promotes a Panglossian belief that all is for the best, and we live in the best of all possible worlds. Movements, one and the same with a 'multitude' recoded as a 'people', cannot but accomplish progressive change. Technology, the desires of networked individuals immanent within it, cannot but deliver postcapitalist utopia. Here there is no appreciation of the fateful objectification of human activity in a reality that increasingly enslaves us. Rather that activity is taken as existing always already for itself, a positivity constrained only by a negativity seen as external to, rather than inherent in, the conditions of possibility of that activity. And, despite all appearances to the contrary, this radically revisionist strand of post-Marxism actually remains wedded to the 'fetters' theory of history that constitutes a key tenet of the orthodox tradition from which it would seem to escape. The rediscovery of new portions of Marx's posthumously repackaged oeuvre, such as the more sophisticated but no less 'fettered' few pages of the 'Fragment of Machines', do nothing to buck this historically determinist hangover.[53]

~~~

From a critical Marxian perspective, in contrast to those recounted above, the contradiction between the forces and relations of production is not regarded as being a transhistorical dynamic which is able to explain the whole of historical development, acting as the guarantor for the coming of communism. Rather it is – like class as a social relation – something specific to capitalism itself. The forces of production do not exist somehow outside of or prior to capitalist social relations but are constitutive of and constituted by them. Indeed, the ability to analytically separate the 'forces of production' as such is only possible from the perspective of a society in which production appears as something to be pursued for its own sake. And the pursuit of production for its own sake – or rather, the production of *value*, or socially-validated labour, for the sake of more value – is unique to capitalism, as we have seen in the previous chapter. As such, while persistent social relations specific to capitalist society do indeed constrain the development of the forces of production, it is not the 'bourgeois state,' private property or the 'capitalist class' which does so, but rather the social necessity that production takes the form of value.

Production which does not meet the standards set by the abstract workings of value is, in real terms, useless in capitalist society, bringing with it only the risk of bankruptcy and ruin. This ensures that production is kept within the limited bounds set by the law of value. And it is the constant competition between everyone living in such a society to ensure that the labour they buy or sell is validated as part of the abstract social whole mediated by money, a situation engendered by the universal separation from direct access to the means of subsistence, which generates the drive to increase productive capacity through technology. Accelerating production – without overcoming the social form that production is forced to take, or the radical state of separation that underpins it – is not the key to overcoming capitalist social relations. It is rather the means by which they are reproduced, in ever more dominant form.

This means the removal of the 'superstructural' elements traditionally assumed to constitute the relations of production – as is the case when the state or workers themselves take over responsibility for production and distribution from the market – does not in itself constitute or even point to a future beyond capitalism. As Moishe Postone summarises,

> Marx's notion of the structural contradiction
> between the forces and relations of production
> should not be interpreted in the traditional way,
> wherein 'relations of production' are understood
> only in terms of the mode of distribution, [authors:
> by which he means the market and 'bourgeois'
> property relations] and the 'forces of production' are
> identified with the industrial mode of production,
> seen as purely technical process. Within such an
> interpretation, the results of liberating those 'forces'
> from their relational 'fetters' would presumably
> be an acceleration of the dynamic of production
> based on the same concrete form of the process
> of production and of the structure of labour...
> [Instead the contradiction of capitalism should be
> understood] as a growing contradiction between the
> sort of labour people perform under capitalism and
> the sort of labour they could perform if value were
> abolished and the productive potential developed
> under capitalism were [self-]reflexively used to
> liberate people from the sway of the alienated
> structures constituted by their own labour.[54]

For Postone, the reproduction of the contradiction between capitalist production and its social form is understood as constituting capitalist society. By contrast, the orthodox accounts which permeate the Corbyn worldview see the forces and the relations of production as representing forces external and opposed to one another – thesis and antithesis. They are not, therefore, antagonistically contained within and conditioned by one another in the 'negative dialectical' way Marx characterised capitalist social relations and their 'real appearances' in social forms.[55] The primary concern of the orthodox 'historical materialist' method is causality. The causality, in this case, flows *from* the forces of production *to* the relations of production – in other words, from the base to the superstructure.[56] But, as Georg Lukács notes, it is not 'the primacy of economic motives in historical explanation' that characterises Marxism against other modes of thought, but rather 'the point of view of totality'.[57]

Indeed, it is somewhat ironic, given the vitriol hurled at 'liberals' by the more bullish sections of the Corbyn base, that the depiction of history as a singular, unidirectional process driven by productive development which underpins accelerationist notions of 'fully automated luxury communism' is a hangover from the liberal materialism of classical political economy and jurisprudence – precisely that which Marx was to later discard in pursuit of a critical analysis of capitalist society.[58] Searching for transhistorical causality serves to obscure the totality of historically-specific relations that persist within capitalism regardless of direction or effect. It is in this totality that the real contradictions are determined, and in which no one side of the contradiction can be posed as external to or separate from the other, but rather contained within the form each assumes.

The failure to recognise the contradictory totality of the social form of labour in capitalist society – a contradiction that cannot simply be overcome by putting the proletariat in the seat of power – means that the unified sociotechnical state of accelerationist dreams may not be the harbinger of universal freedom. In such a scenario, where the state becomes the wage payer by means of a basic income, the whole of an individual's existence, political, social and economic, is now directly dependent on their relation to a technocratic state responsible for both the production and distribution of the means of subsistence. The recourse to collective bargaining and formalised class struggle for better pay and conditions notionally possible between employees and employers is here prematurely liquidated and replaced by a direct relationship of domination between individual and state. And, moreover, as demonstrated in Labour's recent announcement that a basic income pilot will feature in the next manifesto, these totalising solitions tend to stand in for any more targeted response to the complex challenges confronting the contemporary welfare state. The basic income is a convenient stopgap to fill Labour's lack of any real alternative to the impasses of the Universal Credit and the crisis of social reproduction it conceals. In these abstractly utopian schemas, the contradictory and crisis-ridden workings of capitalist society are – falsely – presumed to be resolved. Yet its abstract social forms are not abolished but merely made the responsibility of the accelerationist state, whose sole priority is to ensure that automated production keeps up with the spiralling demands of the law of value, whatever the human cost. The dystopian potential of accelerationist theory is followed to its logical conclusion by the right-accelerationist current led by Nick Land, the founding father of contemporary accelerationism.[59] Left accelerationism meanwhile rests on the possibility of 'ideologically purifying', through the correct technical management, any latent 'neo-reactionary' tendencies inherent in its theoretical and political programme.[60] There are no technological or technocratic solutions to these contradictions, only their mediation in better or worse ways. Accelerationism offers, in effect, another rendition of the theory of capitalism that is the object of our critique, based on the illusion of control over a system which is by definition out of any single actor's reach.

FROM NATURAL SOCIALISM TO NATIONAL POPULISM

The dynamic ideas covered above have seized the imaginations of generations of leftists and lie behind much of what passes as the most exciting left theory today. But they are not sufficient in and of themselves to communicate a viable political programme to a wider audience. In order to pass muster in the specific configuration of political forces that present themselves today, something more is needed. It is our contention here that what characterises Corbynism is the combination of these traditional Marxist theories of class and historical development with a contemporary left populism that dispenses with class in favour of the 'people' but casts the latter in much the same role as proposed for the proletariat in traditional Marxism. In turn this suggests a surprising overlap between the seemingly antithetical terrain of twentieth-century Marxism and twenty-first century populism. This is exemplified in the 'Rousseauian' Marxism that Tamas skewers in his restatement of the foundations of the Marxist theory of class.[61] Seeing the working class as a subjective force synonymous with the people and sure to assume power, this unburdens class struggle of its fateful objectifications in capitalist social forms. Today this populism coexists in the imaginary of the left with a postcapitalism fixated on the forces of production, and Corbynism is a crucible for this meeting.

In the Introduction we quoted Jan-Werner Müller's depiction of populism as the pitting of a 'pure, innocent, always hardworking people…against a corrupt elite who do not really work.' A theory of capitalism founded upon the image of a unified working class, understood in a cultural, social or political sense, which produces the wealth of the world by its labour and yet is deprived of its rightful inheritance by a non-productive capitalist class, certainly seems to fit with this description. We might say the same of the belief that history has hitherto been a preamble to the final triumph of morality and rationality, when the productive reclaim what is rightfully theirs and the unproductive are vanquished. As we have argued above, both of these positions derive from a critique of capitalism which fails to get to grips with the historically specific and socially-constituted abstract forms which distinguish it from all other modes of social organisation. Instead, capitalist 'concrete labour' is naturalised, regarded as 'production as such,' the means by which humans interact with the external world in order to satisfy their needs, existing in the same way across history. The abstract forms of capitalist society, meanwhile – money, finance, exchange – are treated as artificial interlopers into this essentially natural system.

Socialism is thereby regarded as 'an obvious way of living,' a naturally rational mode of production whose emergence is blocked only by the artificial impediments of the capitalist class, the market, the bourgeois state or international finance. But yet, from the alternative analysis laid out here, it is clear that the assumption that the task of socialism is to salvage 'concrete,' non-capitalistic production from its abstract, artificial capitalist kidnappers is precisely a result of the social conditions which produce the appearance of a bifurcation between 'concrete' and 'abstract,' 'production' and 'money,' or 'nature' and 'artificiality' in the first place. These social conditions are rendered invisible in the Corbyn worldview, in both its Bennite and postcapitalist modes.

This bifurcation of nature and artificiality, which as we saw in earlier chapters underpins the set of theoretical assumptions which unite Corbynism and its apparent intellectual alternative Blue Labour, is expressed through another opposition – that between morality and politics. To view socialism as natural means that the good society is one that *already exists* in the natural inclinations of people, in the way that people interact with one another when left to their own devices. If this is the case then people must be inherently moral and naturally good beings, and 'the people' as a whole a unified, self-sufficient, organic community. And this morality, this natural goodness, needs only subjective verification. It is something that can be discovered merely by looking within oneself, checking one's own motivations and confirming their validity, and finding the necessary assurance of moral purity. It does not require any form of objective validation, or any awareness of the relation between one's subjective existence and the social world from and through which that subjectivity exists in objective form. There is no need for the political working through of contradictions by means of mediations, because the existence of contradiction is denied outright. A direct, unmediated and primordial relationship between the individual and the 'community of the good' is posed.

Tamas traces this naturalised moralism back to Jean-Jacques Rousseau's 'unheard-of provocation of declaring the people – the servants of passion – morally and culturally superior to reasoned and cultured discourse.'[62] Here 'the people' exists as a closed and undivided moral and cultural entity, wholly separate and opposed to the 'society' that surrounds and degrades it. The equality of this pre-social 'people' is thus one based on the universal adherence to a singular inner identity and conception of the good. It is impervious to all outside influences, and rejects as impure any form of difference or debate. As Tamas puts it, such a notion of equality 'is opposed not only to hierarchy, but to variety or diversity as well.' The pursuit of a simplified moral community is, we suggest, the basis of all populisms, both left and right.

The populist inflection placed on this conceptualisation of socialism as a natural fact does not recognise the necessity of politics as a limited but vital sphere in which issues, ideas and interests are discussed, rationally appraised, critiqued and transformed. It thereby fails to grasp that the subjective freedom upon which its own naturalistic vision of socialism is based – a liberal framework of rights and freedoms, limited by the workings of the law of value but real nonetheless – did not drop from the sky fully formed, a gift from nature. It was rather the historical result of a long series of political struggles to build the institutions of formal democracy and a public sphere: impersonal institutions which open up the possibility of a notion of equality based on the recognition and mediation of difference, rather than its denial and expulsion.

Formal liberal democracy cannot, it is true, abolish the law of value or the system of socially mediated labour upon which it is based. But for all its flaws and constraints, it pessimistically leaves open the possibility that something deficient may arise in the innate desires of the 'good' people – or the singular movement of history – that needs to be corrected, and offers the opportunity to do so. The possibility of correction or development entails a politics of critique, self-reflexivity and mediation of the other, rather than immediacy and subjective certainty. It demands the creation of a space in which to reflect upon the evidence and change your mind, and the opportunity to recognise errors and to learn from mistakes and opposing arguments. And it is this space – the space of liberalism – which is 'the necessary but insufficient—or, better, *insufficient but bloody necessary*' prerequisite for any future emancipatory project.[63] It is only through the space opened up by the impersonal structures of formal democracy that demands for higher wages, the right to strike, the right to form trade unions, and freedom from discrimination on grounds of gender, race and sexuality can exist, even if in unsatisfactory and incomplete form. Societies without this form of political freedom – societies which reject, rather than work through, 'liberalism,' whether in the name of communism, theocracy or fascism – close off the possibility of the development of future freedom in the very act of prematurely proclaiming its existence.

A theory of socialism which takes it to be natural and self-evident, deriving from the fixed, essential character of 'good' people, or the inevitable progress of an unilinear history, cannot uphold liberalism's crucial notion of the open development of ideas and theories through self-reflection, critical analysis and the mediation of difference. Instead the task of politics – and on this point both left and right populisms are as one – is rather to draw a line between those regarded as 'friends' and those implacable 'foes,' and then to ensure it is not crossed. Indeed, in the increasingly influential theory of left-populism proposed by Chantal Mouffe, without the existence of this antagonistic – or 'agonistic' – frontier between those within and those without, politics ceases to exist. On this account, the lack of political antagonism is the central, if not fatal, flaw with liberal democracy, or parliamentarianism as traditionally conceived. Without the passionate clash of opposing collective wills, politics decomposes into hollow procedures of interminable discussion and insipid compromise, incapable of satisfying the demands of 'the people' and leading to paralysis.

There is certainly something to said for a critique of bloodless technocracy. Indeed, populism can be said to be technocracy's 'mirror.' As Jan-Werner Müller argues, 'technocracy holds that there is only one policy solution: populism claims there is only one will of the people.'[64] But left populism goes beyond this undeniable point, basing itself on a far more radical conception of 'the political' drawn from the work of Nazi jurist Carl Schmitt.[65] Schmitt conceived 'the political' as a foundational moment of concrete, 'miraculous' decision by a sovereign power which sets the boundaries for collective existence and gives meaning to human life. The boundary between 'friend' and 'enemy' established by the sovereign decision pre-exists any form of rational deliberation, institution or legal structure. For Schmitt, 'the political' is inherently antagonistic and ultimately violent. He does not see the existence of explosive political conflict as being the result of particular historical circumstances, a consequence of the contradictory character of capitalist society, or even something to be avoided if possible. Rather antagonism exists at the core of human existence as such.

From this standpoint, attempts to deny or mediate what must be regarded as the essential, *ontological* status of 'the political' as an intense and violently antagonistic conflict between homogenous groups through the establishment of liberal parliamentary procedures are hypocritical, because they fail to acknowledge the decision that must lie at the root of the liberal norms. They also undermine the true democracy that can only exist within a unified 'concrete order' of land, people and the state. The endless 'debate' of liberal societies, the search for a depoliticised 'consensus', drains the political content from democracy. From this perspective, liberalism and 'the political' are mutually exclusive – 'the political' requires a final decision to be made, one which liberalism is constitutively incapable of providing.

For all his stated commitment to 'dialogue' – a word that Schmitt would have no time for – Corbynism similarly regards politics, in the sense of mediating institutions which are not directly shaped or controlled by the movement and are thus opposed to the unity of 'the political', as being an obstacle to the direct expression of the desires of the community of the good represented by the movement itself. Any form of mediation between the singular, unified desires of the good and their instantiation is seen as illegitimate. This is why reform of the Labour Party's internal structures, or their circumnavigation through Momentum's parallel organisation, is of such crucial importance in the Corbyn worldview. In this Schmittian view of democracy, only a direct, unmediated relation between the membership, the substitute for the people as a whole, and the leadership, as the people's ventriloquist, is acceptable. Anything or anyone who stands in the way of that direct relationship

– existing democratic structures, MPs, non-Corbynite factions in the membership or the electorate itself – are placed in the enemy camp. For all the lip-service paid to 'open debate' within the party, the one criterion that counts when it comes to selection for a parliamentary seat, or a place on a Momentum-backed 'left slate' for internal elections – which is now itself a guarantee of victory in any internal election, regardless of the strengths or experience of any particular candidate – is the extent of a candidate's explicit support for Corbyn.[66] Giving more power to the membership, in a situation where that membership votes solely on the basis of a candidate's loyalty to the leader, radically reduces, rather than expands, the range of permissible views within the party. This majoritarian understanding of democracy does not necessitate the eradication of the representative function within the party altogether, merely the assurance that such representation does not contradict the 'expressive unity' of the 'movement' (standing in for the people) and the leadership.[67] This unity, we suggest, is in the last instance determined by the leadership itself, with the membership's role ultimately reduced to defending *post hoc* decisions taken elsewhere, as we have seen with the issues of immigration, welfare and Brexit.

The fascist origins of Schmitt's undoubtedly powerful critique of liberalism and his purported solutions rarely trouble its modern day left-populist adherents. Much as left accelerationists assume that the reactionary logic of their theory can be assuaged through its correct administration by 'good' people – namely 'labour' as opposed to 'capital,' a perspective which does not grasp that this labour is always-already a form of capital, and vice versa – so do those advocating a left populism, even a left national-populism, argue that by selectively drawing on Schmittian understandings of politics they can co-opt the threat of their right-populist opponents and ultimately strengthen, rather than threaten, democratic practices. But this assumption ultimately rests on a form of economic determinism, in which the reactionary outbursts of right populism are explained simply as a distorted desire for socialism. The idea that nationalism and racism are mere epiphenomena of economic grievances, which the endless 'discussions' of liberalism cannot solve, and thus can be 'bought off' by leftists offering economic reform and a 're-politicised' democratic sphere, is one that carries enormous risks.[68] As we have argued in previous chapters, there is an insatiability to demands for 'control' or 'getting our country back' which overrides economic interest, and which cannot, in an irreversibly globalised and complex world, be assuaged by political reform. Moreover, in the contest to create a unified people through the ascription of a collective enemy, the nationalist right has an inbuilt advantage. They can push the rhetoric of national-popular exceptionalism to its logical conclusion in a way the left, one hopes, will not.

~~~

It is the Corbyn movement's reliance on this kind of hyper-moralised Schmittian identitarian politics of 'friend' and 'enemy' which explains why the Corbyn movement appears at its strongest when it comes under attack from internal or external foes, real or imagined, while dwindling into passivity in their absence. If socialism is a reflexive response to the natural, unchanging, essential desires of ontologically 'good' people, an innate 'goodness' which is embodied in or anchored around the person of Corbyn himself, then calling into question the character of Corbyn in any way casts doubt upon the movement's own position as the prefiguration of the society to come, a society in which all contradiction and difference will be dissolved in the name of humanity's unified moral nature. The need to continually defend Corbyn's moral status from those 'enemies' who would 'smear' it acts as the negative force binding the movement together, preventing its internal contra-dictions from rising to the surface.

This goes some way to explaining the crucial effect the framing of Owen Smith's ill-fated 2016 leadership challenge as an orchestrated 'coup' had in reinvigorating Corbyn's grass-roots support, which had dramatically fallen off after his first year in charge. Rather than treating the contest as a legitimate manoeuvre from a party rival, one clearly sanctioned by the party rule book – indeed, a move very similar to Tony Benn's challenge to Neil Kinnock in 1988, a campaign kickstarted by Corbyn himself – both Corbyn's team and his supporters por-trayed Smith as a conspiratorial traitor, his campaign orches-trated by a shadowy PR firm, Portland Communications.[69] Smith's stint as head of government affairs for the pharma-ceutical company Pfizer led to accusations that he intended to privatise the NHS, with Corbyn going so far as to propose in response that all drug research be undertaken by the state – a nonsensical policy, the suggestion of which was aimed only at drawing a populist dividing line between friend and enemy through the Labour party itself.[70] Nonsense or not, the 'coup' narrative undoubtedly galvanised Corbyn's support for a time, to the extent that John McDonnell tried the trick again a few months later, warning that a 'soft coup' against the leadership – 'perpetrated by an alliance between elements in the Labour Party and the Murdoch media empire...[through an] excep-tionally well resourced 'dark arts' operation' – was underway.[71]

It is this defensive, occasionally paranoiac, form of politics, one where the protection of a fixed, abstract identity from an equally essentialised enemy takes priority over debate, cri-tique or even the principle of economic interest, that signals Corbynism's congruity with the politics of sentiment which has come to dominate British politics in the post-Brexit era, as we saw in the Chapter 1. And it is a dynamic with a life of its own – once unleashed, even those who initially sought to channel it towards their own ends can find themselves on the receiving end of its puritanical force. Witness the treatment of Momentum founder Jon Lansman after he put himself forward as a candidate for the party's General Secretary, against the wishes of the leader's office. No-one, aside perhaps from John McDonnell, has done more to transform Corbynism into a coherent political project than Lansman. And yet by implicitly criticising the innate wisdom of Corbyn, he was faced with a torrent of abuse from Corbyn supporters, much of it antisemitic – some accused Lansman of being 'power mad' and wanting to 'further his own Zionist takeover of the Labour Party.'[72] By challenging Corbyn's infallibility, regardless of his prior commitment to the movement, his act of rebellion demonstrated that he had failed to properly comply with the singular will of the 'community of the good.' He thus faced the full force of the logic of denunciation and excommunication that characterises a populist politics of position and sentiment, and will likely not be the last.

~~~

As we have seen in this chapter, populism works with the pre-existing Marxist elements of the Corbynist intellectual coalition to suffuse their two-campist or forces-and-relations worldviews with a new political dynamism. Populism reduces class analysis to the posing of an elite against the people. This personalises power and forgets that class is a relation between people rather than a category in which one sits. Constructing a people here substitutes for a critique of class society, however much some see populism as a way past it. What is presently on offer in the Labour Party simply represents so many ways to liquidate or resolve the class contradiction without confronting its antagonistic core head-on. There are, no doubt, elements among Corbynism's piecemeal intellectual and political coalition that recognise the tenacity and aporetic character of class struggle in a society founded upon it, and the dangerous futility of seeking to liquidate it in utopian schemes or authoritarian short-circuits. But unfortunately, the dominant theoretical and strategic twists and turns of the left today largely express the pursuit of a popular subject that cannot exist in a world criss-crossed by the class relation. Nothing unites us beyond the abstract economic rule to which we are all subject, elites included. A unified 'people' may or may not spring from its destruction, but cannot preexist it.

Corbynism does not provide a critique of things as they are from *within* things as they are, but remains bewitched by the world of fetishized appearances. As such, its critique adopts an external standpoint which sacrifices the present on the altar of essentialised moral golden rules dividing the world into camps of good and bad. Such a move swaps the flawed but vital gains of political mediation through an impersonal liberal order for the essentialised character of a falsely unified moral community. As such it lays the foundation for its own destruction by those willing to push this logic to its reactionary conclusions – the resonances of which we will explore in the next and final chapter.

6

THE RIGGED SYSTEM: CORBYNISM AND CONSPIRACY THEORY

While the rest of the world sat head in hands at Donald Trump's election as US President, one political leader tried to lift the gloom with a statement that was positively cheery. 'Trump's election is an unmistakable rejection of a political establishment and an economic system that simply isn't working for most people,' it read. 'This is a rejection of a failed economic consensus and a governing elite that has been seen not to have listened. And the public anger that has propelled Donald Trump to office has been reflected in political upheavals across the world.' Only the last sentences would let you know it was Jeremy Corbyn and not, say, Marine Le Pen speaking. 'But some of Trump's answers to the big questions facing America, and the divisive rhetoric around them, are clearly wrong', he said. 'I have no doubt, however, that the decency and common sense of the American people will prevail.'[1]

For most observers, especially on the liberal and socialist left, Trump's victory was a catastrophe, posing a genuine threat to the foundations of democratic society. For Corbyn and his team however, it was – along with the Leave victory in the Brexit referendum – to provide the first glimmer of hope for their project after a torrid first year, as well as the outline of a new political strategy that would come to fruition in the 2017 General Election. A few weeks after Trump's victory, it was reported that Corbyn was set to take 'direct inspiration from the U.S. president-elect's aggression against mainstream TV networks and newspapers' which, his advisers hoped, would 'whip up support among those already distrustful of the media.' The Labour press team would make 'greater use of Twitter and Facebook to attack the media rather than attempting to manage it,' drawing attention to Corbyn's 40 years 'taking on the establishment'. And, as with Trump, this flurry of anti-elitist social media zingers would be buttressed with a neo-Keynesian economic policy of infrastructure investment, Corbyn's team 'inspired' by the U.S. President's planned stimulus which they claimed 'parallel[ed] their own £500 billion spending pledge'.[2]

The first fruits of this Trump-inspired strategy could be seen in Corbyn's speech to the Fabian Society in January 2017. The central refrain, repeated again and again, was that for too long the political and economic system has been 'rigged' in favour of 'a moneyed class', who line their pockets while everyone else struggles. 'The people who run Britain have been taking our country for a ride,' Corbyn said.

> They've stitched up our political system to protect
> the powerful…They've rigged the economy and
> business rules to line the pockets of their friends…
> the Leave and Trump campaigns succeeded because
> they both recognised the system was broken and the
> people weren't being listened to…Labour is going
> to call time on this rigged system. Because power is
> in the wrong hands'.[3]

The next few months saw the 'rigged system' line honed into Labour's rhetorical weapon of choice, one reached for at any and every opportunity, both by Corbyn himself as well as his online army of supporters and alternative media outlets. By the time Theresa May finally called her 'snap election,' it had become the foundation stone upon which Labour's entire campaign would be built. At the press conference launching Labour's campaign, Corbyn intensified the rhetoric even further. He railed against the 'cosy cartel' who have constructed 'a rigged system set up by the wealth extractors, for the wealth extractors,' pinning the blame for Britain's travails on the 'morally bankrupt' elite who 'extract wealth from the pockets of ordinary working people...the true wealth creators' by means of a corrupt 'racket.' Only a Corbyn government would 'take on the cosy cartels that are hoarding this country's wealth for themselves', he said.[4]

The trope of the 'rigged system' was directly borrowed from Trump's campaign, who in turn had taken it from the leftist Democrat Bernie Sanders. For Trump, it was the rhetorical glue which brought the various parts of his electoral coalition together, allowing him to connect his rabid racism and misogyny with an economic programme that appealed to both right and left. Through this left-right reach, Trump secured the Republican nomination with the votes of 20 per cent of registered Democrats in some states.[5] Trump's siren-call of protectionism appealed as much to Democrat-leaning trade unionists as did it to traditional Republicans.[6] Anti-immigration policies aside, two of the three legs of his apparently anti-Wall Street 'America First' platform – restrictions on free trade and a non-interventionist, isolationist foreign policy – stole from a left-wing playbook to appeal beyond the reach of the conventional right.[7]

The free trade element was particularly dynamic, projecting the rigged economy outward. Throughout his campaign

Trump argued that American workers had been 'betrayed' by politicians who 'have aggressively pursued a policy of globalization – moving our jobs, our wealth and our factories to Mexico and overseas.' This decision had 'made the financial elite who donate to politicians very wealthy,' in full knowledge that the consequences for working people would be nothing but 'poverty and heartache.' Trump claimed that the 'people who rigged the system for their benefit will do anything – and say anything – to keep things exactly as they are.' And he left his audience in no doubt who was responsible for that 'rigged system' – 'Hillary Clinton and her friends in global finance.' He directly invoked Sanders, Clinton's rival for the Democratic nomination, who had condemned her for 'vot[ing] for virtually every trade agreement that has cost the workers of this country millions of jobs.'[8]

Trump's alternative to this 'rigged system' was an economic programme of national protectionism. He promised to rip up a whole host of international trade deals agreed by previous administrations. He would build a wall along the Mexican border to keep out the hordes of migrants – 'drug dealers, criminals, rapists' – he claimed were undermining the pay and conditions of US workers.[9] The US would no longer act as a 'global policeman' when it came to foreign affairs. Instead America would turn inward in order to prioritise the well-being and security of its own citizens, starting with a $1 trillion investment plan in infrastructure, which he promised would provide millions of jobs for American workers.

Both Trump's political diagnosis and his proposed solutions carried the clear influence of Steve Bannon, the former editor of 'alt-right' news site *Breitbart*, and Trump's strategic advisor during his first year in the White House. Unlike many on the more traditional right, Bannon has no problem critiquing capitalism. And he does so in the way that has become very familiar throughout this book – on the basis of personal morality. Just as those theories on the left which focus their aim entirely on 'neoliberalism' as a set of ideas conjured up in rightwing think tanks and unilaterally imposed on an unsuspecting world, comparing it negatively with the welfare Keynesianism which preceded it, so does Bannon contrast the 'enlightened capitalism' of the post-war consensus with the degraded and amoral form dominant today.[10] A new species of 'crony capitalist' has emerged, intent on winning monopolistic economic power through the capture of state institutions. This has resulted in 'a brutal form of capitalism that is really about creating wealth and creating value for a very small subset of people.' No longer beholden to local communities held together by moral ties, these 'crony capitalists' view themselves as a separate global community more powerful than any single state, bounded by 'this elite mentality that they're going to dictate to everybody how the world's going to be run' via free trade agreements and supranational institutions such as the EU and NATO.

Bannon's vision found powerful expression in Trump's final campaign broadcast, in which Trump railed against 'a global power structure that is responsible for the economic decisions that have robbed our working class, stripped our country of its wealth, and put that money into the pockets of a handful of large corporations and political entities', illustrated – tellingly, as we will go on to see – with images of a series of prominent Jews: George Soros, the Hungarian-American investor, Goldman Sachs CEO Lloyd Blankfein, and Janet Yellen, the then-Chair of the Federal Reserve.[11]

Trump's reference to Bernie Sanders was not coincidental – as mentioned above, Trump had borrowed the 'rigged system' conceit from the latter's campaign for the Democratic nomination. Sanders' message was summarised in one of his TV commercials: 'It's called the rigged economy, and this is how it works. Most new wealth flows to the top 1%. It's a system held in place by corrupt politics, where Wall Street banks and billionaires buy elections.'[12] Sanders' solutions to this 'rigging' were not a million miles away from Trump's either, albeit with the overt racism and misogyny removed. Like Trump, Sanders called for the end of free trade deals – which he blamed for the loss of 'millions of decent paying jobs' in America – and the limiting of immigration, which Sanders argued had resulted 'in more unemployment and lower wages for American workers'.[13] For Sanders, like Trump, and indeed Corbyn, the role of the nation-state is to protect nationally produced wealth and prevent jobs 'sliding away from localities', as the Alternative Models of Ownership report put it.

It is interesting to note the differences between contemporary arguments against globalisation made by the Sanders-Corbyn left and those of the 'alter-' or 'anti-globalisation' movements in the late 1990s and early 2000s. While in its original form, arguments against globalisation stressed the negative impact global free trade was having on the global south, today the emphasis has shifted onto the problems afflicting formerly dominant countries facing competition from economies once-deemed to be 'developing.' In light of this shift, it is not surprising to see supporters of Corbyn's calls for a reinvigorated national economy admit that it 'is a programme to save democracy, democratic institutions and values in the developed world by reversing the 30-year policy of enriching the bottom 60% and the top 1% of the world's population. It is a programme to deliver growth and prosperity in Wigan, Newport and Kirkcaldy – if necessary at the price of not delivering them to Shenzhen, Bombay and Dubai', as Paul Mason recently put it. For all the brickbats Mason received from the left for saying this, he is simply openly acknowledging what remains implicit in the political programme other Corbynists support.[14]

The nationalist and genuinely imperialist tenor of such sentiments, which given an American inflection could sit quite happily in a Trump speech, and the ease with which the 'rigged system' trope has shifted from Sanders on the left, to Trump on the right, and back again to the left with Corbyn, alerts us to a troubling political ambivalence that exposes continuities between Corbyn, Sanders and Trump on key questions that seem to transcend a simple left-right divide. There are clearly substantial differences that should not be overlooked – certainly Trump has no intention of extending workplace democracy or the right to strike. Nor does he have any real concern with reducing economic inequality. Nevertheless the shared use of the 'rigged system' trope indicates at the very least that the respective analyses of Corbyn, Sanders and Trump and the political movements around them are not so different that they cannot utilise the same structural logic in their arguments. And no man is so all-powerful as to control how the resonant logic of their ideas and rhetoric is received once unleashed into the world at large.

There is something very specific about the description of a system or an economy as 'rigged' in its entirety. It differs considerably from a critique which points to particular institutional, legislative or workplace structures and practices that privilege one social group over another. And it is qualitatively distinct from both the analysis of class as a social relation, and that of capitalism as a system of socially-mediated labour, a society dominated by the movement of abstract social forms. A critique of a 'rigged system' implies that capitalist social relations are consciously and covertly designed by a minority of individuals or groups in order to exploit everyone else. That system is regarded as monolithic, entirely oppressive, and devoid of contradiction. Given the numerical disparity between 'the many' and 'the few,' the only way the system can retain its 'rigged' character is either through direct violence or ideological trickery. Thus it is not only the political and economic system which is regarded as 'rigged,' but the media too – or the 'mainstream media' (MSM) at least – if not political and civic culture in its entirety. As we shall see, this can often lend such analyses a conspiratorial edge, even at their most sophisticated.

THE RIGGED SYSTEM AND PERSONALISED CRITIQUE

Tracing the theoretical roots of the conceptualisation of a 'rigged economy' makes it clear that Corbyn's populist turn following Trump's election should have come as no surprise. As we have seen, Corbyn's 'left populism,' like its counterpart on the right, rests upon the construction of 'a political frontier between an 'us' and a 'them.'"[15] The origins of this binary worldview lie in the particular way of thinking about capitalism, 'the people', class and history that has come to dominate both the Labour Party and the broader radical intellectual and activist milieu that surrounds it. As such the populist turn was always a latent possibility embedded deep within the Corbyn worldview. Together the suffusion of Leninist and postcapitalist political outlooks within a left populist dynamic contributes to a critique of capitalism that can best be described as 'truncated' or 'foreshortened'.[16]

Not everything that purports to be a critique of capitalism is actually a critique of capitalism. An analysis based on the separation of the greedy, neoliberal '1%' from the innocent '99%,' or 'the people' from 'the elite,' might make for a powerful slogan, but it is not a critique of capitalism. At best it recognises some of the surface effects of capitalist development, in particular the centralisation and concentration of wealth, but has no means to explain them. It therefore mistakes the part for the whole, attributing full responsibility for the latter to the former.

A personalised or truncated critique of capitalism is one which regards the existence of economic crises, poverty, unemployment and inequality as the direct responsibility of identifiable people or institutions, rather than identifying them as the result of the abstract economic compulsions to which worker and capitalist alike are subject. They do not critique capitalism as a historically specific form of social relations dominated by the intangible yet deadly workings of the law of value – precisely Marx's purpose in his 'critique of political economy.' Instead, personalised critiques are content to merely condemn the pursuit of profit in moral terms, as a matter of individual greed. They thus encourage the naming and shaming of those who are particularly repellent in this regard. In this way the capricious movements of value – the intangible abstract force which compels everyone in capitalist society to jump to its tune, or face the devastating consequences – are 'concretised' or 'reified' in the form of those individuals who end up on top. This negative 'concretisation' of abstract forms mirrors the positive concretisation which lies behind the 'substantialist' Marxian theories which view value as something physically implanted in objects by workers, rather than as a social relation between objects. The central thesis of all personalised critiques is that if only the wrongdoers, those who are attributed the characteristics of the law of value, could be somehow identified and overcome, the rest of us would be fine.

In the hands of the left, such critiques focus on the person of the capitalist, rather than capital as a social relation. But, as we have seen throughout this book, personalisation comes in many different forms, on both left and right: the constant cry that 'immigrants' and 'scroungers' are draining the life out of the economy; the idea that membership of the EU is the source of all the UK's problems; the opposition between 'productive', 'authentic' forms of 'local' capitalism, and 'parasitic' or 'predatory' forms of money-making.

The personalisation of capitalist social relations has long been a favoured tactic within the workers' movement, and not without reason. At some level, personalisation is a prerequisite for building support for political action, and may be apt in workplace disputes or corrupt or dictatorial regimes. But the distinction of liberal society is that it contains such power relations within formal processes, so that, say, collective bargaining and the legal procedure of taking industrial action, with the possibility of independent arbitration, mediates the direct relationship of control and resistance between worker and boss. One feature of an increasingly 'post-liberal' society is that this is breaking down in personalised and precarious employment relationships characterised by a situation of 'neo-villeiny', and plebiscite politics.[17] Moreover, there is a crucial difference between specific criticisms of specific actions of specific people in specific conditions, and a totalising theory which claims to explain everything about the world through the prism of personalisation.

Marx himself criticised those who 'make the individual responsible for relations whose creature he socially remains.'[18] But subsequent generations of Marxists, or those influenced by him, have sought against all good advice to pin the blame for the capricious, uncontrollable movement of capital as a social relation on the individuals and states who appear to embody its power. In this respect, the roots of such 'personalised critiques' of capitalism can be traced back, in part, to vulgar understandings of Marx's so-called 'labour theory of value' outlined in earlier chapters. Indeed, Marx himself was no stranger to analyses which veered close to truncation, particularly in the posthumously repackaged parts of his work which posit a singular line of historical development based on the transhistorical development of the forces of production coming into contradiction with the relations of production – precisely that aspect taken over into postcapitalist and accelerationist thinking.

What links all forms of personalised critique, whether of the right or left, are their naturalistic (or, in Marxian terms, fetishised) premises. If the drive for profit can be explained by the personal moral failings of individuals, attributed to their ontological identity or some libidinal desire for power or money, then the question of a society which *necessitates* the prioritisation of profit over need – a society in which needs can only be fulfilled through profits – requires no further investigation. It is a result of the machinations of the morally deplorable. And its effects are manifest within analyses and solutions which regard themselves to be, in political terms, implacably opposed to one another. Regardless of its political provenance, left or right, in structural terms any form of analysis built on the assumption that its object – in this case, society based on mediated labour and production – is essentially natural and timeless must necessarily regard anything that blocks its smooth running as 'unnatural' and artificial, an illegitimate presence corrupting an otherwise well-functioning whole. The precise identity of that unnatural presence can change according to circumstances. For Trump it is immigrants, free trade deals and the 'global power structure' of the shadowy globalist powers. For the movement around Corbyn it is international finance, the 'wealth extractors,' the market and the imperialist nations. But the logic of the analysis is fundamentally the same.

~~~

Personalising critiques of class and capitalism contain an implicit, although by no means inevitable, tendency towards conspiracy theory and, more dangerously, antisemitism. As scholars like David Hirsh, Brendan McGeever, Robert Fine and Philip Spencer have documented, a specifically left variant of antisemitism has a long history in the socialist and labour movements.[19] There is something in certain forms of thinking about and critiquing capitalism that contains an immanent (but not inevitable) tendency towards it. When taken to extremes, theories which oppose 'productive,' 'natural' and 'local' forms of industry to 'unproductive,' 'artificial' and 'global' modes of finance can slip into antisemitic tropes of 'Jewish bankers' or a 'Jewish lobby' controlling the economy and media in order to manipulate states into doing their bidding. This is not to say that all forms of personalised critique are destined to end up as antisemitism, but that a confluence of historical and theoretical prejudices can combine to place Jews in the frame.

The politically ambivalent tendency to antisemitism latent in these forms of critique is clearly visible in the way that Steve Bannon's theory of the 'global power structure' draws upon various theories of so-called 'globalism' that have floated around the edges of both the hard right and conspiratorial left since the collapse of the Soviet Union. 'Globalism' is construed as a deliberate political strategy cooked up by the international financial, political and media elite at the end of the Cold War as a means to ensure their continued domination. It actively aimed to destroy traditional national communities, and indeed the nation-state itself, in order to establish a deracinated 'new world order' characterised by free trade and open borders for capital, goods and labour. This integrated global system was to be ruled over by transnational institutions such as the UN, NATO, and the European Union, themselves in hock to global finance. Relentlessly promoted by hard right talk show hosts like Alex Jones, over the past two decades the theory has expanded to explain everything from 9/11 and ISIS to the banking bailouts.

It is not difficult to see the parallels between the 'globalism' narrative and early twentieth century antisemitic conspiracy theories such as the 'Protocols of the Elders of Zion', which purported to reveal a plot for world domination concocted by a secret international cabal of Jews and freemasons, devoid of loyalty to any nation state or settled community. The influence of the 'globalism' thesis rang out in Trump's aforementioned eve-of-election broadcast advertisement placing Jewish political and financial figures at the centre of the rigged system.

The appeal of the anti-'globalist' narrative is, unfortunately, by no means limited to the hard right. Its building blocks, if not its full ramifications, are also felt elsewhere.

Corbyn himself has pejoratively used the term 'globalism.'[20] He once described the first Gulf War as 'a curtain-raiser for the New World Order,' and argued, in language very similar to Bannon, that 'the aim of the war machine of the United States is to maintain a world order dominated by the banks and multinational companies of Europe and North America.'[21] The appeal of conspiracy theories to those on the left derives from the way they 'reflect a critical impulse' and a suspicion about the world and its forms of power – this is part of the reason that they recommend themselves to people otherwise concerned with challenging the way the world works.[22] But they do so by personalising abstract social forms of which people are really just the personification.

When combined with the reflexive 'anti-imperialist' stance which, as we argued in Chapter 2, is increasingly the default position amongst the contemporary left, the antisemitic potential in personalised critiques is expressed on a geopolitical level through the attribution of the traditional role of the 'scheming Jew' in classic conspiracy theories to the State of Israel. Israel, the 'Israeli lobby' and 'Zionists' in general, are hereby deemed to be the all-powerful, malicious, and secretive force pulling the strings behind global affairs, responsible for everything from American foreign policy to staging 'false flag' attacks, and even founding ISIS.[23] It is here, at the intersection of personalised critique and Manichean two-campist anti-imperialism, where we suggest the roots of the antisemitism scandals that have plagued Corbyn's leadership can be found.

THE SPECIFICITIES OF LEFT ANTISEMITISM

The debate over Labour and antisemitism has, as we have seen, been consistently rumbling on since Jeremy Corbyn's leadership victory.[24] This has been thanks in the main to a history of dubious associations struck, by no means inevitably, in the course of his lifelong support for the Palestinian cause. But the increasing prominence of claims of antisemitism within Labour was also a result of the actions of a sizeable number of so-called Corbyn supporters online. It first came to a head in the wake of Jackie Walker's aforementioned suspension from the party for accusing Jews of 'funding the slave trade,' and then again following former London Mayor (and historical Corbyn ally) Ken Livingstone's repeated claim that Hitler 'supported' Zionism – with the insinuation that Israel and the Nazis are in some way comparable, a common trope amongst some wings of the anti-Zionist movement.[25]

This build-up of bad choices reached a tipping point in March 2018. A furore arose around Corbyn's 2012 defence of a virulently antisemitic graffiti artist, Mear One. His excuse for doing so was that he was merely defending the right to free speech, and had unfortunately failed to examine the picture closely enough.[26] When in November 2015 the *Jewish Chronicle* first raised the issue of Corbyn's support for Mear One's crude depiction of a cabal of 'Jewish' financiers counting money on the backs of the poor, Corbyn's supporters accused the paper of manufacturing a politically-motivated antisemitism scandal in order to 'smear' his good name.[27] This had been the standard response to every question raised about Corbyn's past activities, issued by everyone from Len McCluskey to Diane Abbott, Seumas Milne and Corbyn himself.[28] At that time, the story did not even merit a response from the Labour leadership. But when it was raised again three years later, it caught fire, perhaps due to it swiftly following evidence of Corbyn's active participation in, and friendship with the founder of, an anti-Zionist Facebook group which regularly hosted Holocaust denial and viciously antisemitic conspiracy theories.[29]

Many of Corbyn's supporters reacted to the mural story, and the subsequent 'Enough is Enough' protest against Labour antisemitism led by Jewish activists outside Parliament, by reverting to the 'smear' allegation. A group of academics wrote a letter to the *Guardian* arguing that antisemitism had been 'weaponise[d]...just ahead of important [local council] elections,' while more than 2000 Corbyn supporters signed a letter portraying the protest as the work of a 'very powerful special interest group' who had used their 'immense strength' to sabotage Corbyn's leadership.[30] Other wings of the Corbyn coalition however recognised, for the first time, that reflexive response of 'smears' to such a clearcut example of antisemitism – with the implication that the whole graffiti story had been cooked up by some nefarious group – actually epitomised the problem, rather than mitigated it.

Three alternative responses commonly followed. First, any potential capacity on the part of Corbyn for thinking or acting in ways considered antisemitic – and by extension, that of the left more generally – was denied on the grounds that someone who has spent his life opposing 'all forms of racism' could not possibly be receptive to antisemitic representations of the world. Corbyn's track record of anti-racist activism – exemplified, as we have seen, by his supposedly exceptional opposition to South African apartheid – precluded him from trading in or tacitly supporting antisemitic forms of thought or action. Therefore, if on this occasion he had inadvertently failed to recognise what was a clearly antisemitic image, this must have been a momentary aberration, an unfortunate mistake, the gravity of which is far outweighed by his otherwise flawless history of anti-racism.[31] In this way the politics of position was called into action in Corbyn's defence.

This led to the second response. Expressions of antisemitism on the left were dismissed as aberrations from the norm. Corbyn himself suggested that, whilst antisemitism sadly does exist within 'pockets' of the party, they are not at all representative of the whole.[32] The removal of these pockets would therefore annul the problem. The widespread portrayal of antisemitism as a 'virus' or 'disease' on the left exemplified this response. It was seen as something completely alien and incompatible with a leftist worldview, something which invades the left from the outside. As such its origins do not require serious consideration, merely its effects.

Third, incidences of antisemitism were diminished with reference to examples of antisemitism on the right. Former Bennite MP Chris Mullin asserted that antisemitism is a societal issue of which Labour's problem was only one part, and as such the significance of its left variant is vastly over-exaggerated by a media out to score easy hits on Corbyn.[33] This argument is regularly backed up by reference to a Campaign Against Antisemitism study which showed antisemitism amongst Labour voters was no higher than in the rest of society.[34] Unfortunately, the survey did not show the level of antisemitism amongst Labour *members*, and in particular the members who joined in the wake of Corbyn's leadership. It is within this cohort that most of the reported problems lie, rather than Labour supporters or voters per se. The widespread misrepresentation of the Campaign Against Antisemitism's research by Corbyn supporters – it was even included in a briefing note issued to Labour MPs by the leadership – led to the organisation issuing a statement condemning the 'appalling misuse' of its work.[35]

Mounting an effective challenge to this common portrayal of leftist antisemitism as merely an unfortunate error or a minor problem requires more than blanket accusations of racism. Doing so merely replicates the superficial analysis which explains antisemitism as an inexplicable disease generated by the innate character of bad people. It fails to grapple with the real contradiction inherent in a situation whereby individuals and groups who otherwise attest to a belief in equality and solidarity among peoples regardless of race could at the same time indulge remarkably frequent and increasingly confident expressions of antisemitism. A coherent explanation is required to combat and convince those whose concern is to protect the Corbyn project from what they incorrectly see as a smear campaign of little real-world consequence.

~~~

One way out of this impasse is offered by a key figure in critical Marxism, Moishe Postone. Postone was known for his innovative theory on the relation between antisemitism and the development of capitalist modernity, relating it to the fetishised (or 'productivist') readings of capitalist society that we have criticised throughout this book.[36] He begins his analysis by making a distinction between modern antisemitism and 'other forms of racism,' one which Corbyn has, at least until very recently, found notoriously difficult to express. Plenty of other racial and ethnic groups are discriminated against. But, Postone suggests, of all groups despised on racial grounds, it is only Jews who are both regarded as 'cockroaches' *and* suspected of secretly controlling the world. A mural of Mexican migrants or black people counting money on the backs of the oppressed would make no sense to a racist. But, it might be suggested, the portrayal of Jews at the table could escape Corbyn's scrutiny because this representation of how power works resonates with the logic of his worldview: his understanding of capitalism as a 'rigged system.'

At the core of the 'rigged system' scheme is the opposition of tangible, visible, concrete 'production' against the parasitical ephemerality and mysteriousness of global finance and money. Jews, historically precluded from certain professions and property ownership, turned to interest-bearing activities at the inception of capitalist society. Ever since they have become subject to an antisemitic critique of capitalism, one which carries traces of traditional religious antisemitism, in which Jews are characterised as the personal bearers of responsibility for the monetary mediation of life under capital.[37] Adorno and Horkheimer, whose work on the relationship between the Enlightenment, capitalism and antisemitism was a key influence on Postone, comment that the contemporary guise of this conspiracy theory thrives on a shift from the rule of aristocrats who resented work to industrialists who championed their productiveness.[38] The latter became synonymous with production in a shared enterprise with workers. Industry was the productive force in society, and as capitalism developed the class antagonism in production was further elided in legal equivalence between the buyers and sellers of labour power. This bore consequences for how the activities of circulation were understood. The class antagonism centred on the wage relation was transported to the buying of goods with that wage. Exploitation, where obscured in the workplace, becomes apparent in how far (or not) the wage goes to meet the price asked. As such, groups who had a historical association with the activities of circulation (shopkeeping, merchants and so on) – in this case, Jews – carried the force of a distorted confrontation with the class antagonism filtered through an antisemitic critique of capitalism that poses what is deemed to be productive against that which is not.

Contemporary critiques of capitalism and class by means of a critique of financiers, bankers or the 'elite' carry this background, calling into service appeals to the 'national community of hard-working people' affronted by the parasitical powers of a class without.[39] This way, conspiracy theory critiques the personifications of economic categories – bankers, traders etc – through personalising them rhetorically and ideologically. Whilst his Shadow Chancellor concurrently gladhands the selfsame financiers at City meetings, Corbyn himself has directly engaged in this kind of thing. In one viral social media video, Corbyn called out 'bankers like Morgan Stanley' (itself a tellingly personalised slip of the tongue), those 'speculators and gamblers who crashed our economy in 2008 and…whose greed plunged the world into crisis…when they say we're a threat, they're right!'.[40]

For all the rhetorical fire of such populist missives, when it comes to criticising capitalism, '[t]he critique of the banker […] misses the object of critique.'[41] By focusing on the bearers of economic categories in such a personalised way, the actual human practice reified in money, wealth and interest as forms of self-valorising value in a system of socially-mediated labour disappears from view. Such a perspective fetishizes both the process of 'real' capitalistic concrete labour, and the movement of abstract, intangible forms which constitutes the other side of capitalist production. The former, concrete labour, and its representatives are extolled as standard-bearers for the society to come, while the latter – the abstract forces of money and value – are first concretised in particular persons (bankers, neoliberals, Jews) who are then demonised as the forces holding back the productive utopia. But the concrete and abstract forms of capitalist society are two halves of the same coin. Concrete labour is no more 'natural' or 'real' than finance, and no less 'the root of all evil' than money. They are both historically specific social forms, and mutually constitutive.

In opposing 'real' production to 'artificial' finance, or chasing the externally-wielded power of one class over another, conspiracy theories of class miss the true nature of the class antagonism as a constitutive contradiction of the society they seek to save from its assailants. At once the conspiracy theory of class suggests that the world is compelled by powerful hidden forces – half true, with regard to the real, unavoidable pull of the law of value – but simultaneously history unfolds according to the will of personalised individual representatives of finance and political power. Conspiratorial theories of capitalism naturalise the capricious movements of the law of value by suggesting those unpredictable yet all-powerful movements are conducted by particular individuals and groups surreptitiously pulling the strings behind the back of society. This fetishised analysis exposes the lack of any sense of real antagonism or contradiction *within* society. Instead, a super-competent elite is posited from without, leeching upon or manipulating the innocent masses. By contrast, critical theories of class understand class as a constitutive relationship immanent to society, rather than an antagonism produced by a confrontation between forces 'inside' society and those 'outside.'

That said, although we are all 'ruled by abstractions,' the wealthy experience this as 'a source of great enrichment and power.'[42] But their position is safe as long as those who get the short end of the bargain ascribe the causes of their misery to the individuals who benefit most. In ineptly addressing the unequal distribution of rewards and spellbound character of capitalist society, conspiracy theory captures some element, however falsely, of the true state of things. Indeed, conspiracy theory grasps that 'the world is really the opposite of how it appears'.[43] But it does not square the circle to inquire what the essence of that appearance is, nor how it is expressed. Indeed, from a purported 'anti-elitist' perspective, it uses an 'elitist' epistemology to suggest the ability to unpick appearances is the preserve of an enlightened few – those who belong to the 'community of the good.' But, as usual, those who claim to be alone privy to the truth are most bereft of it, the more deluded the greater their purported escape from delusion. What this conspiracist rendering of the concept 'class' suggests is that all those living in a society constituted by class need to do is correctly capture their situation in thought. But class is an objective and not a subjective or conscious relation. Workers and capitalists bear class interests only as personifications of economic categories, as a matter not of hidden truth but of the very character of the 'false society' that is capitalist society.[44] The closer conspiracy theories of class purport to penetrate this falsity, the further from its truth they find themselves.

~~~

This function of conspiracy theory as a foreshortened critique of capitalist power, and the ease with which it can spill over into antisemitism, is further complicated by the ascribed position of Jewish people in the left's taxonomy of racism. As David Feldman and Brendan McGeever note, 'the success of Jewish integration in contemporary Britain [means that]... British Jews are poorly positioned to evoke sympathy from those anti-racists who imagine that poverty, exclusion and racism always line up neatly together.'[45] This can lead to the deracination of Jews and the incorporation of Jewish identity into a generic and totalising concept of 'whiteness,' which leaves antisemitism as the poor relation – of concern once, but no longer – in comparison with racisms against Black and Asian people. This move is given additional credence by leftist attempts to force the founding of Israel into a pre-given paradigm of European 'settler-colonialism' – one which not only ignores the long history of Jewish presence in the region but is, in a post-Holocaust context, wholly inappropriate and ahistorical – so as to sustain the simplistic integrity of the 'imperialist' – 'anti-imperialist' dualism.[46] The insistence that the *concept* of a Jewish state is inherently imperialist and racist – as opposed to using such terms only with reference to, for example, the illegal expansion of settlements in the West Bank or East Jerusalem – may go some way to explaining Labour's reticence regarding the International Holocaust Remembrance Association's (IHRA) definition of antisemitism. One of the illustrative examples which Labour declined to adopt indicates that treating the State of Israel itself as a 'racist endeavour' (rather than any particular Israeli law or policy) is antisemitic, as it

denies Jewish people – and Jewish people alone – the right
to national self-determination. This denial is precisely what
is implied in much of the anti-Zionist rhetoric that Corbyn
and his milieu have engaged in over the years. The decision
not to adopt the definition and examples in full thus leaves
the Labour Party with a higher bar for what constitutes antisemitism than British law.[47] At the time of writing, Labour's
rejection of certain IHRA examples relating to Israel had
kickstarted another explosive row over Corbyn's antisemitic
connections. A 2012 interview with Corbyn on Press TV (of
which more below) showed him speculating that 'the hand
of Israel' lay behind the deaths of 16 Egyptian policemen in
a Islamist terror attack. He went on to query the conviction
of a Hamas operative responsible for the death of seven Jews
in a suicide bombing in an Israeli cafe, calling him 'brother.'

The combination of the depiction of Jews as white and
Israel as nothing but a racist European colonial project or US
imperial outpost shows one of the fundamental dangers of
left-wing antisemitism – that those who engage in it genuinely
believe themselves to be fighting the powerful on behalf of
the oppressed. In this, left antisemitism is the mirror image
of those on the right (including the right of the Labour party)
who compete to demonise migrants in the name of the 'white
working class.' As David Hirsh puts it,

> today's antisemitism incorporates the notion that
> those who complain about antisemitism are the
> racists...In the wake of the Brexit and Trump
> movements, we are seeing opponents of other kinds
> of racism too being designated as the powerful
> ones, while racism itself is interpreted as the cry of
> the oppressed.'[48]

The connection between the two forms has become increasingly apparent. The most rabid Brexiteers, faced with the

disintegration of their utopian dreams in the face of political and economic reality, have increasingly sought to outsource the blame for their failures, with George Soros – who now finds himself roped into virtually every conspiracy theory in existence, on both left and right – once again the target, supposedly responsible for a 'secret plot' to halt Brexit.[49] The ease with which such rhetoric passes from left to right and back again means that to dismiss the existence of antisemitism on the left as a minor problem compared with that of the right is to fail to heed the risks that the two forms can, on occasion, complement and confirm each other. In a time of intense political volatility, forms of 'left' critique which mimic or can be easily adopted by the right come laden with serious dangers.

THE CASTING OF DOUBT

The fetishised portrayal of capitalism as a 'rigged system' which underpins the respective worldviews of Trump, Sanders and Corbyn is not merely a matter of academic debate. The way that the world is interpreted by political actors shapes the forms of political action which follow. Whilst this does not mean that the left and the right are identical, as is claimed by proponents of so-called 'horseshoe theory', the formal similarity between the programmes of Trump and Corbyn is not coincidental. Despite differences in content, each focuses upon the use of the nation-state to protect the economic interests of the national community against a variety of 'outsiders'. It is the logical but by no means irresistible conclusion of a particular way of grasping capitalist social relations. And while such truncated critiques of capitalism do not inevitably lead to full-on conspiracy theory or antisemitism, the risk of stumbling from one to the other is ever-present, especially when the reflexive 'anti-imperialism' of the two-campist worldview is added to the mix. This creates a space of commonality between left and right, a space which is currently expanding across a range of political issues, particularly when it comes to undermining liberal democratic norms held to be directly responsible for economic stagnation and political stasis.

We can see the coincidence of left and right ways of thinking in an article by the Keynesian economist Robert Skidelsky published a few days after Trump's election victory. Skidelsky argues that there was 'positive potential' in Trump's 'head-on challenge to the neoliberal obsession with deficits and debt reduction.'[50] As such, liberals should not allow their 'disgust' at Trump's crude racism and sexism to put them off 'engag[ing]' with his economic programme. This captures the growing complexity that characterises the links between Keynesian stimulus and the state in an age of authoritarian populism. That authoritarianism should accommodate itself to the levers of monetary policy to stimulate effective demand is no surprise. Skidelsky greets Trump's election with a call for the Keynesian left to embrace Trumpist economics, whilst holding its nose at what else Trumpism implies. But, far from their separability, what this communicates is the crossover of Keynesian and proto-fascist economics. The latter arises as a solution to problems of capitalist reproduction unresolvable under liberal democracy, resolving those contradictions at a different level of abstraction- of the race, or of the nation, or the people. Meanwhile, the former does so concretely with reference to the free market by setting men to work digging holes and filling them back up again. Indeed, Keynes himself associated his 'general theory' with the early economic policies of Nazism.[51]

In this respect, the 'economic' and 'cultural' explanations of the recent national populist explosions – Trump, Brexit and so on – elide the implication of the one within the other. Nationalism's cultural appeal to a national people has an economic purpose for capitalist reproduction and the over-coming of class antagonisms. And this always plays out on the plain of the never-never, the world of plenty that is always just around the corner. National populism, eking out favours for its national people, makes insatiable and sublime prom-ises like Trump's infrastructure plans and provision of jobs for all.[52] The cultural and the economic are sublated within one another.

In states the world over the realisation appears to be dawn-ing that liberal democracy and transnational cooperation may not be the optimum way of organising capital so as to meet its currently configured conditions of reproduction. Rather, the authoritarian political systems of China and Russia inspire new spheres of influence and dynamic econo-mies all of their own. In line with this, for Skidelsky, 'Trump-ism could be a solution to the crisis of liberalism, not a portent of its disintegration,' even if the price was at 'some cost' to 'liberal values.' He suggests that previous attempts to pursue Keynesian solutions to the 2008 crisis (such as those of Ed Miliband, outlined in Chapter 1) had failed because they had not combined the argument for stimulus with a sufficiently biting critique of liberal globalisation – 'the free movement of goods, capital, and labour, with its conjoined tolerance of financial criminality' – held to be to blame for the crash.[53]

Skidelsky argues that the 'inequality of economic out-comes' caused by globalisation had stripped away 'the demo-cratic veil that hides from the majority of citizens the true workings of power.' It was the addition of Trump's perspica-cious critique of 'the true workings of power' – in Trump's terms, the 'rigged system' imposed by the 'global power struc-ture' – which had legitimised his Keynesian programme of investment, and he was now reaping the electoral rewards. For Skidelsky, the one is not possible without the other. Thus the difference between Skidelsky on the left and Trump on the right is not based on a fundamentally divergent worldview, a genuinely distinct form of social analysis. It is reduced to merely drawing different conclusions from the same premises, conclusions whose divergence rests entirely on the level of personal morality, the respective level of 'cost' to 'liberal values' each is willing to tolerate.

A nominally left argument based on a fetishised understanding of society, made manifest in a personalised critique of capitalism, which regards liberalism as, at best, incidental to the good society, and at worst an active obstacle, can – while ostensibly aiming at very different goals – end up not only being unable to challenge structurally similar arguments of the right but actually strengthening them. The risk is that by pushing the conspiratorialist narrative of a 'rigged system,' and proposing protectionist, nationalist solutions, the left ends up providing a set of argumentative tools that the right can easily take advantage of at a later date, and turn to its own ends. Worse, such shared critiques open up a space for potential political collaboration, however cynical, between those who purport to be political enemies.

~~~

This plays into a wider convergence between right and left over the rejection of liberalism. This convergence is either conveniently elided, as with Corbyn and Trump, or celebrated, as in the statement of the controversialist 'Marxist' philosopher Slavoj Zizek that '[a]lt-right Trump supporters and left-wing Bernie Sanders fans should join together to defeat capitalism'.[54] This goes into darker and arguably more dangerous terrain the less contained it is by the formal niceties of electoral politics, and the closer it comes to a 'red-brown' alliance between the far-left and far-right.[55] The potential for a combined left-right pincer attack on 'liberal values' is particularly pronounced when it comes to the media and the civic culture of liberal democracies.

The collapse of old models of media consumption has been matched by the concomitant rise of 'alternative' news sources propagating out-and-out conspiracy theories on virtually every topic, from the Grenfell fire to Assad's chemical weapons attacks. What is disturbing is the extent to which these conspiracies are not only being given oxygen by the political agendas of those movements claiming to represent 'the people' – whether arraigned around Trump, the Leave campaign or Corbyn – but actively encouraged by them. There is no doubt that such tactics are increasingly effective. As we have seen, Corbyn's leadership and general election campaigns greatly benefitted from the rewriting of his personal history undertaken by his supporters on social media. But the long-term effect of this casual, if politically expedient, attitude to truth is by no means benign, and poses an enormous threat to the democratic norms which are the bedrock of any successful emancipatory movement – specifically, as we shall see, insofar as it relates to the so-called 'mainstream media' or 'MSM'.

~~~

Even Corbyn's fiercest critics would find it hard to deny that he has faced relentless media criticism since his election. Supportive academics – many of whom would later sign the letter complaining of Corbyn's 'trial by media' over antisemitism – produced reports claiming unprecedented bias, arguing that the coverage amounted to a systematic and deliberate 'process of delegitimization,' by means of a 'lack of or distortion of voice...ridicule, scorn and personal attacks; and through association, mainly with terrorism.'[56] Another report suggested that even (or especially) the BBC, bound by statutory codes of impartiality, 'persistently talked about [Corbyn and his supporters] in terms that emphasised hostility, intransigence and extreme positions.'[57]

Leaving aside the question of the extent to which this attitude was merited by Corbyn's past and present associations,
given this background it is perhaps not surprising that, as
mentioned at the start of this chapter, Corbyn's team would
explicitly take inspiration from Trump's 'aggression against
mainstream TV networks and newspapers.'[58] Like Corbyn,
Trump had faced almost universal hostility from all but the
most right-wing television networks and newspapers. Yet his
campaign seemed to feed off it, rather than collapse under its
weight. Even the most critical networks could not turn their
gaze away. Trump's message was thus boosted far beyond the
audiences normally reached in primary campaigns, even if
the coverage was negatively framed. Trump then turned the
tables on his critics by refusing to rebut negative stories in
time-honoured fashion, instead incorporating the MSM as a
whole into his depiction of the 'crooked establishment.'

The further reaches of the Republican right had long flirt-
ed with the discourse of the 'MSM'. Indeed, the idea that the
media is directly controlled by shadowy – and often, fantasti-
cally, Jewish – elites has long been a staple of antisemitic and
anti-'globalist' conspiracy theories in general. But no Republican Presidential candidate hitherto had placed full-frontal
attacks on 'the MSM' at the centre of his campaigning strategy. Trump had no such qualms. As such the 'crooked media'
joined Clinton, the Federal Reserve, Goldman Sachs, and
supranational institutions as founding members of the 'global
power structure' responsible for America's ills, and against
whom only Trump was willing to stand up. In this way any
media criticism of his behaviour or policies was not only del-
egitimised from the start, but actually strengthened the narrative of the 'rigged system.' Corbyn's team hoped to pull off the
same trick. As *Politico* put it, '[instead] of trying to rebut or
kill a negative story that might appear in the press, Corbyn's
team now plan to highlight such articles, making greater use of

Twitter and Facebook to attack the media rather than attempting to manage it.'[59] And on a strategic level, such a move made sense. Perhaps it was the only option left open to him.

But, in truth, Corbyn's adoption of Trumpian strategies aimed at delegitimising the media as a whole cannot be entirely explained as a tactical response to specific examples of press hostility. It was rather the expression of an impulse with far deeper roots in the proto-Corbynist left, one which, once again, we suggest can be ultimately traced back to the truncated grasp of capitalist society. There were more immediate causes too. For Corbyn's supporters, most of whom had been involved in, or were sympathetic to, the various anti-austerity campaigns during the Cameron–Clegg coalition, the treatment meted out to Corbyn by the media was merely an extension of the difficulties they had experienced in communicating a counter-narrative to the 'austerity populism' discussed in Chapter 1. From the left's perspective, as we have seen, austerity was a completely irrational response to the crisis. They could be forgiven for thinking that the only way to explain its popularity with much of the public – who gave Cameron an unexpected majority in 2015 after a campaign explicitly fought on the basis of its continuation – was that the public had been fooled by a hopelessly biased media.

This was just the latest iteration of a 40-year battle during which the left had pinned the blame for its failure to defeat first Thatcherism and then Blair – indeed neoliberalism itself – on the media. Like austerity, it was inexplicable to the Bennite left that anyone, let alone working people themselves, could actually rationally choose to vote for Thatcher. Indeed, the 1980s debates on the Eurocommunist and 'cultural studies' left that led eventually to Blairism were in part a response to this failure to comprehend Thatcherism's social and political power.[60] For the trad-left, meanwhile, the only possible answer was that they had been duped. Many on the left therefore turned to a very similar theory to that propagated by the Trumpian right about the 'MSM', convincing themselves that political reporting was systematically manipulated by journalists, editors and proprietors in order to prevent the general public from questioning the decisions of the 'establishment.' This often comes granted theoretical cover by the work of American linguist Noam Chomsky, which is taken to show how the 'corporate media' cynically 'manufactures' the 'consent' of a hoodwinked public, at the behest of its owners and political powers.[61]

The issue with this theory is not that the UK media is a paragon of objective, scrupulously neutral political reporting. It clearly is not. The Labour Party and its leaders have been on the sharp end of preposterously overblown scare stories from right-wing papers with an unabashed partisan stance since its formation. And, as we argued in the Chapter 1, the hyper-moralistic character of media discussion around austerity was in itself an early sign and source of the politics of sentiment which has exploded in the wake of Brexit and Trump. But the problem comes when a valid critique of specific media outlets, journalistic practices and ownership models turns into the kind of totalising theory which rejects outright the very notion of rigorous journalistic standards or practices that attempt to ensure some form of impartiality in news reporting, however flawed. Such theories are not therefore focused on critiquing news outlets to the extent that they fail to live up to those standards or practices. They rather work from the assumption that the standards themselves – centring on criticism, scepticism and analysis – are fraudulent, nothing but a trick to disguise the real underlying interests of the powerful – and thus worthless. This is the foundation for specifically left-wing brand of 'post-truth' that uproots itself from reality precisely because it is, often rightly, opposed to the way that reality is.[62]

From this perspective, no information emanating from the 'MSM' can ever be trusted in any circumstances, and no distinction of any real significance can be made between different outlets; all are tainted with the original 'MSM' sin of containing the capacity to negate. Critical questioning of favoured politicians from 'MSM' journalists is thus no longer seen as being a fundamental part of a functioning democratic polity. It is rather regarded as a partisan attack from implacable ideological opponents, and thus an affront to be ruthlessly combatted. This attitude is increasingly apparent amongst Trump supporters, hardline Brexiteers, and the more zealous elements of Corbynism's grassroots support. Journalists who ask questions deemed to be inappropriate at Corbyn's press conferences are regularly booed and hissed (a feature of Trump's press appearances too).[63] Indeed, the hounding of BBC Political Editor Laura Kuennsberg, routinely labelled a closet Conservative by Corbyn-supporting alternative media outlets such as *Skwawkbox* and *The Canary*, reached such intensity that she was assigned a bodyguard for the 2017 Labour Party conference (as well as at the Conservative one that followed, due to the presence of leftist protestors).[64]

The generalised attack on journalists – which goes far beyond legitimate critique, and which is now routine on all sides of the political spectrum – is a key example of how the emergence of a politics of position, in which the truth and validity of statements are not rationally appraised but prejudged by the perceived character of the person who states them, is corroding the pillars of a liberal polity. Ironically considering the self-professed aspirations of those who rail against the so-called 'MSM', this focus on persona over standards does nothing to correct for the abuses of journalistic practice common amongst what was once termed the 'yellow' press – it merely poisons what remains of the public sphere further.

Highlighting this irony, one common outcome of the total rejection of 'MSM' journalistic practice as a whole is a situation where 'alternative' news sources are regarded as reliable purely on the basis that they are not part of the 'MSM', regardless of their own lack of journalistic standards, click-bait commercial models or ownership structures. As media theorist Gavan Titley puts it, 'systemic distrust of the western 'MSM' results in nothing more than displaced fidelity to its 'alternative' mirror image.'[65] This is essentially the position that Corbyn himself adheres to, one derived from the 'two campist' view of politics which, as we have seen, structures the Corbyn worldview. Corbyn's own media activity during his years on the backbenches was concentrated in the alternative left-wing press, particularly the *Morning Star*, for whom he wrote a weekly column from 2004 to 2015.

The *Morning Star* is a daily paper owned by the Stalinist-hangover Communist Party of Britain, and historically funded by the Soviet Union. Over the course of its history, initially as the *Daily Worker*, it has supported the Nazi–Soviet Pact, supressed critical coverage of the 1956 Soviet invasion of Hungary, and reacted to the fall of the Berlin Wall with the headline 'GDR unveils reform package.'[66] More recently, the paper greeted as a 'liberation' the fall of Aleppo to Bashar Al-Assad's Russian-backed Syrian army, following a brutal four-year siege of the city.[67] It also implied that the chemical gas attack on the Damascas suburb of Douma in April 2018 was a 'false flag,' set up to incriminate Assad, using the same pseudocritical 'cui bono' logic that led Tony Benn to speculate about Bosnian Muslims bombing themselves in Sarajevo market.[68] While the paper has undoubtedly carried more rigorous reporting than these examples over its lifetime, especially on industrial disputes, the idea that it should be regarded as inherently superior to the 'bourgeois media' does not stand up to scrutiny.

A similar pattern emerges when it comes to Corbyn's attitude the broadcast media. In 2011, Corbyn tweeted to a follower complaining about the BBC that they should 'try Russia Today. Free of Royal Wedding and more objective on Libya than most.'[69] Russia Today – now RT – is owned and run directly by the Russian state. Since his election as leader, Corbyn-supporting shadow ministers and MPs, including Corbyn himself, as well as high profile supporters such as Ken Loach, have made more than 40 appearances on the channel.[70] It is regarded by much of the Corbyn left as a space open to political arguments which are systematically suppressed by the 'MSM' – although the typically savvier John McDonnell has made clear-voiced appeals for Labour figures to refrain from future engagement with Russian state media.[71]

The politically ambiguous character of the space offered by RT is amply demonstrated not so much by its amplification of certain left perspectives favourable to the regime's attempts to sow political confusion in Western states, but by the other content which routinely fills it. RT's coverage since its English-language launch in 2005 has included indulgent interviews with various leading figures of the 'nativist international', from Marine Le Pen to former BNP leader Nick Griffin, who rather predictably took the opportunity to rail against 'globalism'.[72] Conspiracy theories (including claims that 9/11 was an 'inside job') are regularly presented as straight up news stories.[73] One of RT's own presenters described the channel's coverage of the Russian invasion and annexation of Crimea in 2014 as 'whitewashing', before resigning on air.[74] As for the 'objectivity' when it came to Gaddafi's Libya and the NATO intervention in 2011 that won Corbyn's admiration, this included programmes claiming that Libya had been the 'African Switzerland' before the war, and promoting goldbug conspiracy theories that the war was fought to prevent Gaddafi introducing a pan-African 'gold Dinar' to rival the dollar and the Euro – a theory very similar to that which Corbyn claimed was behind the first Gulf War.[75]

This pseudocritical stance – one for which every 'MSM' report is assumed to be propaganda, and any counter-narrative 'casting doubt' is granted legitimacy, however implausible – has been something of a Corbyn trademark throughout his career. In 2003, he seemed to echo far-right 9/11 'truthers' in a *Morning Star* column in which he argued that the media had been 'manipulated' by 'claims that bin Laden and al-Qaida had committed the atrocity' in order to justify the US-led attack on the Taliban, itself then 'subtly' turned into 'regime change' in Afghanistan.[76] Similarly, in an interview soon after Bin Laden had been killed by US forces in 2011, Corbyn gave credence to conspiracy theories surrounding his death by asking, with respect to the supposedly un-Islamic nature of the body's disposal, 'why the burial at sea – if indeed there was a burial at sea – and indeed if it was Bin Laden?'[77] The latter interview was aired on Press TV, a cable channel owned and run by the Iranian state, which was shut down in the UK by broadcasting regulator Ofcom in 2012 after a number of breaches of the broadcasting code.[78] The most notable of these was the broadcast of what was essentially a forced, scripted 'interview' with Mazier Bahari, a *Newsweek* journalist imprisoned and tortured for his reporting on the 2009 Iranian presidential election.[79]

Corbyn had been sporadically employed by Press TV as a stand in presenter for George Galloway on his regular phone-in show – including shows filmed after the hostage interview had been broadcast. Corbyn was paid £20,000 for the privilege.[80] During one show, a caller described the BBC as 'Zionist liars,' while another described Jewish people as a 'disease' and suggested the Arab states 'throw them out' of the Middle East. Corbyn not only failed to challenge this clear antisemitism, but then thanked him for his call.[81] When he was criticised for working for the station, Corbyn claimed he had 'raised human rights issues' – the footage of this has unfortunately never been found – and stopped immediately after the Green

Revolution had been brutally put down by the Iranian regime in 2009. This was not true – Corbyn's last appearance on the station was in 2011, six months after the channel had had its licence revoked for broadcasting the hostage interview.[82]

What is the purpose of the somewhat idiosyncratic attitude to the truth displayed by outlets like RT and Press TV – and by extension the state powers of Russian and Iran? It ultimately rests on a general strategy of destabilisation, the blurring of the lines between fact and fiction, particularly when it comes to the foreign policy of those states, such as Russia's support for Assad's regime in Syria. As media analyst Muhammad Idrees Ahmad puts it, '[the] aim is less to persuade than to obfuscate. RT doesn't have to tell a credible or coherent story as long as it can cast doubt on competing ones,' gradually undermining the legitimacy of a fragmented world order in which Russian influence is easier to exert.[83]

The threat of Russian destabilisation should not be exaggerated, so as to simply replace conspiracy theories of, say, an all-powerful Israel with their Russian equivalents. But neither should it be dismissed out of hand on the basis of nothing more than the utterly patronising two-campist insight that every Russian action is merely a response to the 'Western imperialism.' It is perfectly possible to acknowledge that Russia has its own independent political – or indeed imperialist – objectives, the pursuit of which may involve attempts to prise apart the 'Western alliance,' the financial or propaganda support of hard right movements across the globe, or even direct interference in democratic processes in Europe and the US, without falling down a rabbit hole of conspiratorial scare stories that seek to explain every vaguely surprising event through secretive Russian manoeuvres.

~~~

The post-truth strategy of 'casting doubt' is by no means limited to RT or Press TV alone. It is rapidly becoming the first tool in the media management box of tricks across the political spectrum, epitomised by Trump's now ubiquitous cry of 'fake news' at every critical story, regardless of its provenance or accuracy. Similarly, the Corbyn-supporting news site *Skwawk-box* – regularly granted exclusive interviews with Corbynist rising stars such as MPs Chris Williamson and Laura Pidcock – has made the 'casting of doubt' on reported stories, without ever quite crossing the line into making an outright claim, its *modus operandi*. A significant example of this cynical ambiguity was in the aftermath of the Grenfell Tower fire, when *Skwawkbox* suggested that the government had issued a secret 'D-notice' banning the media from reporting the true number of victims.[84] The story rapidly spread across social media, boosted by high profile Corbyn supporters. This lent credence to the various conspiracy theories about the blaze that had been circulating in the days following the fire.

After it was categorically proven that no 'D-notice' had been issued, and that the official tally of the dead was rising slowly due to the difficulties in identifying the victims rather than a government plot, *Skwawkbox* issued a disingenuous retraction in which it argued that the original article had not actually claimed a D-notice had been issued, but only that it would be scandal *if* it had been.[85] This mealy-mouthed 'correction' went on to imply that other means of restricting information were being used, even if a D-notice was not one of them, thus perpetuating the insinuation of conspiracy over the disaster. The dangers of conspiratorial thinking when it comes to a disaster such as Grenfell – understandable perhaps from those immediately affected, but not by disinterested 'commentators' – were reiterated a week later when, at the Iranian-sponsored Al-Quds march in London, at which Corbyn was once a speaker, and where Hezbollah flags are flown and antisemitic chants invariably heard, one speaker claimed that 'Zionists' were 'responsible for the murder of the people in Grenfell.'[86] *The Times* later reported that one leading activist in a 'Justice4Grenfell' group – most of the members of which were not themselves residents – had claimed the people in the tower had been 'burnt alive in a Jewish sacrifice.'[87] Beyond the clear antisemitism, such thinking does nothing to help the process of getting to the truth about the fire, nor holding people to account – indeed, it blocks it.

It would be an overstatement to say that Corbyn's personal naivety when it comes to 'alternative' news sources – which extends to his support for homeopathy and scepticism of vaccinations, both standard conspiracy fare – is universally shared by the entirety of the movement behind his leadership.[88] But the willingness of both the Corbynist grassroots and its intelligentsia to accept the switch to a Trumpian media strategy, one which takes as axiomatic the belief that the 'MSM' is a homogenous bloc intent on ideological indoctrination, does indicate the spread of a troublingly credulous stance dressed up as independent, critical thinking – as the popularity of dubious sites like *Skwawkbox* and *The Canary* also attests. Moreover, it is a stance that can terminate in 'false flag' readings of terrorism, the denial or justification of war crimes when committed by 'anti-imperialist' states, and even, as in the case of Kosovo, outright genocide denial.

In the first few months of 2018 alone, a loud and sizeable portion of the Corbyn base pushed several lines of conspiracist rumour elevated to the level of alternative truth. First, that the 'novichok' nerve agent attack on a former Russian spy in Salisbury may have been the work of Mossad, the Israeli secret service, or a 'false flag' by the British secret services.[89] Second, that the chemical attack on the Syrian city of Douma either never happened at all, and that videos of children choking were faked – or that the attack was the result of anti-government rebels gassing their own territory.[90] Third, that the US, UK and France bombed chemical weapons sites in Syria in order to distract from political troubles at home.[91] Fourth, that accusations of antisemitism within the Labour party were a concocted 'smear' pushed by Corbyn's political opponents.[92] And fifth, finally, and perhaps most absurdly, that the BBC had digitally manipulated an image of Corbyn to make his hat look 'more Russian'.[93] Many of these arguments were not only tolerated, but actually reiterated by Corbyn and members of his front bench in interviews, during speeches at demonstrations and on social media.[94]

Pushed to its limits this uncritical stance develops into a general refusal to believe any news story or fact whatsoever, and the total abandonment of faith in the ability to distinguish truth from fiction. In this way the very possibility of a factual account of an event is rejected altogether, or, alternatively, replaced by the willingness to believe anything, just as long as it contradicts the 'mainstream' narrative and/or *feels* like it *must be* true. The politics of position meets the politics of sentiment. The effect of this is to leave concrete forms of power completely unchallenged and effectively unchallengeable.

LEFT–RIGHT CROSSOVER

One outcome of the forms of analysis common to Corbynism outlined in this chapter is that there are now substantial areas in which the conspiratorial wing of Corbynism – which is not merely tolerated but encouraged by the leadership – overlaps and gives credence to political positions and conspiratorial narratives pushed by the far right. This is particularly visible when it comes to Syria. Corbyn's refusal to straightforwardly condemn the violence of the Assad regime, responsible for approximately 92% of deaths of the 207,000 civilians killed during the conflict so far, his repeated efforts to 'cast doubt' on the clear evidence of the regime's use of chemical weapons, and the depiction of rebel forces in their entirety as 'jihad-ists' by leading members of the Shadow Cabinet, echoes and amplifies the conspiracy theories pushed by bloggers on both the far right and the nominal 'left.'[95]

We can see how these ideas switch between left and right by tracing the roots of a claim which appeared in a 2016 campaign speech by Donald Trump, where he suggested that 'Barack Hussein Obama' was personally responsible for 'founding ISIS.'[96] This ludicrous claim originated in a declassified Pentagon report published on a rightwing site in 2015.[97] The report, written in 2012, warned that one consequence of the Syrian rebels' attempt to overthrow the Assad regime might be the creation of a 'Salafist principality' in eastern Syria. Despite the very next paragraph of the report describing this eventuality as a 'grave danger', the 'anti-imperialist' leftist journal *Jacobin* ran a piece entitled 'How the US helped ISIS,' based on the argument that any support, however limited, for those struggling for democratic rights in Syria was tantamount to 'empowering' ISIS.[98] Two days later, the *Guardian* published a comment piece making essentially the same point, albeit stripped of any remaining nuance, headlined 'Now the truth emerges: how the US fuelled the rise of ISIS in Syria and Iraq.'[99] Its author was none other than Seamus Milne, Corbyn's chief strategist. A year later, as the Democratic primary campaign came to a head, the story leapt back across the political spectrum, with Steve Bannon's *Breitbart* publishing an article claiming that 'Hillary Clinton Received Secret Memo Stating Obama Admin 'Support' for ISIS.'[100] A few weeks later, the same claim began to appear in Trump's speeches.

This left–right crossover – which was repeated in Corbyn's refusal to directly implicate Russia in the Salisbury poisoning – draws upon the same resources as that which took place in the mid-90s when it came to Serbia, Bosnia and Kosovo. At its most extreme this led to the downplaying and even outright denial of the Srebrenica massacre of Bosnian Muslims and the genocide of Kosovan Albanians.[101] And it is no coincidence that a leading advocate of revisionist histories of both the Yugoslavia and Syrian conflicts is Noam Chomsky, the author of the 'propaganda model' of media analysis that has been hugely influential on Corbyn's wing of the pseudocritical left.[102] The simplistic logic of *cui bono* – which as we have seen, lay at the heart of Tony Benn's latter-day approach to geopolitics, taken over wholesale by Corbyn – generated by Chomsky's analysis is unable to recognise the mediated character of capitalist society and, as such, encourages the kind of reductive and fetishistic pseudo-criticism increasingly common amongst both right and left.

At the root of this conspiratorial historical revisionism is a reflexive anti-Americanism or anti-Atlanticism which is the foundation of two campist 'anti-imperialism,' and which, as we have seen, is the price of entry into Corbyn's Stop the War milieu. Such essentialised anti-Americanism must be distinguished from the critique of any particular American government or policy, Trump more than anyone. Anti-Americanism in this sense derives from 'a relentless critical impulse toward American social, economic, and political institutions, traditions, and values,' and in particular the inauthenticity of American culture, the inexorable spread of which is regarded as corroding the original purity of superior cultures. As Andrei S. Markovits and Heiko Beyer put it

> *there is a sense of inevitability to this process,*
> *a kind of helplessness befalling the victims of*
> *Americanization, a loss of agency in the face of this*
> *all-powerful onslaught that breeds resentment.*[103]

Anti-Americanism was traditionally a feature of far right nationalism, stemming from resistance to what was regarded as American-instigated liberalism, commericialisation and globalisation – in short, another form of personalised critique of capitalism. Virulent Anti-Americanism continues to characterise various forms of ethnic nationalism, from the French Front Nationale to the German 'New Right', as well as Arab nationalisms and the 'National Bolshevism' or 'neo-Euroasianism' of the hard-right Russian nationalist Alexsander Dugin, an intellectual influence on Putin.[104] According to Markovits and Beyer there is an 'affinity with anti-American conspiracy theories and antisemitic narratives':

> *Jews, just like Americans, are also seen as corrosive, as undermining an entity's authenticity, as subverting its original purity. Both Jews and Americans are deemed to be particularly powerful even though they are almost always considered culturally inferior and somehow artificial, most assuredly inauthentic.*

With this in mind, it is not surprising that a preoccupation with Israel, 'Zionism' and the power of the 'Israeli lobby' – which, again, goes beyond legitimate critique of any particular Israeli government, the occupation of the West Bank, or other Israeli policy, and instead obsessively delegitimizes and demonises Israel as a unique evil in the world – also marks a space in which left and right can cohere. This leads to a downplaying or outright denial of antisemitism on the left, particularly when it is found within movements regarded as 'objectively anti-imperialist' – such as Hamas or Hezbollah – despite their often genocidal intentions.[105]

In each of these cases right and left come together in agreement that the US, Israel, NATO, the European Union, free trade, global finance and the international rule-based liberal order *in toto* represent the greatest threat to world peace, and the first obstacle to be removed in the building of an

emancipated society. This shared analysis results in similar
(though not identical) conclusions too, which rest at present
in an imaginary of a national-popular programme of economic protectionism and isolationism. This, we have suggested, is dangerously mistaken in both diagnosis and prognosis.
As such the contemporary left of Corbyn, Sanders and the
similarly inclined Jean-Luc Melenchon of the 'La France
Insoumise' movement risks repeating the catastrophic mistakes
of the left in the 1920s and 30s. Trapped in a fetishised worldview, much of today's left makes the fatal error of conflating
liberal political forms with capitalism as a system of socially
mediated labour. It thus regards any threat to the former as an
attack on the latter. Hence the widespread ambivalence amongst
the left when it comes to a contest between a 'neoliberal' such
as Emmanuel Macron and an actual fascist like Marine Le Pen,
with Melenchon refusing to endorse the former against the latter after being eliminated in the first round of voting.[106]

The common idea that liberalism inevitably and inexorably leads to fascism is precisely the kind of deterministic illusion which obscures the political tasks which need
to be undertaken in order to ensure that it does not. The
failure to make a clear distinction between liberal and
authoritarian forms of capitalism – a failure which, as we
have shown, stems from an inability to grasp the mediated
character of capital as a social form – is the sign of a 'syn-
cretic agreement between the revolutionary left and ultra-
nationalist far right to overthrow the liberal centre.'[107] It
is this agreement, and not liberalism per se, which is itself
the mark of incipient fascism – or, better, 'post-fascism' as
GM Tamas has termed it, a fascism without jackboots and
uniforms, but one where even the 'tempered universality'
of formal liberal nationalism is rejected in favour of the
politics of position and essentialised identity.[108] And it is

this we see today in what Kyrylo Tkachenko calls the 'geo-political turn' taken by an international red-brown alliance of far-left and far-right united by 'the single factor of anti-liberalism'.[109]

Our argument is not, to be clear, that Corbynism itself is fascist, either implicitly or embryonically. What is at stake here is the ability of a Corbyn-style left to effectively combat a rising hard right, now effectively sublated in the ruling parties of government on both sides of the Atlantic. This chapter has highlighted the tendency within Corbynism – conscious or not – to echo far right conspiracy theories about capitalist society, from the role of international finance to geopolitical conflict. Such a fetishised worldview is manifest in Corbyn's reflexive and essentialised 'two campist' anti-imperialism, what is – at best – a failure to recognise antisemitism and at worst a structurally antisemitic worldview, a fetishised critique of international finance, a casual attitude to authoritarian, nationalist and theocratic regimes, a conflation of liberalism and capitalism, and an economic programme that is in its essence one of protectionist nationalism. The parallels between such a programme and that offered by the populist right should, at the very least, give leftists pause for thought. The ease with which the terminology of the 'rigged system' has travelled along the political spectrum, put to various uses by politicians ostensibly opposed to one another, is clear signal of a worrying political ambivalence in rhetoric and, ultimately, worldviews.

In an era characterised by intense political volatility, the creation of a cross-political anti-liberal consensus, built upon a fetishised form of pseudo-criticism that regularly tips over into full-on conspiracy theory, and placed in the service of a protectionist programme of national renewal, can rapidly spiral out of control and in unexpected directions. There is a real danger that by uncritically cheering on these developments, the reactionary potential of which is assuaged solely by the absolute faith in Corbyn's moral exceptionalism, Corbynism is part of a wider political consensus that heightens the risk that the undoubtedly flawed liberalism of the present will be replaced by something much worse.[110]

Conclusion

A POLITICS OF PESSIMISM

In late April 2018, Jeremy Corbyn's byline appeared in the *Evening Standard* setting out what he was doing to 'banish' anti-semitism from the Labour Party.[1] There was a seriousness in the article entirely lacking in his previous attempts to address the issue. The 'few bad apples' theory was definitively dispatched with, as Corbyn instead focused explicitly on how conspiracist understandings of both capitalism and imperialism create an environment in which antisemitism takes root and thrives:

> *there are people who have come to see capitalism and imperialism as the product of conspiracy by a small shadowy elite rather than a political, economic, legal and social system. That is only a step from hoary myths about "Jewish bankers" and "sinister global forces". These views do no service to the struggle for a just society. Instead, they reproduce the sort of scapegoating that we recognise when directed at ethnic or religious minorities.*[2]

Shortly before, Momentum had also released a statement acknowledging the scale of the problem, proposing a programme of political education to 'move people away from conspiratorial thinking and towards a systematic understanding of how society works'.[3] In so doing, both Corbyn and Momentum spoke in terms recognisable to readers who have reached this far in the book. We, too, have argued for a systemic critique of capitalism to replace the foreshortened and personalised critiques among which left antisemitism spreads.

The month before Corbyn's statement, we had published an op-ed in the *New Statesman* on antisemitism in the Labour Party and how it could be understood, challenging the incomplete critique of capitalism it rests upon with the critical Marxism covered here. It appeared at the beginning of a week in which many key figures on the Corbynist left went on to significantly change their tune on the very real problem confronting the Labour Party, not least, it would seem from the timing, because Corbyn himself had begun to noticeably shift his own position in the days following the Mear One mural controversy.[4]

The evolving response of the Labour leadership and its praetorian guard created a more open environment for the exchange of views of Labour's antisemitism crisis and how to fix it. But, despite the calls of the former for more systematic critiques of capitalism capable of challenging and replacing the kinds of personalised critiques that lead to left antisemitism, our piece received a number of responses that struck a more defensive posture. The critiques to which we were subject are worth considering here not least because they pose questions of our approach that some readers may be left asking should they have stuck with us until now. The critical reactions to our argument have been, for the most part, insightful, knowledgeable and have helped move the whole debate forward to a much more productive and progressive footing.

It has to be said that we were also on the receiving end of some more knockabout, *ad hominem* stuff.[5] The more intemperate responses appeared to have been provoked by our attempt to communicate to a wider audience a Marxian analysis not by rights ours to understand or share in the first place, let alone attempt to creatively interpret in new ways. Here the self-nominated gatekeepers of what is and is not authentic Marxist theory have sought to impugn our own use of Marx and his ideas, taken as an adornment or subterfuge, a sleight of hand to deceive the reader into supposedly non-Marxist political conclusions. As merely 'self-described Marxists' – we must remember to seek approval in future! – we have been charged with manhandling 'Marxist categories to mystify the social world instead of rendering it intelligible and knowable' – something of a conspiracy theory in itself.[6]

The milder accusation of having 'a strange reading of Marx', on the other hand, is one to which we plead happily and wholeheartedly guilty. Our guilt is all the more profound if the measure of this strangeness is how far we travel from a redundant orthodoxy erected around a series of largely unfinished and unpublished texts cleverly repackaged and sold as scripture.[7]

This policing of what is and is not Marxist, often on the flimsiest of textual interpretations, somewhat undermines the tendency of our critics to suggest that it is us who are offering an 'authoritarian' reading of Marx that selfishly protects our own orthodoxy from outsiders, and places us in the position of its sole and exclusive purveyors. Thus, we are criticised for employing what is merely 'Marxist ornamentation' as a 'phony gesture of authority' based on 'a domineering application of theory'.[8] Of course, the term 'authoritarian' is too loosely applied here, especially by those who should know better its political implications. But if we are to apply the term in such a way, what could be more 'authoritarian' than seeking to say what is and is not *really* Marxism and what is really only ornamental? This is, perhaps, an outwards projection of defensiveness and liturgical insecurity on the part of the authors.

In any case, we are not interested in defending actually existing Marxism. Nor do we wish to scold others over the uses and abuses of Marx. We are interested instead in promoting an open Marx freed from orthodoxy and the political objectives forced upon his fragmentary and unfinished intellectual project, in full recognition that other thinkers and theories are necessary to fill in the gaps. In this spirit, our concern is with sharing a theoretical orientation we have found useful in navigating the contours of a topic of public debate.

One of the most sustained critiques of our approach – that of the *New Socialist* – exposes the real basis for this professed concern with our fidelity to Marxism. This is the notion that there is some imperative upon us to make our theory 'practical' by subordinating it to the end of political action. This rests on an assumption of 'the radical externality' of us and our critique 'to the experience of the movement.'[9] Here we see the full force of the dogmatism retroactively applied to Marx by his ill-fated followers on the basis of the contested legacy of the *Theses on Feuerbach,* whereby what is important is not to interpret the world but to change it.[10] This has the effect of suggesting that practice trumps theory, whereas in our view the latter is in fact always-already dialectically the former, and vice versa. Placing theory at the beck-and-call of practical expediency has only encouraged mindless intellectual conformity to a higher cause that has, and almost certainly will continue to, come up short.

The supposed political utility or otherwise of our approach has also been hauled over the coals by commentators of a left-populist or Polanyian bent. An impeccably clear example by Michaela Collard suggests that the specificity of 'a left critique of elite power' is that it is 'properly *political.*'[11] It argues that we 'delegitimate' this 'kind of left analysis' focused on elite power at a time where apparently, such forms of analysis are 'already widely viewed suspect' – even though, as we have seen, railing at 'elites' is the dominant political discourse of our time on both right and left. On one hand, Collard's response argues that our approach overlooks real empirical issues, leading to an impoverished analysis. There is indeed a danger of this when engaging in work based upon the critique of abstract forms – but, we would suggest, it is impossible to understand *why* so-called 'elite' actors do the things they do without a prior grasp of the abstract economic compulsion that impels them. More problematic is Collard's claim that doing away with personalised critiques would 'lose the power of the Corbyn project – its willingness to hold elites to account'. On this front, 'Corbyn's 'rigged system' narrative' is *necessary* 'for the left to be politically effective'. Hence any critique of the analysis, whether right or wrong, is once again subordinated to the predetermined political goal.

Also from a broadly left-populist perspective, Jeremy Gilbert similarly focuses on both the analytical and practical-political implications of our approach.[12] His reading is based on the seeming misapprehension that we posit an inevitable relationship or, in his words 'resemblance', between genuine critiques of 'agency or interests' and antisemitic critiques of capitalism. Yet it is precisely the purpose of our argument to make clear the distinction between the two. Gilbert remains stuck at the level of discussions of 'discourse', when for us ideology is a question of the 'real appearances' taken by the material structure of society at a given time. This is a question not of 'ideas' uprooted from reality, but ideas as material parts of society itself, the critique of which is a critique of that society in turn. In this sense, the claim made elsewhere that we are 'idealists' gets things half right.[13] The missing half is the material side that for us the ideal is inextricably intertwined with.

Gilbert also poses the important question of how anti-capitalism can be differentiated from antisemitism not only in theory but in practice. One thing is for sure: as far as anti-capitalism is concerned, suspending any critical judgement focused inward on the left itself so that Corbynism can be let to run its course will do little to aid its chances. In fact, for various reasons raised in this book, Corbynism maintains a commitment to nation, people and state that actively militates against its capacity to create any substantial theoretical or practical alternative to capitalism.

~~~

It was strange, in sight of all these wagons circling Project Corbyn in the name of anticapitalism and anti-imperialism, to see Corbyn himself come out with such an explicit recognition that it was partly abstract opposition to capitalism and imperialism that fostered the conditions for a specifically left antisemitism. Corbyn argued essentially in support of the key idea we put forward about the relationship between a 'rigged system' critique of capitalism and the spread of antisemitism. In this, he somehow surpassed his more intellectual supporters in seemingly advancing his position whilst others were lodged squarely in a reflexive mode of defending him and his project at all costs.

The extent to which Corbyn's *volte face* was anything more than a public relations exercise aimed at quelling a media storm remains to be seen. Events since, in particular the needless and provocative row over Labour's refusal to adopt the IHRA definition of antisemitism with all indicative examples, on the quasi-conspiratorial basis that it is intended to prevent criticism of the Israeli government or occupation, does not give much ground for hope.[14] Regardless, the greater problem here is, as we have argued, that once unleashed, the kind of politically ambivalent and conspiratorial worldview that is epitomised in the rhetoric of a 'rigged system' quickly takes on a life of its own, with unexpected consequences.

Thus even when Corbyn himself criticised truncated forms of anti-capitalism and anti-imperialism, some among his supporters seemingly refused to listen, and instead doubled-down on the original position. What this goes to show is that, whatever the likelihood of an end to the rigged system schtick, the conceit around which it was constructed was only the expression of an underlying set of ideas specific to the age. Uncaged, Corbyn and his core support were powerless to resist not only the convenient convergence this rhetoric struck with external political reality, but moreover the uses to which it is put by those whose own foreshortened and personalised critiques it grants the ideological and institutional room to move. In his response to these events, Paul Mason proposes that Labour should

> build a vibrant political culture where anti-Semitism
> is combated, where any illusions about Vladimir
> Putin's Russia are punctured and the truth is told
> about the crimes of Stalinism; a culture where people
> are educated in the values of the Labour movement
> and its diverse traditions – social democracy,
> syndicalism and democratic Marxism – not just given
> a manifesto, a rulebook and a list of doors to knock.
> We need a movement that helps people develop a
> belief in their own agency – not the agency of states,
> religions, autocrats or, for that matter, iconic Labour
> leaders. That part is up to us.[15]

Mason here grasps how antisemitism segues with a wider political culture that is increasingly dangerous and to which the Labour Party under Corbyn is far from immune. This recognition, we would argue, demands some kind of reconciliation with tenets of liberalism as a bulwark against something much worse. Against this, Jeremy Gilbert contends that 'centrist liberalism' has no response 'adequate to the task' of combatting antisemitism because it cannot sustain the class politics necessary to do so.[16] However, in this book we have argued that one of the selling points of 'holding the centre' at the current juncture is precisely that liberalism creates the space for the working through of the contradictions of class society. It does this not by means of mass subjective politics but by providing an objective legal and deliberative framework through which antagonisms can play out with no false promise of their resolution. It is precisely by giving room to the expression of class struggle through collective bargaining and legal mediation that the role of personalised force is pushed back from employment and political relations, and the dangerous politics of anti-elite populism is contained. But now from within the cracks of a broken liberal order a workplace and labour market characterised by personalised 'neo-villeiny' arises, teamed with insurgent authoritarian nationalisms blossoming in the political sphere. In the face of this perhaps liberalism does, after all, have something to offer the construction of a new left intellectual and political agenda able to overcome some of the impasses of Corbynism, whilst keeping space open for the positive development of its dynamic contradictions – rather than shutting them down in the name of loyalty to an omnipotent 'movement' that condemns the basis of its own existence.

An interesting feature of the past few years has been the dawning realisation on the Corbyn-sympathetic left that the crisis of liberalism may not be all it is cracked up to be. One of the clearest, although heavily caveated, expositions of the imperative for leftists to think seriously about liberalism at a time of its decline comes from left commentator Richard Seymour. Seymour considers the extent to which Judith Shklar's concept of a 'liberalism of fear' – which we have already encountered in Chapter 3 – might provide orientation to a left able to confront the 'cruelty' inherent in a crumbling political, legal and global order, and an increasingly intemperate climate of public and intellectual debate.[17] In the face of this looming reality, liberalism 'at its *best*' is

> *anti-populist, anti-majoritarian, against what*
> *Michael Mann calls the 'dark side of democracy', in*
> *favour of a regime of rules, procedures, limits and*
> *so on. It is against arbitrary power, for a predictable*
> *framework of government action. It distrusts*
> *massifications, suspects causes, and sees nothing*
> *holy in majorities. It says…if I had to choose*
> *between betraying my country, and my friend, I*
> *hope I have the guts to betray my country.*

This represents a viable alternative to many of the targets of our critique – nationalism, authoritarianism, populism, isolationism. What gives the 'liberalism of fear' its edge is its pessimistic appraisal of why liberalism is necessary in spite of, as Seymour is at pains to stress, its inherent limitations and record of past and present misdemeanours. This is because the alternative to liberalism is usually, and in the absence of any convincing transformative agenda suggesting otherwise, much worse. The 'liberalism of fear' is 'a liberalism motivated by a fear of authoritarian alternatives.'[18] Therefore, a reconciliation with liberalism in an apparently post-liberal age of political opportunity, a rearguard attempt to ensure the centre holds at a time of its dissolution, may instil the cognisance necessary for the left to articulate an emancipatory programme of political change – without seeking the false resolution of contradictions in foreshortened forms of theoretical critique and practical action. Liberalism compels us think and act under the cloud of a realistic but radical pessimism about the persistence of contradiction and imperfectability, and the limits of our capacity to change it. But are any of the competing intellectual forces in the contemporary

Labour Party capable of taking up this challenge? If the intellectual and political project of Corbynism is blighted in the
ways we have surveyed in this book, what is the alternative?

~~~

The theoretical alternative proposed here is one already close
at hand, looming in the left's subconscious waiting to be
(re)discovered. It is present in Marx's dialectical unfolding of
contradictions in *Capital*, most notably in his understanding
of how liberal niceties of right and market constitute a real
appearance expressing antagonistic class relations.[19] Stepping
out of the shadow of Bolshevism that still looms over the UK
left, it finds common cause instead with the Menshevik critique
of Lenin.[20] It resounds in the defence of bourgeois rule of law as
a carrier of the fruits of class struggle found in the work of E.P.
Thompson and the latter-day Nicos Poulantzas.[21] It is vented
in Adorno and Horkheimer's increasingly pessimistic appraisal
of the prospects of revolutionary totalitarianism and attendant
appreciation of the United States as a bulwark against it.[22] It
is found elsewhere on the fringes of the Frankfurt School as its
intellectuals reckoned with the positive contradictions of the
rule of law against the totalising experience of fascism.[23]

It is fought for in the 'two-and-a-half-campist' American
democratic socialist tradition represented in *Dissent* magazine,
a watering hole for what Michael Walzer calls the 'decent left'.[24]
Elsewhere, it appears in Claude Lefort's radically democratic
and anti-totalitarian advocacy of human rights.[25] It is commu-
nicated in Robert Fine's critical cosmopolitanism inspired in
equal parts by Marx, Hegel, the Frankfurt School and Hannah
Arendt.[26] It gains one of its most forceful advocates in Norman
Geras's Marxian defence of liberal internationalism.[27]

Today, it attains a new edge from the fierce critique of
antisemitic nationalism, reactionary forms of 'anti-capitalism'
and fascism found in the 'New Reading of Marx' forged from

the post-war German new left, and upon whose theorists this book has heavily relied.[28] Moreover, the suggestive vision of Marx on which all of these variants are to some extent based achieves new exegetical resonance in Terrell Carver's intellectually liberating presentation of the man himself as a political operator engaged in bourgeois coalitions for liberal reform, as well as the recent biographical work of Gareth Stedman Jones, which gives a fine-grained portrayal of Marx's cognisance of the opportunities and affordances of liberalism.[29]

Further practical, political and theoretical work will undoubtedly be necessary to draw out the implications of the subterranean tradition represented here. But we can already discern some of what a wider and more robust theoretical alternative would entail in practice.

It would deny the so-called 'will of the people'. It would instead recognise and protect the space of pluralist dialogue and debate, acknowledging the right to and inevitably of difference, and the importance of democratic structures and institutions which facilitate its articulation. It would view the democratic space of negotiation between formal equals as an achievement won through struggle rather than an obstacle or fetter to be casually cast aside in the name of a chimerical 'real' or 'concrete' democracy– something in evidence in Labour's support for the repeal of the 2016 Trade Union Act but not always so much in evidence elsewhere

It would see national borders as no barrier to the building of practical solidarity with individuals who, like most, have no choice living under the state they find themselves in. It would understand that the kind of sovereignty it seeks is not something realisable in this world, and that stringing people along in its search is selling a dangerous political stimulant. It would instead seek to work with other states in the hope of someday abolishing their necessity altogether. Even at the level of transnational cooperation, control cannot be 'taken back' from capital, but a more cosmopolitan approach would at least get to grips with capitalism's global character in a way the nation state alone is incapable of. In line with this any alternative would welcome interaction with what is 'outside' and aim for the abolition of any gap between inside and out to begin with, rather than suspecting it on the basis of nationalist conspiracies.

It would not side with authoritarian dictators or theocratic fascists on the grounds that they are objectively 'anti-imperialist.' It would recognise the complexity and multisided agency of world events, and refuse to explain away the existence of genocidal forces by reference to one-size-fits-all foreign policy determinism. It would acknowledge the dangers inherent in reactionary forms of anticapitalism that contain the structural preconditions for antisemitism, worldviews from which 'good' leftists are by no means immune.

It would also not misrepresent how power works in contemporary society by building political coalitions of homogenous 'people' against omnipotent and parasitical 'elites', each of which do not exist, and instead of persecuting their personalisations, build political movements posed against the abstract forces that do dominate us: money, capital, commodities. It would do so in the first instance by seeing what others see as abstract rights as concretely constituted results of struggle, defending freedom of movement of labour as the freedom to move itself in a world where we live only through labour.

The challenges that face the left as the certainties of the neoliberal era slowly collapse are inescapably transnational in character. They can only be grappled with through the protection, reform and expansion of the democratic transnational institutions that do currently exist – with the EU, in the British context, being of course the most pertinent – rather than turning away from internationalism in the false belief that a resuscitated national sovereignty provides the means to 'take back control' in a world shaped by the contradictory, abstract power of capital.

This call for a reinvigorated internationalism may appear no less 'utopian' than the schemes put forward by competing post-liberal wings of the Labour Party today. But the difference is that insofar as this alternative is utopian at all it regards utopia in the sense of a realistic and pessimistic 'minimum' utopia along the lines proposed by Norman Geras.[30] In putting forward such a 'minimum' utopia, this seeks to protect liberalism as an unsatisfactory but essential system for the management of contradictions, but one which stands as the necessary precursor to any socialist politics intent on the avoidance of authoritarianism. It would therefore seek to confront and articulate contradictions deliberatively and democratically, rather than falsely abolishing them in utopian schemes of national or popular renewal.

In all this it would not offer either the false hope of optimism about history's unfolding or a blanket rejection of the current practical forms and real abstractions through which humans relate to one another. And, by doing all the above, it would overcome flawed worldviews unable to mount a sustained defence of the hard-won gains of the liberal order from the barrage of attacks of a rising reactionary right because they ultimately share many of its premises. Specifically, such an alternative would resist the headlong rush into a politics of the abyss prepared to take the economy, and thus society itself, down with it. It would give nothing to the racists and nationalists to whom Nigel Farage appeals in his assault on economic rationality that we saw in the opening chapter. In resisting calls for controls on immigration it would recognise but not respect the irrationality of political actors whipped up by populists and racists, and not genuflect to a fictional caricature of the dispossessed out of fear for the electoral consequences. It would not engage any further in the reckless politics of pure sentiment that tells an imaginary people it can have everything it wants on a plate without reservations.

Whether such an unsentimental alternative can stem the rising tide of ruin is still to be seen. Any left project contends with the historical fate that its best intentions will turn into something monstrous, but this is the way of all subjective activity, where we subsist and realise our desires in and through alien things – money, wages, the state – that spring from our activity but come to dominate us all the same. This sublation of the subject in the object is the price paid for all political action in a world shaped by capital. The only way to live and act in these circumstances is to recognise the intractability of contradiction in a society built upon it, including the contradictions that run through ourselves and our own worldviews, and thus work in and through the situation whereby we can only achieve what we want imperfectly and incompletely. The alternative is the fantasy world of populisms right and left, and the authoritarianism that must surely follow in the effort to force a divided reality into the straitjacket of a premature identity.

The historic task confronting leftists today is that of defence against the forward march of fascism and national populism. Liberalism is the sea in which socialists in capitalist democracies swim. So much of what the labour movement knows and does rests on liberal legal and political forms. At the moment the sea is leaking out the side of the basin. It is imperative that the left attempt to plug the holes, and not try and surf the resulting tidal wave for electoral success when society itself is at stake. It is perilous folly to regard the loss of the 'liberal' aspects of 'neoliberalism' as a sign of the impending downfall of the rest.

But in swimming this sea, social democrats should have no illusions. A pessimistic politics would face up to the extent to which our fortunes are tied up with those of institutions that are the products of our own activity but come to dominate, cajole and harry us. As bad as they are, we subsist through these institutions of capital and of liberal democracy all the same, and it is by accepting this contradiction and working within it, critically, that a radical social democratic politics can stand for itself in what is saved. Liberated from the illusion that the false resolution of contradictions is possible or desirable, we face the choice between better and worse means for their mediation. Increasingly, Corbynism strikes compromises with contemporary reality. The question a critical approach raises is the character of the world with which these compromises are struck, and whether other, better compromises and other, better worlds are possible.

ENDNOTES

PREFACE

1. Alex Nunns, *The Candidate: Jeremy Corbyn's Improbable Path to Power*, (London: OR Books, 2018); Richard Seymour, *Corbyn: The Strange Rebirth of Radical Politics*, (London: Verso, 2017); Mark Perryman (ed.), *The Corbyn Effect*, (London: Lawrence and Wishart, 2017); Simon Hannah, *A Party with Socialists in it*, (London: Pluto, 2018); Leo Panitch, *The Socialist Challenge Today: Syriza, Sanders, Corbyn*, (London: Merlin, 2018)

2. For a discussion of 'good conversation' based in the Hegelian idea of 'mutual recognition', see Richard Gunn, "Marxism and Philosophy: A Critique of Critical Realism," Capital and Class, 13 (1989), 1–30

3. For a brief attempt to articulate differences on this issue through the work of Werner Bonefeld, written in the months before Corbyn entered the leadership race, see Frederick Harry Pitts, "The critique of political economy as a critical social theory," *Capital and Class*, 39(3) (2015), 537–544.

4. Rowena Mason, 'Labour voters in the dark about party's stance on Brexit, research says,' *The Guardian,* 30 May 2016, https://www.theguardian.com/politics/2016/may/30/labour-voters-in-the-dark-about-partys-stance-on-brexit-research-says [Accessed 21 May 2018]; Sarah Pine, 'Corbyn: "Article 50 has to be invoked now",' *LabourList*, 24 June 2016, https://labourlist.org/2016/06/corbyn-article-50-has-to-be-invoked-now/ [Accessed 21 May 2018]

5. Matt Bolton, 'The Terrifying Hubris of Corbynism,'
    Medium, 14 July 2016, https://web.archive.org/
    web/20171021172346/https://medium.com/@matatatatat/the-
    terrifying-hubris-of-corbynism-6590054a9b57; 'Corbynism
    without Guarantees,' *Medium*, 10 August 2016, https://web.
    archive.org/web/20170119153138/https://medium.com/@
    matatatatat/corbynism-without-guarantees-310d760ea5a6;
    F H Pitts, 'Corbynism changes the political centre – but
    can it convert it?,' *Disclaimer*, 27 July 2016, http://www.
    disclaimermag.com/politics/corbynism-changes-the-political-
    centre-but-can-it-convert-it-3727; 'Popular delusions:
    Corbynism constructs its people,' *Open Democracy*, 2 August
    2016, https://www.opendemocracy.net/uk/f-h-pitts/popular-
    delusions-corbynism-constructs-its-people; [All accessed 21
    May 2018]

6. See https://twitter.com/marxists4owen

7. Owen Jones, 'Questions all Jeremy Corbyn supporters need
    to answer,' *Medium*, 31 July 2016, https://medium.com/@
    OwenJones84/questions-all-jeremy-corbyn-supporters-need-to-
    answer-b3e82ace7ed3 [Accessed 21 May 2018]

8. Paul Mason, 'Corbyn: the summer of hierarchical things,'
    Medium, 12 July 2016, https://medium.com/mosquito-ridge/
    corbyn-the-summer-of-hierarchical-things-ab1368959b80
    [Accessed 18 July 2018]

9. Matt Bolton and Frederick Harry Pitts, 'Corbynism and Blue
    Labour: Post-liberalism and national populism in the British
    Labour Party' *British Politics*, forthcoming.

INTRODUCTION: TAKING CORBYNISM SERIOUSLY

1. Owen Jones, 'Back to calling Corbyn supporters delusional
    and thick, are we,' *Medium*, 19 March 2018, https://medium.
    com/@OwenJones84/back-to-calling-corbyn-supporters-

delusional-and-thick-are-we-fdc9d5a6668a [Accessed 7 May 2018]

2. Abbas Panjwani, 'How are Theresa May and Jeremy Corbyn doing in the polls?', *Full Fact*, 2 May 2018, https://fullfact.org/news/how-are-theresa-may-and-jeremy-corbyn-doing-polls/ [Accessed 10 May 2018]

3. Joshua Chaffin, 'Communist Party of Britain embraces Comrade Corbyn,' *Financial Times*, 10 May 2018, https://www.ft.com/content/ee215d4a-4ebf-11e8-a7a9-37318e776bab [Accessed 10 May 2018]

4. Frederick Harry Pitts and Ana Cecilia Dinerstein, 'Corbynism's conveyor belt of ideas: Postcapitalism and the politics of social reproduction,' *Capital and Class*, 41:3 (2017), 423-434; Deborah Hermanns, 'Labour's reinvention needs to come from the bottom up,' *The Guardian*. 7 March 2017. : https://www.theguardian.com/commentisfree/2017/mar/07/labour-reinvention-comes-from-bottom-up [Accessed 10 May 2018]; Ewan MacAskill and Alex Hacillo 'Momentum plans relaunch to end factional infighting,' *The Observer*. 4 March 2017, https://www.theguardian.com/politics/2017/mar/04/momentum-relaunch-factionalism-jon-lansman-labour [Accessed 10 May 2018]

5. Paul Mason, *Postcapitalism: A Guide to Our Future* (London: Allen Lane, 2015), Nick Srnicek and Alex Williams, *Inventing the Future* (London: Verso, 2015), Aaron Bastani, *Fully Automated Luxury Communism* (London: Verso, 2018). For how these ideas function in Corbynism see Pitts and Dinerstein, 'Corbynism's conveyor belt of ideas'. For an account of the role Fully Automated Luxury Communism plays in Corbynism see Ben Judah, 'Momentum: inside Labour's revolutionary movement,' *Financial Times*. 27 April 2018, https://www.ft.com/content/0e99fc98-4872-11e8-8ae9-4b5ddcca99b3 [Accessed 9 May 2018]. For general overviews of post-work and accelerationist thinking in the contemporary UK left see Andy Beckett, 'Accelerationism: How a fringe

philosophy predicted the future we live in,' *The Guardian*, 11 May 2017, https://www.theguardian.com/world/2017/may/11/accelerationism-how-a-fringe-philosophy-predicted-the-future-we-live-in [Accessed 9 May 2018]; 'Post-work: the radical idea of a world without jobs,' *The Guardian*. 19 Jan 2018. https://www.theguardian.com/news/28/jan/19/post-work-the-radical-idea-of-a-world-without-jobshttps://www.theguardian.com/news/2018/jan/19/post-work-the-radical-idea-of-a-world-without-jobs [Accessed 9 May 2018]

6.   Frederick Harry Pitts, 'Beyond the Fragment: postoperaismo, postcapitalism and Marx's 'Notes on machines', 45 years on,' *Economy and Society*, 46: 3–4 (2018): 324–345

7.   Paul Mason, 'Labour must become the party of people who want to change the world, not just Britain,' *Open Democracy*, 26 April 2018, https://www.opendemocracy.net/neweconomics/labour-must-become-party-people-want-change-world/ [Accessed 9 May 2018]; cf. Daniel Randall, 'Why class still matters: a reply to Paul Mason,' *Open Democracy*, 3 May 2018, https://www.opendemocracy.net/neweconomics/class-still-matters-reply-paul-mason/ [Accessed 9 May 2018]

8.   Ashley Cowburn, 'Labour sets up 'working group' to investigate universal basic income, John McDonnell reveals,' *The Independent*, 5 February 2017, http://www.independent.co.uk/news/uk/politics/labour-sets-up-working-group-to-investigate-radical-idea-of-basic-income-john-mcdonnell-reveals-a7563566.html [Accessed 10 May 2018]; Annabelle Dickson, 'Jeremy Corbyn to address challenge posed by robots,' *Politico*, 26 September 2017, https://www.politico.eu/article/jeremy-corbyn-labour-leader-post-brexit-to-address-challenge-posed-by-robots/ [Accessed 10 May 2018]

9.   Decca Aitkenhead, Heather Stewart and Jessica Elgot, 'Labour: Corbyn camp hits back at Tom Watson 'Trotsky entryists' comments,' *The Guardian*. 9 August 2016, https://www.theguardian.com/politics/2016/aug/09/trotskyists-young-labour-members-jeremy-corbyn-tom-watson [Accessed 9 May 2018]

10. Media Diversified, 'Stand Up To Racism: Stand Up To Rape Culture,' *Media Diversified*, 6 October 2016, https://mediadiversified.org/2016/10/06/stand-up-to-rape-culture [Accessed 16 July 2018]

11. Daniel Randall, 'The Third Camp, Socialism From Below, and the First Principle of Revolutionary Socialism,' *New Politics*, Winter 2018, http://newpol.org/content/third-camp-socialism-below-and-first-principle-revolutionary-socialism [Accessed 9 May 2018]

12. See Justin Reynolds, 'Acid Corbynism, left accelerationism and Brighton sunshine – The World Transformed 2017,' *Justin Reynolds- Writer*, 3 October 2017, http://justinreynoldswriter.com/2017/10/03/acid-corbynism-left-accelerationism-brighton-sunshine-world-transformed-2017/ [Accessed 9 May 2018]

13. George Eaton, 'The Meaning of Corbynism,' *New Statesman*, 5 March 2018, https://www.newstatesman.com/politics/uk/2018/03/meaning-corbynism [Accessed 9 May 2018]

14. Jeremy Gilbert, *The Progressive Alliance: Why Labour Needs It* (London: Compass, 2017)

15. Jeremy Gilbert and Alex Williams, *Hegemony Now* (London: Verso, 2018)

16. For a summary of key works see Jeremy Gilbert, 'Acid Corbynism: The Story So Far,' *jeremygilbertwriting*, 10 November 2017, https://jeremygilbertwriting.wordpress.com/2017/11/10/acid-corbynism-the-story-so-far/ [Accessed 9 May 2018]

17. For an idea of its main influences, see Tom Blackburn, 'The Labour Party: A Socialist Reading List,' *New Socialist*, 28 August 2017, https://newsocialist.org.uk/the-labour-party-a-socialist-reading-list/ [Accessed 10 May 2018]

18. Joe Guinan and Thomas M. Hanna, 'Full Corbynism: Constructing a new left Political Economy beyond Neoliberalism,' *New Socialist*, 19 June 2017, https://newsocialist.org.uk/full-corbynism-constructing-a-new-left-

political-economy-beyond-neoliberalism/ [Accessed 10 May
2018]

19. Economist, 'Preston, Jeremy Corbyn's Model Town,' *The
Economist*, 19 October 2017, https://www.economist.com/
news/britain/21730421-how-one-city-became-unlikely-
laboratory-corbynomics-preston-jeremy-corbyns-model-town
[Accessed 28 April 2018]

20. Jessica Elgot, 'How Momentum stopped vote on single market
at Labour conference,' *The Guardian*, 25 September 2017,
https://www.theguardian.com/politics/2017/sep/25/how-
momentum-stopped-vote-single-market-labour-conference
[Accessed 10 May 2018]

21. Rowena Mason, 'Jeremy Corbyn seeks grassroots Labour
support for stance against bombing Syria,' *The Guardian*, 27
November 2015, https://www.theguardian.com/politics/2015/
nov/27/jeremy-corbyn-labour-bombing-syria-isis-airstrikes
[Accessed 10 May 2018]

22. Anushka Asthana, 'Big majority of Labour members 'want UK
to stay in single market'',' *The Guardian*, 17 July 2017, https://
www.theguardian.com/politics/2017/jul/17/most-labour-
members-want-uk-to-remain-in-single-market [Accessed 10
May 2018]

23. Maxine Molyneux and Thomas Osborne, 'Populism: A
Deflationary View,' *Economy and Society* 46.1 (2017) 1–19

24. Chantal Mouffe, 'Jeremy Corbyn's Left Populism,' *Verso*, 16
April 2018, https://www.versobooks.com/blogs/3743-jeremy-
corbyn-s-left-populism [Accessed 14 May 2018]

25. Jan-Werner Müller, *What is Populism?* (Philadelphia:
University of Pennsylvania Press, 2016) 19

26. We have learnt a lot in particular from lynchpins of the
principled left blogosphere Bob from Brockley and Tendance
Coatesy (see http://brockley.blogspot.co.uk/ and https://
tendancecoatesy.wordpress.com/)

27. Michael Chessum, 'Labour has quietly shifted right on immigration – with troubling consequences. *New Statesman*,' 16 June 2017, https://www.newstatesman.com/politics/staggers/2017/06/labour-has-quietly-shifted-right-immigration-troubling-consequences [Accessed 15th October 2017]; Michael Chessum, 'Labour has a path to power – but only if it stands up to the Tories on Brexit,' *New Statesman*. 18 April 2017, https://www.newstatesman.com/politics/uk/2017/04/labour-has-path-power-only-if-it-stands-tories-brexit [Accessed 15th October 2017]; Speak Out on Syria, 'Jeremy Corbyn: Speak Out on Syria,' 3 October 2016, https://speakoutonsyria.wordpress.com/ [Accessed 15th October 2017]

28. QQ and Mike Harman, 'The Poverty of Luxury Communism,' *Libcom*, 5 April 2018, https://libcom.org/blog/poverty-luxury-communism-05042018 [Accessed 10 May 2018]; Dyjbas/International Communist Tendency, 'Back to the Future: Rebranding Social Democracy,' *Libcom*, 12 April 2018, https://libcom.org/blog/back-future-rebranding-social-democracy-12042018 [Accessed 10 May 2018]; Ravings of a Radical Vagabond, 'An Investigation Into Red-Brown Alliances: Third Positionism, Russia, Ukraine, Syria, And The Western Left,' *Libcom*, 1 Feb 2018. : https://libcom.org/library/investigation-red-brown-alliances-third-positionism-russia-ukraine-syria-western-left [Accessed 10 May 2018]; Cautiously Pessimistic, 'Syria seen from the Viewpoint of imperial purity: the crushing narcissism of empire', *Libcom*, 20 Feb 2018. : https://libcom.org/library/syria-seen-viewpoint-imperial-purity-crushing-narcissism-empire [Accessed 10 May 2018]; Daphne Lawless, 'The Red-Brown "zombie plague": how fascist ideas are becoming popular on the Left,' *Fightback*, 9 May 2018, https://fightback.org.nz/2018/05/09/the-red-brown-zombie-plague-part-one [Accessed 16 May 2018]; see also Critisticuffs, 'We Don't Share Anything,' *Occupied Times*. 3 April 2016.: https://theoccupiedtimes.org/?p=14219 [Accessed 10 May 2018]

29. Theodor W Adorno, Adorno, *Prisms* (Cambridge, MA: MIT Press, 1983) 32

30. Jonathan Rutherford, 'Labour must choose between two fundamentally different understandings of the human condition,' *New Statesman*. 26 September 2017, https://www.newstatesman.com/politics/staggers/2017/09/labour-must-choose-between-two-fundamentally-different-understandings [Accessed 15th October 2017]

31. From a similar but crucially divergent perspective as that put forward by Rutherford, see Jon Cruddas, 'The humanist left must challenge the rise of cyborg socialism,' *New Statesman*. 23 April 2018: https://www.newstatesman.com/politics/uk/2018/04/humanist-left-must-challenge-rise-cyborg-socialism [Accessed 10 May 2018]

32. For post-liberalism see Adrian Pabst, 'Brexit, Post-Liberalism and the Politics of Paradox,' *Telos,* 176, Fall 2016, 189-201; and Jonathan Rutherford, 'Goodbye to the liberal era,' *New Statesman,* 6 Feb 2017, https://www.newstatesman.com/politics/2017/02/goodbye-liberal-era [Accessed 10 May 2018]

33. See Maurice Glasman, Jonathan Rutherford, Marc Stears, M, and Stuart White (eds.) *The Labour Tradition and the Politics of Paradox.* (London: Lawrence and Wishart, 2011)

34. Jonathan Rutherford, 'Labour has lost its identity,' *New Statesman*. 31 October 2016, https://www.newstatesman.com/politics/2016/10/labour-has-lost-its-identity [Accessed 15th October 2017]

35. For a likeminded comparison of the two, with a specific focus on how Corbynism effectively liquidates Blue Labour by subsuming some of its thinking, see J. A. Smith, 'Blue Labour in the Age of Corbyn,' *LSE Review of Books*, 26 September 2016, http://blogs.lse.ac.uk/lsereviewofbooks/2016/09/26/the-long-read-blue-labour-in-the-age-of-corbyn-by-j-a-smith/ [Accessed 10 May 2018]

36. Jonathan Rutherford, 'Why the left should support Brexit,' *New Statesman*, 26 November 2017, https://www.newstatesman.com/politics/brexit/2017/11/why-left-should-support-brexit [Accessed 10 May 2018]

37. Full Brexit, "Founding Statement," https://www.thefullbrexit.com/ [Accessed 28 July 2018]

38. Adrian Pabst, 'Brexit, Post-Liberalism and the Politics of Paradox'

39. For a statement of this ethical humanism that critiques accelerationism in terms similar, although divergent in crucial respects, to our own, see Cruddas, 'The humanist left must challenge the rise of cyborg socialism'

40. Danny Postel, discussion comment in '30 years of the Islamic Revolution in Iran,' *Platypus Review*, 20 (February 2010), https://platypus1917.org/2010/02/18/30-years-of-the-islamic-revolution-in-iran [Accessed 9 May 2018]

41. Michael Walzer, 'The Historical Task of the Left in the Present Period,' *Dissent*, 2 January 2017, https://www.dissentmagazine.org/online_articles/historical-task-of-left-present-period-trump [Accessed 15 October 2017]

42. Werner Bonefeld, *Critical Theory and the Critique of Political Economy*, (London: Bloomsbury, 2014), Chap. 9; Moishe Postone, 'Antisemitism and National Socialism,' in *Germans and Jews Since the Holocaust*, eds. Anson Rabinbach and Jack Zipes (New York, London: Holmes and Meier, 1986); Moishe Postone, 'History and Helplessness: Mass Mobilization and Contemporary Forms of Anticapitalism,' *Public Culture*, 18(1), (January 2006): 93–110; Michael Heinrich, *An Introduction to the three volumes of Karl Marx's Capital*, New York: Monthly Review Press, 2012), Chap. 10; Moishe Postone, 'Zionism, anti-semitism and the left,' *Solidarity* 3/166, 4 February 2010, http://www.krisis.org/2010/zionism-anti-semitism-and-the-left [Accessed 9 May 2018]

43. Richard Gunn, 'Against Historical Materialism: Marxism as First-Order Discourse,' *Open Marxism Volume II: Theory and Practice*, eds. Werner Bonefeld, Richard Gunn, and Kosmas Psychopedis. (London: Pluto Press, 1992), 1–45.

CHAPTER 1: EXPLAINING 2017: THE RISE AND FALL OF AUSTERITY POPULISM

1. Channel 4 News, 'Jon Snow's *Game of Thrones* take on the general election,' Facebook, 9 June 2017, https://www.facebook.com/Channel4News/videos/10154921679231939/

2. Michael Savage and Alex Hacillo, 'How Jeremy Corbyn turned a youth surge into general election votes', *The Observer*, 10 June 2017, https://www.theguardian.com/politics/2017/jun/10/jeremy-corbyn-youth-surge-votes-digital-activists [Accessed 10 May 2018]

3. Theresa May, 'Theresa May's Conference speech in full,' *Daily Telegraph*, 5 October 2016, https://www.telegraph.co.uk/news/2016/10/05/theresa-mays-conference-speech-in-full [Accessed 9 May 2018]

4. Jason Groves, 'Crush the Saboteurs,' *Daily Mail*, 19 April 2017, https://www.pressreader.com/uk/daily-mail/20170419/281479276290041 [Accessed 9 May 2018]; Tom Newton Dunn, 'Blue Murder,' *The Sun*, 19 April 2017, https://www.thesun.co.uk/news/3360452/theresa-may-vows-to-crush-tory-brexit-rebels-and-labour-party-with-snap-general-election [Accessed 9 May 2018]

5. Jessica Elgot, 'Success for Labour Party would be 200 seats, says Len McCluskey,' *The Guardian*, 16 May 2017, https://www.theguardian.com/politics/2017/may/16/success-for-labour-in-election-would-be-200-seats-says-mccluskey [Accessed 9 May 2018]

6. See, for example, Sally Campbell, 'European Bosses Club,' *Socialist Review*, December 2014, http://socialistreview. org.uk/397/european-bosses-club [Accessed 9 May 2018]. For a critique of the 'bosses' club' rhetoric, see Aufheben, 'Brexit means… what? Hapless ideology and practical consequences,' 5 November 2016, https://libcom.org/library/ brexit-means%E2%80%A6-what-hapless-ideology-practical-consequences [Accessed 9 May 2018]

7. Stephen Bush, 'The Sleaford and North Hykeham by-election shows Labour has more than Ukip to fear,' *New Statesman*, 9 December 2016, https://www.newstatesman.com/politics/ staggers/2016/12/sleaford-and-north-hykeham-election-shows-labour-has-more-ukip-fear [Accessed 9 May 2018]

8. Agnes Chambre, 'Jeremy Corbyn: In the last election Labour was offering austerity-lite,' *Politics Home*, 12 July 2015, https://www.politicshome.com/news/uk/social-affairs/politics/ media-interview/50619/jeremy-corbyn-last-election-labour-was [Accessed 9 May 2018]. For an opposing view, drawn from the Blue Labour wing of the party, see Jon Cruddas, Nick Pecorelli and Jonathan Rutherford, *Labour's Future: Why Labour lost in 2015 and how it can win again,* (London: One Nation Register, 2016) https://www.scribd.com/doc/313245238/ Labour-s-Future-19-05-16 [Accessed 9 May 2018]

9. Kate Forrester, 'The Corbyn Effect: Huge Vote Share Boost Where Labour Leader Held General Election Rallies,' *Huffington Post*, 9 June 2017, https://www.huffingtonpost. co.uk/entry/the-corbyn-effect-huge-vote-share-boost-where-labour-leader-held-general-election-rallies_ uk_593ab69ee4b0b13f2c69bcb1 [Accessed 10 May 2018]

10. Dan Hancox, "There is no unwinnable seat now'– how Labour revolutionised its doorstep game,' *The Guardian*. 13 June 2017, https://www.theguardian.com/politics/2017/jun/13/ there-is-no-unwinnable-seat-now-how-labour-revolutionised-its-doorstep-game [Accessed 10 May 2018]

11. Chris Giles and Jim Pickard, 'Fiscal deficit: The big silence at the heart of election campaigning,' *Financial Times*, 5 June 2017, https://www.ft.com/content/0f6f6430-4a00-11e7-a3f4-c742b9791d43 [Accessed 9 May 2018]; Speakers Corner, 'What happened to the deficit?' *The Economist*, 12 May 2017, https://www.economist.com/blogs/speakerscorner/2017/05/deficit-deniers [Accessed 9 May 2018]

12. Bagehot, 'The culture wars arrive in Britain,' *The Economist*. 9 June 2017, https://www.economist.com/news/britain/21723197-election-reveals-astonishing-changes-political-landscape-culture-wars-arrive; David Evans, 'Who are the diehard Conservative voters behind Theresa May?,' *New Statesman*, 1 June 2017, http://www.newstatesman.com/politics/june2017/2017/06/who-are-diehard-conservative-voters-behind-theresa-may [Accessed 9 May 2018]

13. Jonathan Hopkin, "The Brexit vote and General Election were both about austerity and inequality," *LSE Brexit Blog*, 28 June 2017, http://blogs.lse.ac.uk/brexit/2017/06/28/the-brexit-vote-and-general-election-were-both-about-austerity-and-inequality/ [Accessed 10 May 2018]

14. See Owen Hatherley, "Lash out and cover up': Austerity nostalgia and ironic authoritarianism in recession Britain,' *Radical Philosophy* 157 (Sep/Oct 2009), https://www.radicalphilosophy.com/commentary/lash-out-and-cover-up [Accessed 28 Apr 2018]; Tom Whyman, 'Beware of cupcake fascism', *The Guardian*, 8 April 2014, https://www.theguardian.com/commentisfree/2014/apr/08/beware-of-cupcake-fascism [Accessed 10 May 2018]

15. Hatherley, "Lash out and cover up"

16. For 'national community of hard-working people' see Bonefeld, *Critical Theory*, 197

17. David Cameron, "The real choice in British politics," Speech given 12 Feb 2010, https://conservative-speeches.sayit.mysociety.org/speech/601534 [Accessed 7 May 2018]

18. George Osborne, "George Osborne's speech to the Conservative conference: full text," *New Statesman*, 8 Sep 2012, https://www.newstatesman.com/blogs/politics/2012/10/george-osbornes-speech-conservative-conference-full-text [Accessed 28 Apr 2018]

19. Will Heaven, 'George Osborne: the politically homeless ex-chancellor,' *The Spectator*, 12 Oct 2017, https://blogs.spectator.co.uk/2017/10/george-osborne-the-politically-homeless-ex-chancellor/ [Accessed 28 Apr 2018]

20. Kate McCann and Tom Morgan, 'Nigel Farage: £350 million pledge to fund the NHS was 'a mistake',' *Daily Telegraph*, 24 June 2016, https://www.telegraph.co.uk/news/2016/06/24/nigel-farage-350-million-pledge-to-fund-the-nhs-was-a-mistake/ [Accessed 28 Apr 2018]

21. John Aziz, 'Did Osborne Pause Austerity in 2013?,' *Coppola Comment*, 19 May 2015. Available from: http://www.coppolacomment.com/2015/05/did-osborne-pause-austerity-in-2013.html [Accessed 28 Apr 2018]; Simon Wren-Lewis, 'Osborne's Plan B,' *Mainly Macro,* 17 December 2013. Available from: https://mainlymacro.blogspot.co.uk/2013/12/osbornes-plan-b.html [Accessed 28 Apr 2018]

22. Another Angry Voice, 'How Ed Balls' austerity-lite agenda ruined Labour's election chances,' *Another Angry Voice,* 8 May 2015, http://anotherangryvoice.blogspot.co.uk/2015/05/ed-balls-austerity-lite-labour.html [Accessed 9 May 2018]

23. Patrick Hennessey, 'David Cameron: We'll get the deficit down – but it won't be easy,' *Daily Telegraph*, 5 February 2011, https://www.telegraph.co.uk/news/politics/david-cameron/8305818/David-Cameron-Well-get-the-deficit-down-but-it-wont-be-easy.html [Accessed 10 May 2018]; David Cameron, 'David Cameron: We've saved the economy from ruin – don't let Ed Miliband spoil it,' *Daily Telegraph*, 25 April 2015, https://www.telegraph.co.uk/news/politics/david-cameron/11561628/David-Cameron-Weve-saved-the-economy-from-ruin-dont-let-Ed-Miliband-spoil-it.html [Accessed 10 May 2018]

24. Ezra Klein, 'Who are the 99%?' *The Washington Post*, 4 October 2011, https://www.washingtonpost.com/blogs/ezra-klein/post/who-are-the-99-percent/2011/08/25/gIQAt87jKL_blog.html?utm_term=.67d5c69e7092 [Accessed 9 May 2018]

25. See, for example, Michael Hudson, *Killing the Host: How Financial Parasites and Debt Destroy the Global Economy*, (Islet, 2015)

26. John McDonnell, "Austerity is a political choice," Speech given 11 March 2016, https://labourlist.org/2016/03/austerity-is-a-political-choice-full-text-of-john-mcdonnells-speech/ [Accessed 7 May 2018]

27. Cf Werner Bonefeld, *The Strong State and the Free Economy* (London, New York: Roman and Littlefield International, 2017)

28. Werner Bonefeld, "Authoritarian Liberalism, Class and Rackets," *Logos: a journal of modern society and culture*, (2017), http://logosjournal.com/2017/authoritarian-liberalism-class-and-rackets/ [Accessed 10 May 2018]

29. For a summary see Will Davies, 'The difficulty of 'neoliberalism", *Political Economy Research Centre Blog*, 1 January 2016, http://www.perc.org.uk/project_posts/the-difficulty-of-neoliberalism/ [Accessed 10 May 2018]

30. Owen Jones, 'Labour's shift has been vindicated. The public is tired of austerity,' *The Guardian*, 28 June 2017, https://www.theguardian.com/commentisfree/2017/jun/28/labour-vindicated-public-tired-austerity-jeremy-corbyn [Accessed 10 May 2018]

31. Labour Party, *For the Many Not the Few: The Labour Party Manifesto 2017*, p10. https://labour.org.uk/wp-content/uploads/2017/10/labour-manifesto-2017.pdf [Accessed 9 May 2018]

32. Kamal Ahmed, 'Labour announces 'fiscal credibility rule,' *BBC News,* 11 March 2016, http://www.bbc.co.uk/news/business-35780703 [Accessed 9 May 2018]

33. Michael Segalov, 'These Rebel MPs Are Planning a War with Labour Austerity,' *Vice*, 20 April 2015, https://www.vice.com/

en_uk/article/dp9w3w/jeremy-corbyn-john-mcdonnell-interview-election-2015-labour-party-674 [Accessed 9 May 2018]

34. Gordon Rayner and Steven Swinford, 'Labour manifesto would 'bankrupt Britain' with £250bn debt and biggest tax burden since 1950s,' *Daily Telegraph*, 16 May 2017, https://www.telegraph.co.uk/news/2017/05/16/labour-manifesto-would-bankrupt-britain-250bn-debt-biggest-tax [Accessed 9 May 2018]

35. Tom Newton Dunn, 'Leaf it Out,' *The Sun*, 2 June 2017, https://www.thesun.co.uk/news/3704055/jeremy-corbyns-far-fetched-election-promises-would-blow-a-300bn-hole-in-britains-finances [Accessed 9 May 2018]

36. Daniel Boffey and Toby Helm, 'Vote Leave embroiled in race row over Turkey security threat claims,' *The Observer*, 22 May 2016, https://www.theguardian.com/politics/2016/may/21/vote-leave-prejudice-turkey-eu-security-threat [Accessed 9 May 2018]

37. Heather Stewart and Rowena Mason, 'Nigel Farage's anti-migrant poster reported to police,' *The Guardian*, 16 June 2016, https://www.theguardian.com/politics/2016/jun/16/nigel-farage-defends-ukip-breaking-point-poster-queue-of-migrants [Accessed 9 May 2018]

38. Sarah Pine, 'Corbyn: 'Article 50 has to be invoked now',' *Labour List,* 24 June 2016, https://labourlist.org/2016/06/corbyn-article-50-has-to-be-invoked-now/ [Accessed 10 May 2018]

39. John Harris, 'They voted Brexit in a cry of pain. What happened to the left-behind?,' *The Guardian,* 5 November 2017, https://www.theguardian.com/commentisfree/2017/nov/05/brexit-theresa-may-economic-austerity-leave-voting [Accessed 10 May 2018]

40. Andrew Flood, 'Making sense of the Brexit tide of reaction and the reality of the racist vote,' *Libcom*, 27 Jun 2016, https://libcom.org/news/making-sense-brexit-tide-reaction-reality-racist-vote-andrew-flood-27062016 [Accessed 10 May 2018]

41. Kevin Rawlinson, 'Farage blames immigration for traffic on M4 after no-show at Ukip reception,' *The Guardian*, 7

December 2014, https://www.theguardian.com/politics/2014/
dec/07/nigel-farage-blames-immigration-m4-traffic-ukip-
reception [Accessed 10 May 2018]

42. Georgia Graham, 'Nigel Farage: 'Massive oversupply' of
    foreign labour is forcing British wages down,' *Daily Telegraph*,
    5 January 2014, https://www.telegraph.co.uk/news/politics/
    ukip/10551704/Nigel-Farage-Massive-oversupply-of-foreign-
    labour-is-forcing-British-wages-down.html [Accessed 10
    May 2018]. For a debunking of this argument see Jonathan
    Portes, 'How small is small? The impact of immigration
    on UK wages,' National Institute of Economic and Social
    Research, 17 January 2016, https://www.niesr.ac.uk/blog/how-
    small-small-impact-immigration-uk-wages#.V1wpqPkrJpk
    [Accessed 10 May 2018]. See also Martin Ruhs and Carlos
    Vargas Silva, 'The Labour Market Effects of Immigration,'
    The Migration Observatory, 24 February 2018, http://www.
    migrationobservatory.ox.ac.uk/resources/briefings/the-labour-
    market-effects-of-immigration/ [Accessed 10 May 2018]

43. Richard Bagley, "Into the archives: Tony Benn on the true
    power of democracy," *The Morning Star,* 30 April 2014,
    https://morningstaronline.co.uk/a-7a6a-into-the-archives-tony-
    benn-on-the-true-power-of-democracy [Accessed 28 Apr 2018]

44. Ken Loach, *The Spirit of '45* (Sixteen Films, Fly Film
    Company, 2013); cf Owen Hatherley, *The Ministry of
    Nostalgia* (London: Verso, 2015).

45. Ben Quinn, 'TTIP deal poses 'real and serious risk' to NHS,
    says leading QC,' *The Guardian,* 22 February 2016 [Accessed
    10 May 2018]. Cf Vincenzo Scarpetta, 'There's no basis for
    claims that the NHS is under threat from TTIP,' *Open Europe*,
    20 May 2016, https://openeurope.org.uk/today/blog/theres-no-
    basis-claims-nhs-threat-ttip/ [Accessed 10 May 2018]

46. Christopher Hope, 'Health tourists cost UK taxpayers nearly
    £6billion in eight years,' *Daily Telegraph*, 5 April 2016, https://
    www.telegraph.co.uk/news/2016/04/04/health-tourists-cost-uk-
    taxpayers-nearly-6billion-in-eight-years [Accessed 10 May 2018];
    Vote Leave, 'UK gives £5.8 billion more to EU countries for

medical costs than it gets back,' *Vote Leave Take Control*, 5 April 2016, http://www.voteleavetakecontrol.org/uk_gives_5_8_billion_ more_to_eu_countries_for_medical_costs_than_it_gets_back. html [Accessed 10 May 2018]; cf Georgia Graham, 'Does health tourism cost the NHS billions?' *Channel 4 Fact Check*, 15 June 2016, https://www.channel4.com/news/factcheck/factcheck-health-tourism-cost-nhs-billions [Accessed 10 May 2018]

47. Jon Cruddas was one of the first to recognise the significance of Farage's statement. He makes a somewhat different argument about its relevance to Corbynism in an op-ed for the Financial Times, in which he counterposes Corbyn's alleged economism to Farage's apparent attack on it. See Jon Cruddas, "The mortal threat to Labour," Financial Times. 24th July 2016, https://www.ft.com/content/cbbd860c-4a98-11e6-8d68-72e9211e86ab?siteedition=uk [Accessed 10 May 2018]. See also John Harris, 'It's not about the money: what Ed Miliband and David Cameron can learn from Nigel Farage,' *The Guardian,* 10 January 2014, https://www.theguardian. com/commentisfree/2014/jan/10/farage-political-nose-gdp-immigration [Accessed 10 May 2018]

48. Matthew Holehouse, 'I'd rather be poorer with fewer migrants, Farage says,' *Daily Telegraph*, 7 January 2014, https:// www.telegraph.co.uk/news/uknews/immigration/10555158/ Id-rather-be-poorer-with-fewer-migrants-Farage-says.html [Accessed 10 May 2018]

49. Nick Timothy, 'What does the Conservative Party offer a working class kid from Brixton, Birmingham, Bolton or Bradford?' *Conservative Home*, 22 March 2016, https://www. conservativehome.com/thecolumnists/2016/03/nick-timothy-what-does-the-conservative-party-offer-a-working-class-kid-from-brixton-birmingham-bolton-or-bradford.html [Accessed 10 May 2018]

50. George Parker, Robert Wright and Henry Mance, "May's manifesto chief held talks with former Miliband aide," *Financial Times.* 9 May 2017, https://www.ft.com/ content/f810ffc6-34ae-11e7-99bd-13beb0903fa3 [Accessed 17th October 2017]

51. Theresa May, 'Statement from the new Prime Minister Theresa May,' 13 July 2016, https://www.gov.uk/government/speeches/statement-from-the-new-prime-minister-theresa-may [Accessed 10 May 2018]

52. For Mayism see William Davies, "Home Office Rules," *London Review of Books*, 3 November 2016, https://www.lrb.co.uk/v38/n21/william-davies/home-office-rules [Accessed 10 May 2018]; Jason Cowley, "The May Doctrine," *New Statesman*, 8 February 2017, https://www.newstatesman.com/2017/02/-theresa-may-method-interview-jason-cowley [Accessed 10 May 2018]

CHAPTER 2: THE PRECONDITIONS OF CORBYNISM: ON TWO-CAMPISM

1. The Labour Party, 'The Labour Party Manifesto 2015,' p. 65

2. Christopher Hope, 'Ed Miliband's 'shameful' immigration mug attacked by Diane Abbott,' *The Daily Telegraph*, 29 March 2015, https://www.telegraph.co.uk/new s/general-election-2015/11502577/Ed-Milibands-sham eful-immigration-mug-attacked-by-Diane-Abbott.html [Accessed 28 April 2018]

3. Mikey Smith, 'Jeremy Corbyn says we should 'celebrate' record immigration and slams Labour manifesto pledge as 'appalling',' *The Daily Mirror*, 27 August 2015, https://www.mirror.co.uk/news/uk-news/jeremy-corbyn-says-should-celebrate-6331301 [Accessed 28 April 2018]

4. Martin Kettle, 'For Labour the choice is stark: purity, or power,' *The Guardian*, 25 June 2015, https://www.theguardian.com/commentisfree/2015/jun/25/labour-leadership-purity-power-benn-corbyn-lib-dems-farron [Accessed 10 May 2018]

5. Rowena Mason and Josh Halliday, 'Gordon Brown urges Labour not to be party of protest by choosing Jeremy Corbyn,'

The Guardian, 17 August 2015, https://www.theguardian.com/politics/2015/aug/16/gordon-brown-warning-against-jeremy-corbyn-labour-leadership [Accessed 10 May 2018]

6. Mikey Smith and Nicola Bartlett, 'No, Jeremy Corbyn wasn't dancing a jig on his way to the Cenotaph,' *Daily Mirror*, 13 November 2016, https://www.mirror.co.uk/news/uk-news/no-jeremy-corbyn-wasnt-dancing-9252300 [Accessed 10 May 2018]; Dan Lomas, 'Was Jeremy Corbyn a Czech spy? The reality is far more mundane,' *Prospect*, 19 February 2018, https://www.prospectmagazine.co.uk/politics/was-jeremy-corbyn-a-czech-spy-the-reality-is-far-more-mundane [Accessed 10 May 2018]

7. Laura Kuenssberg, 'Corbyn office 'sabotaged' EU Remain campaign – sources,' *BBC News*, 26 June 2016, http://www.bbc.co.uk/news/uk-politics-36633238 [Accessed 10 May 2018]

8. Owen Bennett, 'Chuka Umunna: We Should Be Prepared To Sacrifice Single Market Membership To Axe Freedom Of Movement,' *Huffington Post,* 22 September 2016, https://www.huffingtonpost.co.uk/entry/chuka-umunna-single-market-free-movement-brexit_uk_57e3e201e4b0db20a6e8b057 [Accessed 10 May 2018]; Rachel Reeves, 'Ending free movement should be a red line for Labour post-Brexit,' *New Statesman*, 19 September 2016, https://www.newstatesman.com/politics/economy/2016/09/rachel-reeves-mp-ending-free-movement-should-be-red-line-labour-post-brexit [Accessed 10 May 2018]

9. Caroline Mortimer, 'Labour MP Rachel Reeves: Riots could sweep streets of Britain if immigration is not curbed after Brexit,' *Independent*, 28 September 2016, https://www.independent.co.uk/news/uk/politics/rachel-reeves-brexit-immigration-labour-mp-riots-uk-conference-speech-a7334266.html [Accessed 10 May 2018]

10. The Labour Party, *For the Many Not the Few: The Labour Party Manifesto 2017*, p. 28

11. Tom Whitehead, 'Immigration has fuelled legitimate concerns among voters,' *Daily Telegraph*, 28 April 2010, https://www.telegraph.co.uk/news/uknews/law-and-order/7646987/Immigration-has-fuelled-legitimate-concerns-among-voters.html [Accessed 10 May 2018]

12. Ed Fieldhouse and Chris Prosser, 'The Brexit election? The 2017 General Election in ten charts,' *British Election Study*, 1 August 2017, http://www.britishelectionstudy.com/bes-impact/the-brexit-election-the-2017-general-election-in-ten-charts/#.Wsxck5ch02x [Accessed 28 April 2018]; Matt Zarb-Cousin, 'How Jeremy Corbyn managed to bring Ukip voters back to Labour,' *The Guardian*, 13 June 2017, https://www.theguardian.com/commentisfree/2017/jun/13/jeremy-corbyn-brought-ukip-voters-back-labour [Accessed 16 May 2018]

13. Chris Prosser, Ed Fieldhouse, Jane Green, Jonathan Mellon, and Geoff Evans, 'The myth of the 2017 youthquake election,' *British Election Study*, 29 January 2018, http://www.britishelectionstudy.com/bes-impact/the-myth-of-the-2017-youthquake-election [Accessed 16 May 2018]; Benjamin Kentish, 'Labour's late general election surge driven by middle-aged centrists, not young Corbynites, study finds,' *Independent*, 18 April 2018, https://www.independent.co.uk/news/uk/politics/labour-general-election-surge-older-centrists-young-jeremy-corbyn-policy-network-a8311201.html [Accessed 16 May 2018]

14. Helen Lewis, 'Jeremy Corbyn: 'wholesale' EU immigration has destroyed conditions for British workers,' *New Statesman*, 23 July 2017, https://www.newstatesman.com/politics/staggers/2017/07/jeremy-corbyn-wholesale-eu-immigration-has-destroyed-conditions-british [Accessed 10 May 2018]

15. John McDonnell speaking on *Andrew Marr Show*, BBC One, 21 January 2018, http://news.bbc.co.uk/1/shared/bsp/hi/pdfs/21011802.pdf [Accessed 28 April 2018]

16. To illustrate the latent possibility for a different politics around this issue, during the writing of the book John McDonnell issued an interesting piece with the General Secretary of the Universities and Colleges Union, Sally Hunt, taking a firm stance against the divisive effects of some anti-migrant policies, even whilst his party continued to maintain the same *de facto* platform of an end to free movement. See John McDonnell and Sally Hunt, 'Home Office rules mean immigrants can't go on strike without risking deportation. Post-Brexit, this will include EU workers,' *Independent*, 11 May 2018, https://www.independent.co.uk/voices/home-office-hostile-environment-strike-trade-unions-brexit-a8346461.html. [Accessed 11 May 2018]. For evidence that immigration does not depress wages in the manner suggested, see Portes, 'How small is small?' and Ruhs and Silva, 'The Labour Market Effects of Immigration,'

17. David Pavett, 'A Spectacular Own Goal,' *Labour Futures*, 13 September 2017, http://www.leftfutures.org/2017/09/a-spectacular-own-goal/ [Accessed 16 October 2017]; Paul Mason, 'We can escape Brexit doom with one small tweak to free movement,' *The Guardian*, 16 January 2017, https://www.theguardian.com/commentisfree/2017/jan/16/we-can-escape-brexit-doom-with-one-small-tweak-to-free-movement [Accessed 10 May 2018]

18. Cf Guy Aitchison, 'Are Human Rights Moralistic?' *Human Rights Review* 19.1 (2018) 23-43; Robert Fine, 'Cosmopolitanism and Human Rights,' *Law, Social Justice and Global Development*, 2007 (1), https://warwick.ac.uk/fac/soc/law/elj/lgd/2007_1/fine/ [Accessed 10 May 2018]; Nina Power, 'Defending Rights against the Right,' *Red Pepper*, 22 February 2015, https://www.redpepper.org.uk/defending-rights-against-the-right [Accessed 10 May 2018]; Etienne Balibar, 'On the Politics of Human Rights,' *Constellations* 20.1 (March 2013) 18-26; Paul O'Connell, 'On the Human Rights Question,' forthcoming in Human Rights Quarterly (2018), https://ssrn.com/abstract=3065757 [Accessed 10 May 2018]

19. Tony Benn, *Arguments for Socialism* (London: Jonathan
    Cape, 1979) p. 164–169; Tony Benn, *Against the Tide: Diaries
    1973–1976* (London: Hutchinson, 1989)
    p. 342–349

20. Adam Bienkov, 'John McDonnell backs Brexit as 'enormous
    opportunity for Britain',' *Politics.co.uk*, 15 November 2016,
    http://www.politics.co.uk/news/2016/11/15/john-mcdonnell-
    backs-brexit-enormous-opportunity-britain [Accessed 28 Apr
    2018]

21. Michael Chessum, 'Jeremy Corbyn supporters should stop
    excusing Labour's anti-immigration drift,' *New Statesman*,
    16 March 2018, https://www.newstatesman.com/politics/
    brexit/2018/03/jeremy-corbyn-supporters-should-stop-
    excusing-labour-s-anti-immigration [Accessed 28
    Apr 2018]

22. Joe Guinan and Thomas M Hanna, 'Forbidden Fruit: The
    Neglected Political Economy of Lexit,' IPPR Progressive
    Review 24.1 (2017) 14-24; Thomas Fazi and William Mitchell,
    'Why the Left Should Embrace Brexit,' *Jacobin*, 29 April
    2018, https://www.jacobinmag.com/2018/04/brexit-labour-
    party-socialist-left-corbyn [Accessed 10 May 2018]; Fraser
    Watt, '5 Reasons the Left Should Support Leaving the Single
    Market,' *Novara Media*, 9 March 2018, http://novaramedia.
    com/2018/03/09/5-reasons-the-left-should-support-leaving-
    the-single-market [Accessed 10 May 2018]. Cf Andy Tarrant
    and Andrea Biondi, 'EU law is no barrier to Labour's economic
    programme,' Renewal, 22 September 2017, http://renewal.org.
    uk/blog/eu-law-is-no-barrier-to-labours-economic-programme
    [Accessed 10 May 2018]; Ian Dunt, 'Everything you need
    to know about Lexit in five minutes,' Politics.co.uk, 17
    November 2017, http://www.politics.co.uk/blogs/2017/11/17/
    everything-you-need-to-know-about-lexit-in-five-minutes
    [Accessed 10 May 2018]

23. Annabelle Dickson, 'Jeremy Corbyn calls for 'jobs-first Brexit,'
    Politico, 9 May 2017, https://www.politico.eu/article/jeremy-

corbyn-calls-for-jobs-first-brexit [Accessed 10 May 2018];
Toby Helm, 'Gordon Brown pledges jobs for British workers,'
Daily Telegraph, 11 September 2007, https://www.telegraph.
co.uk/news/uknews/1562791/Gordon-Brown-pledges-jobs-for-
British-workers.html [Accessed 10 May 2018]'

24. For an account of the shifting positions of leading Corbyn
commentator Owen Jones on Brexit, see 'Dear Owen...', *Muse
Aloud Blog*, 23 July 2017, https://musealoudblog.wordpress.
com/2017/07/23/dear-owen/ and 'Dear Owen...A Response,'
Muse Aloud Blog, 24 July 2017, https://musealoudblog.
wordpress.com/2017/07/24/dear-owen-a-response [Accessed
10 May 2018]. See also Matt Zarb-Cousin, 'Corbyn
betraying young people on Brexit? What colossal nonsense,'
The Guardian, 1 August 2017, https://www.theguardian.
com/commentisfree/2017/aug/01/corbyn-betraying-young-
people-brexit-colossal-nonsense-middle-aged-remainers
[Accessed 10 May 2018]; Rhiannon Lucy Cosslett, 'Brexit
will be catastrophic. Yet I still support Jeremy Corbyn,' *The
Guardian*, 7 August 2017, https://www.theguardian.com/
commentisfree/2017/aug/07/brexit-catastrophic-support-
jeremy-corbyn-remainer [Accessed 10 May 2018]

25. Tony Blair, 'The way to fight the Tories in June's election is to
turn Brexit against them', *The Guardian*, 24 April 2017, https://
www.theguardian.com/commentisfree/2017/apr/24/tony-blair-
fight-tories-june-election-brexit-labour-eu; Roy Greenslade,
'Alastair Campbell calls for a second EU referendum', *The
Guardian*, 15 Jul 2016, https://www.theguardian.com/media/
greenslade/2016/jul/15/the-new-european-lands-alastair-
campbell-brexit-scoop; Heather Stewart, 'George Osborne:
Brexit plans do not prioritise the economy,' *The Guardian*, 1
Feb 2017, https://www.theguardian.com/politics/2017/feb/01/
george-osborne-uk-brexit-plans-do-not-prioritise-the-economy
[All accessed 28 Apr 2018]

26. Peter Walker, 'Labour's Long-Bailey: 'we want to have our cake
and eat it' on Brexit,' *The Guardian*, 16 Jul 2017, https://www.

theguardian.com/politics/2017/jul/16/labour-rebecca-long-bailey-brexit-cake-and-eat-it [Accessed 28 Apr 2018]

27. Ed Fieldhouse and Chris Prosser, 'The Brexit election?'

28. Roy Greenslade, 'Tony Benn endured press vilification throughout his political career,' *The Guardian*, 14 March 2014, https://www.theguardian.com/media/greenslade/2014/mar/14/tony-benn-national-newspapers [Accessed 10 May 2018]; Chris Mullin, 'Tony Benn: The radical who never lost his passion,' *Daily Telegraph*, 14 March 2014, https://www.telegraph.co.uk/news/politics/labour/10698209/Tony-Benn-the-radical-who-never-lost-his-passion.html [Accessed 10 May 2018]

29. Tony Benn, *Against the Tide. Diaries 1973–76*, (London: Hutchinson, 1989), 621

30. Lizzie Dearden, 'Labour pressure group claims Jeremy Corbyn would 'destroy chances of electability' as leader,' *Independent*, 11 July 2015, https://www.independent.co.uk/news/uk/politics/labour-pressure-group-claims-jeremy-corbyn-would-destroy-chances-of-electability-as-leader-10382371.html [Accessed 10 May 2018]; Andrew Sparrow and Helen Pidd, 'Yvette Cooper says Labour rival Jeremy Corbyn's policies not credible or radical,' *The Guardian*, 13 August 2015, https://www.theguardian.com/politics/2015/aug/13/yvette-cooper-jeremy-corbyn-policies-not-credible-labour [Accessed 10 May 2018]; Owen Smith, 'For me, it's Labour or nothing: credible, united and electable,' *The Guardian*, 4 September 2016, https://www.theguardian.com/commentisfree/2016/sep/03/labour-or-nothing-owen-smith [Accessed 10 May 2018]

31. For some of this history see Paul Thompson, 'Hard left, soft left: Corbynism and beyond,' *Renewal: A Journal of Social Democracy*, 24(2) (2016), 45–40

32. Andrew Hosken, *Ken: The Ups and Downs of Ken Livingstone* (Arcadia Book, 2008), Ch. 18

33. John Nichols, 'Tony Benn and the Five Essential Questions of Democracy,' *The Nation*, 14 March 2014, https://www.

thenation.com/article/tony-benn-and-five-essential-questions-democracy/ [Accessed 10 May 2018]

34. New Statesman, 'Who's who in Team Corbyn,' *New Statesman*, 27 August 2015, https://www.newstatesman.com/politics/elections/2015/08/who-s-who-team-corbyn [Accessed 28 April 2018]

35. Leila Al Shami, 'The 'Anti-Imperialism' of idiots,' 14 April 2018, https://leilashami.wordpress.com/2018/04/14/the-anti-imperialism-of-idiots [Accessed 10 May 2018]; Cautiously Pessimistic, 'Syria seen from the Viewpoint of imperial purity: the crushing narcissism of empire,' *Libcom.org*, 20 February 2018, https://libcom.org/library/syria-seen-viewpoint-imperial-purity-crushing-narcissism-empire [Accessed 10 May 2018]

36. For an account of Iranian imperialist pretensions in Iraq, Syria and beyond, see Rohini Hensman, *Indefensible: Democracy, Counter-Revolution, and the Rhetoric of Anti-Imperialism* (Chicago: Haymarket, 2018)

37. David Hirsh, *Contemporary Left Antisemitism* (Abingdon: Routledge, 2017) *passim*; David Hirsh, 'The Corbyn left: the politics of position and the politics of reason,' *Fathom Journal*, Autumn 2015, http://fathomjournal.org/the-corbyn-left-the-politics-of-position-and-the-politics-of-reason [Accessed 17 May 2018]

38. Norman Geras, 'The Reductions of the Left,' *Dissent*, Winter 2005, https://www.dissentmagazine.org/article/the-reductions-of-the-left [Accessed 12 May 2018]

39. Vladimir Ilyich Lenin, 'Imperialism, the Highest Stage of Capitalism,' 1917, https://www.marxists.org/archive/lenin/works/1916/imp-hsc/ [Accessed 1 June 2018]

40. Alan Johnson, 'No, Jeremy Corbyn is not antisemitic – but the left should be wary of who he calls friends,' *New Statesman*, 2 September 2015, https://www.newstatesman.com/politics/staggers/2015/09/no-jeremy-corbyn-not-antisemitic-left-should-be-wary-who-he-calls-friends [Accessed 10 May

2018]; Daniel Randall, 'The Third Camp, Socialism From
Below, and the First Principle of Revolutionary Socialism,'
New Politics, XVI-4, Winter 2018, http://newpol.org/content/
third-camp-socialism-below-and-first-principle-revolutionary-
socialism [Accessed 10 May 2018]

41. See, for example, Andrew Coates' summary of much of the
     left's response to 2017 protests against state violence in
     Venezuala, in which protestors were painted as the agents of
     'reaction' or 'imperialism': 'Venezuala, Honesty and the Left,'
     Tendance Coatesy, 28 July 2017, https://tendancecoatesy.
     wordpress.com/2017/07/28/venezuela-honesty-and-the-left/
     [Accessed 10 May 2017].

42. 'Jeremy Corbyn on Hamas and Hezbollah,' *YouTube*,
     uploaded 15 June 2015, https://www.youtube.com/
     watch?v=pGj1PheWiFQ [Accessed 17 May 2018]; 'BBC
     News, 'Gaza: Hamas killed and tortured, says Amnesty,'
     BBC News, 27 May 2015, http://www.bbc.co.uk/news/
     world-middle-east-32894633 [Accessed 17 May 2018];
     Associated Press, 'Hamas executes six suspected informants
     for Israel on Gaza street,' *The Guardian*, 20 November
     2012, https://www.theguardian.com/world/2012/nov/20/
     hamas-executes-informants-israel-gaza [Accessed 17 May
     2018]; Jacob Eriksson, 'Why Hamas still relies on violent
     repression to control Gaza,' *The Conversation*, 8 June 2015,
     https://theconversation.com/why-hamas-still-relies-on-violent-
     repression-to-control-gaza-42461 [Accessed 17 May 2018]

43. Michael Mosbacher, 'The Stalinist Past of Corbyn's Strategist,'
     Standpoint, December 2015, http://www.standpointmag.co.uk/
     node/6327/full [Accessed 28 April 2018]

44. Dave Rich, *The Left's Jewish Problem* (Biteback Publishing,
     2016)

45. Robert Fine and Philip Spencer, *Antisemitism and the Left: On
     the Return of the Jewish Question* (Manchester: Manchester
     University Press, 2017)

46. Marcel Stoetzler, 'Reflections: antisemitism, anti-imperialism and liberal communitarianism,' *Open Democracy*, 26 May 2016, https://www.opendemocracy.net/can-europe-make-it/marcel-stoetzler/reflections-antisemitism-anti-imperialism-and-liberal-communitar [Accessed 1 June 2018]

47. Michael Parenti quoted in Marko Atilla Hoare, 'Genocide in the former Yugoslavia: a critique of left revisionism's denial,' *Journal of Genocide Research* 5.4, (2003), 548

48. Ibid., 549

49. Ibid., 549–560

50. Tuzla municipal branch of the Congress of Independent Trade Unions of the Republic of Bosnia-Herzegovina, 'Open Letter to the 'Committee for Peace in the Balkans',' *Bosnian Institute*, June-August 1995, http://www.bosnia.org.uk/bosrep/report_format.cfm?articleid=1849&reportid=110 [Accessed 16 May 2018]

51. *Balkan Witness*, 'Deniers of Serbia's War Crimes,' http://balkanwitness.glypx.com/articles-deniers.htm [Accessed 28 April 2018]; George Monbiot, 'My fight may be hopeless, but it is as necessary as ever,' *The Guardian*, 21 May 2012, https://www.theguardian.com/commentisfree/2012/may/21/ratko-mladic-genocide-denial [Accessed 28 April 2018]

52. Tony Benn, 'Tony Benn on Bosnia: 'The main enemy is NATO',' *Workers' Liberty*, 2 April 2009. http://www.workersliberty.org/story/2009/04/02/tony-benn-bosnia-main-enemy-nato [Accessed 28 April 2018]

53. 'Early Day Motion 392: John Pilger and Kosovo,' https://www.parliament.uk/edm/2004-05/392 [Accessed 28 April 2018]

54. Seumas Milne, 'Hague is not the place to try Milosevic,' *The Guardian*, 2 August 2001, https://www.theguardian.com/politics/2001/aug/02/warcrimes.serbia [Accessed 28 April 2018]

55. Anonymous, 'An Investigation into Red-Brown Alliances:
    Third Positionism, Russia, Ukraine, Syria, And The Western
    Left,' *Libcom*, 1 February 2018, https://libcom.org/library/
    investigation-red-brown-alliances-third-positionism-russia-
    ukraine-syria-western-left [Accessed 13 July 2018]

56. Seumas Milne, 'They can't see why they are hated,' *The
    Guardian,* 13 September 2001, https://www.theguardian.com/
    politics/2001/sep/13/september11.britainand911 [Accessed 28
    April 2018]

57. Chris Floyd, 'Paris reaps whirlwind of western support
    for extremist violence in Middle East,' *Stop the War
    Coalition.* 14 November 2015, https://archive.is/
    du1n5#selection-637.0-637.78 [Accessed 28 April 2018]

58. See the common argument that Russia's bombing of Syrian
    rebels is legitimate because 'Russia, after all, had been invited
    to intervene by Assad's government, which still holds the
    country's seat at the United Nations'. Jonathan Steele, 'Putin in
    Syria,' *London Review of Books*, 38(8), 21 April 2016, 33-35,
    https://www.lrb.co.uk/v38/n08/jonathan-steele/putin-in-syria
    [Accessed 28 April 2018]

59. BBC, 'Full text of Benn interview with Saddam,' *BBC News*,
    4 February 2003, http://news.bbc.co.uk/1/hi/2726831.stm
    [Accessed 13 July 2018]

60. As Moishe Postone argues, 'The disastrous nature of the war
    and, more generally, of the Bush administration should not
    obscure that...progressives found themselves faced with what
    should have been viewed as a dilemma — a conflict between
    an aggressive global imperial power...and a brutal fascistic
    regime...[Yet there were very few] attempts to problematize
    this dilemma or to try to analyze this configuration with an
    eye toward the possibility of formulating what has become
    exceedingly difficult in the world today — a critique with
    emancipatory intent. This would have required developing a
    form of internationalism that broke with the dualisms of a
    Cold War framework that all too frequently legitimated (as

'anti-imperialist') states whose structures and policies were
no more emancipatory than those of many authoritarian and
repressive regimes supported by the American government,'
'History and Helplessness: Mass Mobilization and
Contemporary Forms of Anticapitalism,' 96

61. Nick Cohen, 'The lesson the left has never learnt,' *New
Statesman*, 21 July 2003. Available from: https://www.
newstatesman.com/node/199924 [Accessed 28 April 2018]

62. Bob from Brockley, 'Eight Reasons not to let George Galloway
back into the Labour Party,' 9 December 2017, http://brockley.
blogspot.co.uk/2017/12/eight-reasons-not-to-let-george.html
[Accessed 10 May 2018]; Connor P, 'Novichok for the Soul,'
Medium, 21 March 2018, https://medium.com/@connorp89/
novichok-for-the-soul-3ff34681cc1 [Accessed 10 May 2018]

63. James Bloodworth, 'The bizarre world of Jeremy Corbyn and
Stop the War,' *Politico*, 12 November 2015, https://www.
politico.eu/article/bizarre-world-of-jeremy-corbyn-and-stop-
the-war-coalition-galloway-rees-iraq-far-left/ [Accessed 28 Apr
2018]

64. Stuart McGurk, 'Jeremy Corbyn interview: 'As far as I know,
my team voted Remain. I haven't asked them',' *GQ* (Jan-Feb
2018), http://www.gq-magazine.co.uk/article/jeremy-corbyn-
gq-interview [Accessed 28 Apr 2018]

65. BBC, 'Outrage over MP's praise of IRA,' *BBC News*, 30 May
2003, http://news.bbc.co.uk/1/hi/england/london/2949688.stm
[Accessed 28 Apr 2018]

66. Ronan Bennett, 'Jeremy Corbyn has been on the right
side of history for 30 years. That's real leadership,' *The
Guardian*, 16 September 2016, https://www.theguardian.com/
commentisfree/2016/sep/16/jeremy-corbyn-leadership-david-
cameron-libya-labour [Accessed 10 May 2018]

67. 'Jeremy Corbyn on Hamas and Hezbollah,' recorded 2009,
YouTube https://www.youtube.com/watch?v=QZAn7ZEvwek
[Accessed 10 May 2018]

CHAPTER 3: ON THE RIGHT SIDE OF HISTORY: THE MORAL MYTHOLOGY OF CORBYNISM

1.   Luke Akehurst, 'Why Jeremy Corbyn should be on the leadership ballot,' *Labour List*, 9 June 2015, https://labourlist. org/2015/06/why-jeremy-corbyn-should-be-on-the-leadership-ballot [Accessed 10 May 2018]

2.   George Eaton, 'How the Labour left triumphed: the inside story,' *New Statesman*, 23 September 2017, https://www. newstatesman.com/politics/uk/2017/09/how-labour-left-triumphed-inside-story [Accessed 10 May 2018]

3.   Adam Smith, 'Diane Abbott gets so much racist abuse her aides update police every week,' *Metro*, 29 April 2018, http://metro. co.uk/2018/04/29/diane-abbott-gets-so-much-racist-abuse-her-aides-update-police-every-week-7508279/ [Accessed 12 May 2018]

4.   Mark Mardell, 'Jeremy Corbyn victory: How hard is it to be authentic?' *BBC News*, 15 September 2015, http://www. bbc.co.uk/news/world-34245926 [Accessed 10 May 2018]; Jeremy Corbyn, 'Jeremy Corbyn's Labour party conference speech 2015: full text,' *New Statesman*, 29 September 2015, https://www.newstatesman.com/politics/staggers/2015/09/ jeremy-corbyns-labour-party-conference-speech-2015-full-text [Accessed 10 May 2018]

5.   BBC, 'Margaret Beckett: I was moron to nominate Jeremy Corbyn,' *BBC News*, 22 July 2015, http://www.bbc.co.uk/ news/uk-politics-33625612 [Accessed 10 May 2018]

6.   Jon Stone, 'Tony Blair says he wouldn't want a left-wing Labour party to win an election,' *Independent*, 22 July 2015, https://www.independent.co.uk/news/uk/politics/tony-blair-says-he-wouldn-t-want-a-left-wing-labour-party-to-win-an-election-10406928.html [Accessed 10 May 2018]

7.   Ronan Bennett, 'Jeremy Corbyn has been on the right side of history for 30 years. That's real leadership,' *The Guardian*, 16 September 2016, https://www.theguardian.com/ commentisfree/2016/sep/16/jeremy-corbyn-leadership-david-cameron-libya-labour [Accessed 10 May 2018]

8. Meyrem Hussein, 'Islington North MP Jeremy Corbyn is the country's lowest expenses claimer,' *Islington Gazette*, 8 December 2010, http://www.islingtongazette.co.uk/news/politics/islington-north-mp-jeremy-corbyn-is-the-country-s-lowest-expenses-claimer-1-748369

9. University of Leicester, 'Research unearths viral image of Labour Party leader,' 15 October 2015, https://www2.le.ac.uk/news/blog/2015-archive-1/october/apartheid-research-project-unearths-viral-image-of-labour-party-leader [Accessed 10 May 2018]; Martin Shipton, 'Peter Hain gets top South African award for campaigning against apartheid,' *Wales Online*, 8 December 2015, https://www.walesonline.co.uk/news/wales-news/peter-hain-gets-top-south-10564731 [Accessed 10 May 2018]

10. RW Johnson, 'Secret Deal with South Africa's Stalinists,' *Standpoint*, April 2011, http://standpointmag.co.uk/node/3803/full [Accessed 30 May 2018]

11. Seumas Milne, 'Left takeover bid for Anti-Apartheid,' *The Guardian*, 27 October 1984

12. Twll Dun, 'The right side of history,' *Medium*, 9 July 2016, https://medium.com/@twlldun/the-right-side-of-history-de2228da346f [Accessed 28 April 2018]

13. Matt Chorley, 'Conservatives should be renamed the 'Workers Party' with a ladder as its logo, says new deputy chairman Robert Halfon,' *Daily Mail*, 19 May 2015, http://www.dailymail.co.uk/news/article-3087429/Conservatives-renamed-Workers-Party-ladder-logo-says-new-deputy-chairman-Robert-Halfon.html#ixzz5F84bjAS5 [Accessed 10 May 2018]

14. For an account of the welfare bill debacle from Harman's perspective, see Rosa Prince, *Comrade Corbyn* (Biteback Publishing, 2016) Chapter 18

15. Chaminda Jayanetti, 'Why Labour's welfare mess matters,' *Politics.co.uk*, 7 June 2017, http://www.politics.co.uk/comment-analysis/2017/06/07/why-labour-s-welfare-mess-matters [Accessed 10 May 2018]

16. Rob Merrick, 'Labour admits it would not end benefits freeze, after day of confusion,' *The Independent*, 16 May 2017, http://www.independent.co.uk/news/uk/politics/general-election-20107-latest-labour-manifesto-benefits-freeze-cap-jeremy-corbyn-a7739471.html [Accessed 28 April 2018]

17. Graeme Demianyk, 'Labour Leadership Candidate Liz Kendall Says Back Benefits Reform or Face 'Decades' Out Of Power,' *Huffington Post*, 2 July 2015, http://www.huffingtonpost.co.uk/2015/07/02/liz-kendall-andy-burnham-yvette-cooper-jeremy-corbyn-benefits-lga-hustings_n_7712740.html [Accessed 28 April 2018]

18. Daily Mail, 'Labour's apologists for terror: The Mail accuses Corbyn troika of befriending Britain's enemies and scorning the institutions that keep us safe,' *Daily Mail*, 6 June 2017, http://www.dailymail.co.uk/news/article-4578716/Apologists-terror-Corbyn-McDonnell-Abbott.html [Accessed 16 May 2018]

19. This dissonance was expressed in the outraged denials and historical revisionism that followed the publication of pictures showing Corbyn supposedly laying a wreath in honour of members of the 'Black September' Palestinian terror group. This revisionism came in spite of the fact that Corbyn's own account of the event in a 2014 *Morning Star*, article indicated he had attended such a ceremony. Cf Jeremy Corbyn, 'Palestine United,' Morning Star, 5 October 2014, https://morningstaronline.co.uk/a-98de-palestine-united-1 [Accessed 18 August 2018]

20. Asa Winstanley, 'Jeremy Corbyn backs boycott of Israeli universities involved in arms research,' *Electronic Intifada*, 2 August 2015, https://electronicintifada.net/blogs/asa-winstanley/jeremy-corbyn-backs-boycott-israeli-universities-involved-arms-research [Accessed 1 June 2018]

21. For a thorough examination of Corbyn's personal brand of 'anti-Zionism' and the relationship of the latter to antisemitism, see David Hirsh, *Contemporary Left Antisemitism*, 40–65

22. Jewish Chronicle, 'The key questions Jeremy Corbyn must answer,' *Jewish Chronicle*, 12 August 2015, https://www.thejc. com/news/uk-news/the-key-questions-jeremy-corbyn-must-answer-1.68097 [Accessed 28 April 2018]

23. Peter Edwards, 'Len McCluskey: Anti-Semitism claims are 'mood music' used to undermine Corbyn,' *LabourList*, 27 September 2017, https://labourlist.org/2017/09/len-mccluskey-labour-anti-semitism-claims-are-mood-music-used-to-undermine-corbyn [Accessed 28 April 2018]

24. Rowena Mason, 'MPs should have no say over who leads Labour, argues shadow minister,' *The Guardian*, 28 August 2017, https://www.theguardian.com/politics/2017/aug/28/make-labour-leadership-rules-more-democratic-urges-shadow-minister [Accessed 28 April 2018]

25. Vice News, *Jeremy Corbyn: The Outsider*, 2016, https://video. vice.com/alps/video/jeremy-corbyn-the-outsider/57488923aa26 43cc23a63890 [Accessed 10 May 2018]

26. Jonathan Freedland, 'Labour and the left have an antisemitism problem,' *The Guardian*, 18 March 2016, https://www. theguardian.com/commentisfree/2016/mar/18/labour-antisemitism-jews-jeremy-corbyn [Accessed 10 May 2018]

27. BBC News, 'Labour activist Jackie Walker 'appalled' by suspension,' *BBC News,* 7 May 2016, http://www.bbc.co.uk/news/uk-england-kent-36236332 [Accessed 17 May 2018]; Henry Louis Gates Jr, 'Black Demagogues and Pseudo-Scholars,' *New York Times,* 20 July 1992, https://www. nytimes.com/1992/07/20/opinion/black-demagogues-and-pseudo-scholars.html [Accessed 17 May 2018]

28. Owen Jones, 'Agree with this statement from the Labour Representation Committee – LRC: Jeremy Corbyn is right to launch an inquiry into anti-Semitism, but the suspension of Jacqueline Walker – a black activist of Jewish heritage, and a proud anti-racist campaigner – has no justification…' Facebook, 5 May 2016, https://web.archive.

org/web/20160929191412/https://www.facebook.com/
owenjones84/posts/1018258411601004 [Accessed 17 May
2018]

29. Emilio Casalicchio, 'Jeremy Corbyn criticised after appearing
     with anti-Semitism row activist,' 6 September 2016, *Politics
     Home*, https://www.politicshome.com/news/uk/political-
     parties/labour-party/news/78700/excl-jeremy-corbyn-criticised-
     after-appearing-anti [Accessed 17 May 2018]

30. Hirsh, *Contemporary Left Antisemitism*

31. Jeremy Corbyn, 'Jeremy Corbyn letter to Jewish leaders: I
     will always be your ally in the fight against antisemitism,'
     Labour.org.uk, 26 March 2018, https://labour.org.uk/press/
     jeremy-corbyn-letter-jewish-leaders-i-will-always-ally-fight-
     antisemitism/ [Accessed 28 April 2018]

32. Ben Weich, 'Thousands of Labour supporters back antisemitic
     open letter to Jeremy Corbyn,' *Jewish Chronicle*, March 29
     2018, https://www.thejc.com/news/uk-news/jeremy-corbyn-
     labour-antisemitism-open-letter-1.461677 [Accessed 10 May
     2018]

33. Andrew Gilligan, 'Revealed: Jeremy Corbyn and John
     McDonnell's close IRA links,' *Daily Telegraph*, 10 October
     2015, http://www.telegraph.co.uk/news/politics/Jeremy_
     Corbyn/11924431/Revealed-Jeremy-Corbyn-and-John-
     McDonnells-close-IRA-links.html [Accessed 28 April 2018]

34. Robert Wright, 'Spotlight falls on Jeremy Corbyn's links with
     Irish republicans,' *Financial Times*, 30 May 2017, https://www.
     ft.com/content/9f833a98-452c-11e7-8519-9f94ee97d996
     [Accessed 28 April 2018]

35. Andrew Gilligan, 'Revealed: Jeremy Corbyn and John
     McDonnell's close IRA links'

36. ITN, 'Jeremy Corbyn: There has to be a political solution in
     Syria,' 10 April 2018, https://uk.news.yahoo.com/jeremy-
     corbyn-political-solution-syria-175128795.html [Accessed 10
     May 2018]

37. Jeremy Corbyn, 'Diplomacy, and not bombing, is the way to end Syria's agony,' *The Guardian*, 15 April 2018, https://www. theguardian.com/commentisfree/2018/apr/15/un-inspectors-not-bombs-peace-syria-jeremy-corbyn [Accessed 10 May 2018]. Cf Oz Katerji, 'If Jeremy Corbyn opposes intervention in Syria, he should have more to say about Russia,' *New Statesman*, 18 April 2018, https://www.newstatesman.com/ politics/uk/2018/04/if-jeremy-corbyn-opposes-intervention-syria-he-should-have-more-say-about-russia [Accessed 10 May 2018]

38. Michael Walzer, 'A Foreign Policy for the Left,' *Dissent*, Spring 2014. Available from: https://www.dissentmagazine.org/article/ a-foreign-policy-for-the-left [Accessed 12 May 2018]

39. Andrew Marr Show, 'Interview with Jeremy Corbyn,' 15 April 2018, http://news.bbc.co.uk/1/shared/bsp/hi/pdfs/15041801. pdf [Accessed 10 May 2018]

40. Channel 4 News, 'Jeremy Corbyn: 'I wanted Hamas to be part of the debate',' *Channel 4 News*, 13 July 2015, https://www. channel4.com/news/jeremy-corbyn-i-wanted-hamas-to-be-part-of-the-debate [Accessed 28 April 2018]

41. Ido Vock, 'Why Jeremy Corbyn's Cozy at an Iranian Revolution Rally, but Not a Balfour Dinner,' *Haaretz* 31 Oct 2017, https://www.haaretz.com/opinion/.premium-why-corbyn-s-cozy-at-a-pro-iran-rally-but-not-a-balfour-dinner-1.5461243 [Accessed 28 April 2018]; Toby Helm, 'Jeremy Corbyn turns down visit to Israel's Holocaust museum,' *The Observer*, 10 Sep 2016, https://www. theguardian.com/politics/2016/sep/10/jeremy-corbyn-israel-yad-vashem [Accessed 28 April 2018]

42. For Corbyn's meeting see Dominic Kennedy, 'Palestinian lobby group paid for Corbyn to meet Assad in Syria,' *The Times*, 29 Oct 2016. Available from: https://www.thetimes.co.uk/ article/palestinian-lobby-group-paid-for-corbyn-to-meet-assad-in-syria-jv5hrsjfl [Accessed 12 May 2018]; For Assad, repression and rendition see Robin Yassin-Kassab and Leila

al-Shami, *Burning Country: Syrians in Revolution and War*. New edition. (London: Pluto Press, 2018), esp. 25-26. For Corbyn's opposition to rendition see Jeremy Corbyn, 'The role of Blair, MI6, CIA and extraordinary rendition will haunt the US and UK establisments [sic] for years to come', *Twitter* 8 Sep 2011. Available from: https://twitter.com/jeremycorbyn/status/111729061151248384 [Accessed 12 May 2018]

43. Jessica Elgot, 'Jeremy Corbyn calls for UK to lead UN push to defuse Syria crisis,' *The Guardian*, 13 April 2018, https://www.theguardian.com/world/2018/apr/13/jeremy-corbyn-calls-for-uk-to-lead-un-push-to-defuse-syria-crisis [Accessed 28 April 2018]

44. Tom Harris, 'Jeremy Corbyn's disingenuous objections to intervention in Syria,' *CapX*, 16 April 2018, https://capx.co/jeremy-corbyns-disingenuous-objections-to-intervention-in-syria/ [Accessed 28 Apr 2018]

45. Gene, 'People of Yarmouk ask: Where's the solidarity?' *Harry's Place*, April 16 2016, http://hurryupharry.org/2016/04/16/people-of-yarmouk-ask-wheres-the-solidarity/ [Accessed 17 May 2018]; Raf Sanchez, 'Palestinian refugee camp in Syria turns 'unimaginably brutal' as Assad regime drives Isil out of Yarmouk,' *Daily Telegraph*, 26 April 2018, https://www.telegraph.co.uk/news/2018/04/26/palestinian-refugee-camp-syria-turns-unimaginably-brutal-assad [Accessed 17 May 2018]

46. Rob Merrick, 'Jeremy Corbyn condemns Western 'silence' over Israel's killing of at least 27 Palestinians on the Gaza border,' *The Independent*, 7 April 2018, https://www.independent.co.uk/news/uk/politics/jeremy-corbyn-israel-killings-palestine-gaza-border-violence-a8293881.html [Accessed 28 April 2018]

47. Tom Whyman, 'Why we all belong to a shared community,' *New Internationalist*, 1 April 2018. Available from: https://newint.org/features/2018/04/01/a-new-universalism [Accessed 12 May 2018]

48. Judith Shklar, 'The Liberalism of Fear,' in Judith Shklar, *Political Thought and Political Thinkers*, ed. Stanley Hoffman (Chicago: University of Chicago Press, 1990) p. 11

49. Jonathan Rutherford, 'Labour must choose between two fundamentally different understandings of the human condition,' *New Statesman*. 26 September 2017, https://www.newstatesman.com/politics/staggers/2017/09/labour-must-choose-between-two-fundamentally-different-understandings [Accessed 28 April 2018]

50. Cf Cautiously Pessimistic, *Syria from the Viewpoint of imperial purity*

51. 'Jeremy Corbyn interview with Hassan Alkatib,' *YouTube*. 25 Jul 2015, https://www.youtube.com/watch?v=ihVLo5cGYEo [Accessed 28 April 2018]

52. Skwawkbox, 'World Exclusive: #Corbyn – Mowlam's Envoy, Met IRA and Loyalists,' *The Skwawkbox*, 25 May 2017, https://skwawkbox.org/2017/05/25/world-exclusive-corbyn-mowlams-envoy-to-ira-and-loyalists/ [Accessed 28 April 2018]

53. Andrew Gilligan, 'Abbott declared support for British defeat in Northern Ireland,' *The Times*, 21 May 2017, https://www.thetimes.co.uk/article/abbott-declared-support-for-ira-defeat-of-britain-rp79dvvmk [Accessed 28 Apr 2018]

54. Maxine Molyneux and Thomas Osborne, 'Populism: A Deflationary View'

55. Ibid.

56. Ibid.

57. Bob from Brockley, 'Islamophobia turns left: Ben Norton and the Grayzone Project,' 8 March 2018, http://brockley.blogspot.co.uk/2018/03/who-is-ben-norton.html [Accessed 10 May 2018]

58. Ashley Cowburn, 'Diane Abbott says it would be 'outrageous' for Theresa May to deny MPs vote on Syria military action,' *The Independent*, 13 Apr 2018. Available from: https://

www.independent.co.uk/news/uk/politics/diane-abbott-
theresa-may-syria-parliament-vote-labour-corbyn-military-
action-a8302411.html [Accessed 28 Apr 2018]

59. Leila Al-Shami, 'The 'anti-imperialism' of idiots,' *Leila's Blog*,
    14 April 2018, https://leilashami.wordpress.com/2018/04/14/
    the-anti-imperialism-of-idiots/ [Accessed 28 April 2018]

60. Stephen Levitsky and Daniel Ziblatt, *How Democracies Die*
    (Viking, 2018)

61. Joe Smallman, 'Corbynism without Corbyn: Time for the left
    to think the unthinkable', *Politics.co.uk*, 9 Apr 2018. Available
    from: http://www.politics.co.uk/comment-analysis/2018/04/09/
    corbynism-without-corbyn-time-for-the-left-to-think-the-unth
    [Accessed 12 May 2018]; Owen Jones, 'Jeremy Corbyn says
    he's staying. That's not good enough,' *The Guardian*, 1 Mar
    2017, https://www.theguardian.com/commentisfree/2017/
    mar/01/corbyn-staying-not-good-enough [Accessed 12 May
    2018]

CHAPTER 4: TAKING BACK CONTROL: CORBYNISM IN ONE COUNTRY

1. George Eaton, 'What is Labour's official Brexit position?' *New
   Statesman*, 15 November 2016, https://www.newstatesman.
   com/politics/uk/2016/11/what-labours-official-brexit-policy
   [Accessed 11 May 2018]

2. Jonathan Lis, 'Brexit: Corbyn is playing a clever long game
   that could benefit us all,' *Politics.co.uk*, 28 December 2017,
   http://www.politics.co.uk/comment-analysis/2017/12/28/
   brexit-corbyn-is-playing-a-clever-long-game-that-could-benef
   [Accessed 11 May 2018]

3. Mariana Mazzucato (@mazzucatom), 'Labour's official
   position on Brexit (supporting it) is why most of the economic

advisors resigned. It defies reason (economic & political),'
Twitter, 24 March 2018, https://twitter.com/mazzucatom/
status/977549293019115521 [Accessed 28 April 2018]

4.   BBC News, 'Jeremy Corbyn backs permanent customs union
      after Brexit,' *BBC News*, 26 February 2018, http://www.bbc.
      co.uk/news/uk-politics-43189878 [Accessed 28 April 2018]

5.   Paul Waugh, 'Norway-Style Brexit Now 'Dead' After Jeremy
      Corbyn Signals To MPs He Won't Back European Economic
      Area Model,' *Huffington Post*, 14 May 2018, https://www.
      huffingtonpost.co.uk/entry/norway-style-brexit-now-dead-
      after-jeremy-corbyn-signals-to-mps-he-wont-back-european-
      economic-area-model_uk_5af9dd09e4b09a94524b1630
      [Accessed 17 May 2018]

6.   Pippa Crerar and Jessica Elgot, 'Ministers selling out UK
      exporters, Corbyn to say,' *The Guardian*, 24 Jul 2018, https://
      www.theguardian.com/politics/2018/jul/24/ministers-selling-
      out-uk-exporters-corbyn-to-say [Accessed 24 Jul 2018]

7.   Anushka Asthana, 'Big majority of Labour members 'want UK
      to stay in single market',' *The Guardian*, 17 July 2017, https://
      www.theguardian.com/politics/2017/jul/17/most-labour-
      members-want-uk-to-remain-in-single-market [Accessed 14
      July 2018]

8.   Jeremy Corbyn, 'Tony Benn: A titan of our movement,'
      Morning Star, 17 March 2014, https://morningstaronline.
      co.uk/a-08f9-tony-benn-a-titan-of-our-movement [Accessed 11
      May 2018]

9.   Dan Bloom, 'Jeremy Corbyn says his £500bn investment
      pledge was an 'approximation',' *Daily Mirror*, 25 September
      2016, https://www.mirror.co.uk/news/uk-news/jeremy-corbyn-
      says-500bn-investment-8910536 [Accessed 28 April 2018]

10.   Nigel Nelson, 'Jeremy Corbyn: If I don't win Labour
      leadership I can always go back to my allotment,' *Daily
      Mirror*, 25 July 2015, https://www.mirror.co.uk/news/uk-news/

jeremy-corbyn-dont-win-labour-6138128 [Accessed 28 April 2018]

11. Official Jeremy Corbyn Channel, '#WeDemand', *Youtube*, 2 June 2017. https://www.youtube.com/watch?v=28-fC6_Byu0 [Accessed 28 April 2018]

12. Antonio Gramsci, *Selections from the Prison Notebooks*, ed. Quintin Hoare (London: Lawrence and Wishart, 2005) p12. For a critique of Gramsci's concept of hegemony and the flawed theory of class upon which it is based, see GM Tamas, 'Telling the Truth About Class,' *Socialist Register*, Vol 42, 2009, and Werner Bonefeld, 'What is the alternative?' *Shift*, 11, January 2011, https://www.weareplanc.org/blog/werner-bonefeld-what-is-the-alternative/ [Accessed 11 May 2018]

13. Cambridge Political Economy Group, *Britain's Economic Crisis* (Spokesman, 1974) p. 6

14. See Jonathan Bearman, 'Anatomy of the Bennite Left,' *International Socialism*, 2:6, (Autumn 1979), 51–70, www.marxists.org/history/etol/newspape/isj2/1979/isj2-006/bearman.html [Accessed 28 April 2018]

15. See John Medhurst, *That Option No Longer Exists*, (London: Zero Books, 2014), 100–109

16. Tony Benn, *Against the Tide. Diaries 1973–76*, (London: Hutchinson, 1989), 621

17. Jeremy Corbyn, 'Jeremy Corbyn's full speech to Scottish Labour conference,' *Labour.org.uk*, 9 Mar 2018, https://labour.org.uk/press/jeremy-corbyns-full-speech-scottish-labour-conference/ [Accessed 28 April 2018]

18. Francis Grove White (ed.), *Busting the Lexit Myths* (Open Britain/Labour Campaign for the Single Market, 2018), https://www.labour4singlemarket.org/busting_the_myths [Accessed 28 Apr 2018]; Andy Tarrant and Andrea Biondi, 'EU law is no barrier to Labour's economic programme,' *Renewal: A Journal of Social Democracy*. 22 Sep 2017. http://www.renewal.org.uk/blog/eu-law-is-no-barrier-to-labours-economic-programme

[Accessed 28 Apr 2018]; Andy Tarrant, 'Negotiating the Red Lines,' *Fabian Society*, 8 May 2018, https://fabians.org.uk/negotiating-the-red-lines/ [Accessed 11 May 2018]

19. Labour Party, *Alternative Models of Ownership*

20. Ibid, p. 5

21. Ibid, p. 6

22. Ibid, p. 7

23. Ibid, p. 6

24. Ibid, pp. 16–17

25. Sharryn Kasmir, *The Myth of Mondragon*, (New York: State University of New York, 1996), 68

26. 'Eric Hobsbawm interviews Tony Benn,' *Marxism Today*, October 1980

27. Labour Party, *Alternative Models of Ownership*, 7

28. Economist, 'Preston, Jeremy Corbyn's Model Town,' *The Economist*, 19 October 2017, https://www.economist.com/news/britain/21730421-how-one-city-became-unlikely-laboratory-corbynomics-preston-jeremy-corbyns-model-town [Accessed 28 April 2018]. Cf Martin O'Neill and Joe Guinan, 'The Institutional Turn: Labour's new political economy,' *Renewal*, 26.1 (2018), http://www.renewal.org.uk/articles/the-institutional-turn-labours-new-political-economy [Accessed 2 June 2018]

29. Philip Mirowski, *More Heat than Light: Economics as Social Physics, Physics as Nature's Economics*. (Cambridge: Cambridge University Press, 1989)

30. Anej Korsika, 'Interview with Moishe Postone: 'Critique and Dogmatism',' *anejkorsika.wordpress.com*, 26 February 2015, https://anejkorsika.wordpress.com/2015/02/26/interview-with-moishe-postone-critique-and-dogmatism [Accessed 17 May 2018]

31. Miroswki, *More Heat than Light*, 148

32. See Joe Guinan, 'Modern money and the escape from austerity,' *Renewal*, 22:3/4 (2014), http://www.renewal.org.uk/articles/modern-money-and-the-escape-from-austerity [Accessed 14 May 2018]. For an application in the context of 'Lexit' see Joe Guinan and Thomas M. Hanna, 'A left-wing Brexit is possible – if we play it right, we could change the whole of society for good,' *The Independent*, 8 August 2017, https://www.independent.co.uk/voices/brexit-lexit-left-wing-economics-end-of-neoliberalism-a7882111.html [Accessed 13 May 2018]

33. Mirowski, *More Heat than Light*, 159

34. Mirowski, *More Heat than Light*, 159–60; Philip Mirowski, Learning the Meaning of a Dollar: Conservation Principles and the Social Theory of Value in Economic Theory. *Social Research*, 57:3 (1990), 689–717 (698)

35. William Clare Roberts, 'The value of Capital. Jacobin. 27 March 2017 https://www.jacobinmag.com/2017/03/marxs-inferno-capital-david-harvey-response/ [Accessed 13 May 2018]

36. For more indepth discussions of the difference between pre-capitalist and capitalist forms of labour, see Ellen Meiksins Wood, *The Origin of Capitalism* (London, New York: Verso, 2002) and Moishe Postone, *Time, Labor and Social Domination* (Cambridge: Cambridge University Press, 1993). See also Michael Heinrich, *An Introduction to the Three Volumes of Karl Marx's Capital* (New York: Monthly Review Press, 2012) Section 1.1

37. Cf Werner Bonefeld, *Critical Theory and the Critique of Political Economy*

38. Frederick Harry Pitts, Critiquing Capitalism Today: New Ways to Read Marx. (New York: Palgrave Macmillan, 2017)

39. Karl Marx, *Capital* Vol 1, Chapter 1

40. Richard Gunn, 'Notes on Class,' *Common Sense* 2 (1987), https://libcom.org/files/notes%20on%20class.pdf [Accessed 28 April 2018]

41. Labour Party, *Alternative Models of Ownership*, 26

42. Joe Guinan and Thomas Hanna, 'Polanyi against the Whirlwind,' *Renewal*, 25:1 (2017), 5-12, http://www.renewal. org.uk/articles/polanyi-against-the-whirlwind [Accessed 28 Apr 2018]

43. Labour Party, *Alternative Models of Ownership*, 32

44. Cf Paul Mason, 'Catalonia, Lombardy, Scotland ... why the fight for self-determination now?' *The Guardian*, 23 October 2017, https://www.theguardian.com/commentisfree/2017/ oct/23/we-need-to-understand-why-catalonia-lombardy-scotland-are-reposing-question-of-self-determination [Accessed 11 May 2018]; Paul Mason, 'The second trench: forging a new frontline in the war against neoliberalism,' *Open Democracy*, 8 May 2018, https://www.opendemocracy.net/neweconomics/ second-trench-forging-new-frontline-war-neoliberalism/ [Accessed 11 May 2018]

45. Karl Polanyi, *The Great Transformation* (Boston: Beacon Press, 2002), p3

46. Maurice Glasman, *Unnecessary Suffering: Management, Markets and the Liquidation of Solidarity* (London: Verso, 1996); Guinan and Hanna, 'Polanyi against the Whirlwind'

47. Wolfgang Streek, *How Will Capitalism End?* (London: Verso, 2016); Aditya Chakrabortty, 'Wolfgang Streeck: The German economist calling time on capitalism,' *The Guardian*, 9 December 2016 https://www.theguardian.com/books/2016/ dec/09/wolfgang-streeck-the-german-economist-calling-time-on-capitalism [Accessed 28 April 2018]

48. Philip Oltermann, 'Germany's left and right vie to turn politics upside down,' *The Guardian*, 22 Jul 2018, https:// www.theguardian.com/world/2018/jul/22/german-leftwingers-woo-voters-with-national-social-stance [Accessed 27 July 2018]

49. The Full Brexit, 'Founding Statement'

50. Adam Tooze, 'A General Logic of Crisis,' *London Review of Books*. 39:1, 5 Jan (2017), 3–8, http://www.lrb.co.uk/v39/n01/adam-tooze/a-general-logic-of-crisis [Accessed 28 April 2018]

51. Maurice Glasman, 'Things don't only get better: why the working class fell out of love with Labour,' *New Statesman*. 3 November 2016, https://www.newstatesman.com/politics/2016/11/things-dont-only-get-better-why-working-class-fell-out-love-labour [Accessed 28 April 2018]

52. Rutherford, 'Labour must choose between two fundamentally different understandings of the human condition'; Jonathan Rutherford, 'Labour has lost its identity,' *New Statesman*, 31 October 2016. https://www.newstatesman.com/politics/2016/10/labour-has-lost-its-identity [Accessed 28 April 2018]

53. Media Mole, 'Momentum criticised by Stella Creasy for sharing 'xenophobic' rail fares hike video,' *New Statesman*, 3 January 2017. https://www.newstatesman.com/politics/media/2017/01/momentum-criticised-stella-creasy-sharing-xenophobic-rail-fares-hike-video [Accessed 28 April 2018]; Nicholas Mairs, 'WATCH: Scottish minister accuses Momentum of 'xenophobia' over SNP attack ad,' *Politics Home*, 24 August 2017. https://www.politicshome.com/news/uk/uk-regions/scotland/news/88448/watch-scottish-minister-accuses-momentum-xenophobia-over-snp [Accessed 28 April 2018]

54. Joe Guinan and Thomas M Hanna, 'A left-wing Brexit is possible – if we play it right, we could change the whole of society for good,' *Independent*, 8 August 2017, https://www.independent.co.uk/voices/brexit-lexit-left-wing-economics-end-of-neoliberalism-a7882111.html [Accessed 11 May 2018]; Thomas Fazi and William Mitchell, 'Why the Left Should Embrace Brexit.' Cf Anthony Barnett, 'The lure of Lexit must be resisted – socialism in one country is a fantasy,' *New Statesman*, 21 September 2017, https://www.newstatesman.com/politics/uk/2017/09/lure-lexit-must-be-resisted-socialism-one-country-fantasy [Accessed 11 May 2018]

55. Bagehot, 'Boris Johnson is wrong: in the 21st century, sovereignty is always relative,' *Economist*, 21 February 2016, https://www.economist.com/blogs/bagehot/2016/02/bojo-breaks-ranks [Accessed 11 May 2018]

56. Andrew Coates, 'Does Galloway Blaze Trail for 'Left' Shift to Align with Nationalist Right?' *Tendance Coatesy*, 17 April, https://tendancecoatesy.wordpress.com/2016/04/17/does-galloway-blaze-trail-for-left-shift-to-align-with-nationalist-right [Accessed 11 May 2018]

57. John Ross, 'The damaging blind alley of US protectionism,' (http://ablog.typepad.com/keytrendsinglobalisation/2017/02/the-dead-end-of-us-protectionism.html). Whilst insightful, the perspectives of Ross and other contributors to the Socialist Economic Bulletin come from an intriguing place politically, carrying links with Russia and China and developed through a policy organ said to be funded, initially at least, by the proceeds accrued from Livingstone's after-dinner speeches to 'bankers and commodity brokers' peppered with the analysis of his Marxist economist advisor. See John Carvel, 'Power that stayed beyond our Ken', The Guardian, 17 Apr 1999, https://www.theguardian.com/uk/1999/apr/17/livingstone [Accessed 11 May 2018]; Jessica Berry and David Bamber, 'Mayor's 'Moscow embassy' angers London taxpayers', Daily Telegraph, 19 Sept 2004, https://www.telegraph.co.uk/news/1472104/Mayors-Moscow-embassy-angers-London-taxpayers.html [Accessed 11 May 2018]; Andrew Coates, 'John Ross: from the International Marxist Group to defending "politically socialist" Chinese regime', Tendance Coatesy, 8th September 2017, https://tendancecoatesy.wordpress.com/2017/09/08/john-ross-from-the-international-marxist-group-to-defending-politically-socialist-chinese-regime/ [Accessed 11 May 2018]

58. Tom O'Leary, 'There is no People's Brexit,' *Socialist Economic Bulletin* (http://socialisteconomicbulletin.blogspot.co.uk/2017/03/there-is-no-peoples-brexit.html)

59. 'Roy Jenkins and Tony Benn debate: The European Communities membership referendum, 1975 – Panorama,' *YouTube*, uploaded 6 July 2016, https://www.youtube.com/watch?v=_zBFh6bpcMo [Accessed 18 May 2018]

60. Tony Benn, *Arguments for Socialism*, p. 43

61. 'Eric Hobsbawm interviews Tony Benn'

62. Andrew Fisher, *The Failed Experiment* (Comerford & Miller, 2014)

63. Jamie Merchant, 'Fantasies of Secession: A Critique of Left Economic Nationalism,' *The Brooklyn Rail*, 7 February 2018, https://brooklynrail.org/2018/02/field-notes/Fantasies-of-Secession-A-Critique-of-Left-Economic-Nationalism [Accessed 12 May 2018]

64. *Economist*, 'Preston, Jeremy Corbyn's Model Town'

65. Philip Blenkinsop, 'EU sets steel import duties to counter Chinese subsidies,' *Reuters*, 9 June 2017, https://uk.reuters.com/article/uk-eu-china-steel-idUKKBN1901KI [Accessed 12 May 2018]

66. Ian Dunt, 'Everything you need to know about Lexit in five minutes'

67. Bruno Waterfield and Lucy Fisher, 'Fear of Jeremy Corbyn-led government prompts tough EU line on Brexit,' *The Times*, 7 May 2018, https://www.thetimes.co.uk/article/fear-of-corbyn-prompts-tough-eu-line-on-brexit-lrcmwgvlx [Accessed 12 May 2018]; Paul Mason, 'Labour needs to wage war on EU neoliberalism to prevent a Brussels sabotage,' *New Statesman*, 9 May 2018, https://www.newstatesman.com/politics/uk/2018/05/labour-needs-wage-war-eu-neoliberalism-prevent-brussels-sabotage [Accessed 12 May 2018]

68. Owen Jones (@owenjones84), 'Attempts by European leaders to prevent an elected socialist government enacting socialist policies for which it has a democratic mandate is a straightforward attack on British democracy: that's if the Tories consent to it. So much for taking back control, eh?'

Twitter, 7 May 2018, https://twitter.com/OwenJones84/
status/993505695394926594 [Accessed 12 May 2018]

69. Marc-William Palen, 'Protectionism 100 years ago helped
    ignite a world war. Could it happen again?' *Washington
    Post*, 30 June 2017, https://www.washingtonpost.com/news/
    made-by-history/wp/2017/06/30/protectionism-100-years-ago-
    helped-ignite-a-world-war-could-it-happen-again [Accessed 12
    May 2018]

70. James Stafford and Florence Sutcliffe Braithwaite, 'Ready
    for Government?' *Renewal*, 25.3–4 (2017), renewal.org.uk/
    articles/ready-for-government [Accessed 12 May 2018]

71. Costas Lapavitsas, 'Jeremy Corbyn's Labour vs the Single
    Market,' *Jacobin*, 30 May 2018, https://www.jacobinmag.
    com/2018/05/corbyn-labour-eu-single-market-economic-policy
    [Accessed 2 June 2018]

72. BBC News, 'US tariffs a dangerous game, says EU,' *BBC News*,
    1 June 2018, https://www.bbc.co.uk/news/business-44324565
    [Accessed 2 June 2018]

73. Brendan Cooney, 'Against Left Economic Populism'

CHAPTER 5: 'THINGS CAN AND THEY WILL CHANGE': CLASS, POSTCAPITALISM AND LEFT POPULISM

1. Poppy Noor, 'At last, real Labour is back – and the working-
   class vote proves that,' *The Guardian*, 14 June 2017, https://
   www.theguardian.com/commentisfree/2017/jun/14/labour-
   stop-pitying-young-people-represent-us-common-sense-
   revolution [Accessed 15 May 2018]; Owen Jones, 'Glastonbury
   is more evidence: Corbyn's appeal crosses classes,' *The
   Guardian*, 26 June 2017, https://www.theguardian.com/
   commentisfree/2017/jun/26/labour-jeremy-corbyn-middle-
   working-class-glastonbury [Accessed 15 May 2018]

2.   See John Holloway, *Change the World Without Taking Power* (London: Pluto Books, 2002)

3.   Dan Hancox, 'Why Ernesto Laclau is the intellectual figurehead for Syriza and Podemos,' *The Guardian*, 9 February 2015, http://www.theguardian.com/commentisfree/2015/feb/09/ernesto-laclau-intellectual-figurehead-syriza-podemos [Accessed 15 May 2018]

4.   Ibid.

5.   Gunn, 'Notes on Class'

6.   GM Tamas, 'Telling the Truth about Class,' *Socialist Register*, Vol 42, 2009

7.   BBC News, 'Labour leadership: Corbyn on austerity and poverty'

8.   Ernesto Laclau and Chantal Mouffe, *Hegemony and Socialist Strategy: Towards a Radical Democratic Politics* (London: Verso, 1985)

9.   Bernard-Henri Levy, 'The politics of Donald Trump and Vladimir Putin will dominate the world post-Brexit,' *New Statesman*, 4 July 2016, http://www.newstatesman.com/politics/staggers/2016/07/politics-donald-trump-and-vladimir-putin-will-dominate-world-post-brexit [Accessed 15 May 2018]

10. Michael Kazin, 'How Can Donald Trump and Bernie Sanders Both Be 'Populist'? *New York Times*. 22 March 2016, http://www.nytimes.com/2016/03/27/magazine/how-can-donald-trump-and-bernie-sanders-both-be-populist.html [Accessed 15 May 2018]

11. For a likeminded critique see Critisticuffs, 'We Don't Share Anything,' *Occupied Times*, 3 April 2016, https://theoccupiedtimes.org/?p=14219 [Accessed 15 May 2018]

12. Jeremy Corbyn, 'My speech at Labour's State of the Economy conference,' 21 May 2016, http://jeremycorbyn.org.uk/articles/jeremy-corbyn-my-speech-at-labours-state-of-the-economy-conference/ [Accessed 28 April 2018]

13. Karl Marx, *Capital* Vol 3 (London: Penguin, 1992) Chapter 48. Cf Simon Clarke, *Marx, Marginalism and Modern Sociology* (Palgrave Macmillian, 1991)

14. See Pitts, *Critiquing Capitalism Today*.

15. Labour Party, *Alternative Models of Ownership*, 13

16. Karl Marx, *Capital* Vol 1, 644

17. Max Horkheimer, quoted in Werner Bonefeld, 'Negative Dialectics and Critique of Economic Objectivity,' *History of the Human Sciences* 29 (2): 60–76

18. For a useful introduction to Miliband's work and that of his various interlocuters, particularly Nicos Poulantzas, see Asad Haider, 'Bernstein in Seattle: Representative Democracy and the Revolutionary Subject,' *Viewpoint*, May 15 2016, https://www.viewpointmag.com/2016/05/15/bernstein-in-seattle-representative-democracy-and-the-revolutionary-subject-part-1/ [Accessed 11 May 2018]

19. Ralph Miliband, *The State in Capitalist Society* (New York: Basic Books, 1973), p. 3, p. 23

20. Ibid, p. 68

21. Ralph Miliband, *The State in Capitalist Society*, p. 146

22. Ralph Miliband, *Parliamentary Socialism* (London: Merlin, 1972), 13

23. Ralph Miliband, 'Socialist Advance in Britain,' *The Socialist Register* (1983), 103–120, https://www.marxists.org/archive/miliband/1983/xx/advance.htm [Accessed 28 April 2018]

24. Ralph Miliband, 'Socialist Advance in Britain'

25. Ralph Miliband, 'The New Revisionism in Britain' *New Left Review,* I/150, March-April 1985. https://newleftreview.org/I/150/ralph-miliband-the-new-revisionism-in-britain [Accessed 28 April 2018]

26. Ibid.

27. Labour Party, *For the Many not the Few: The Labour Party Manifesto 2017*. https://labour.org.uk/wp-content/uploads/2017/10/labour-manifesto-2017.pdf [Accessed 14 May 2018]

28. Jane Dudman, 'Tony Blair: UK civil service has genuine problem with change,' *The Guardian*, 10 August 2017, https://www.theguardian.com/public-leaders-network/2017/aug/10/tony-blair-uk-civil-service [Accessed 26 July 2018]

29. Nicos Poulantzas, 'The Problem of the Capitalist State,' *New Left Review* 58, November-December 1969 (67–78) p. 70

30. Ralph Miliband, 'The New Revisionism in Britain'

31. Karl Marx, *Capital* Vol 1, p. 135

32. Simon Clarke, *The State Debate* (Palgrave Macmillan, 1991) p. 18

33. Eric Hobsbawm and Tony Benn, 'Eric Hobsbawm interviews Tony Benn,' *Marxism Today*, October 1980, http://banmarchive.org.uk/collections/mt/pdf/80_10_05.pdf [Accessed 28 April 2018]

34. Tim Ross, 'Jeremy Corbyn: Britain can learn from Karl Marx,' *Daily Telegraph*, 26 July 2015, https://www.telegraph.co.uk/news/politics/labour/11763640/Jeremy-Corbyn-Britain-can-learn-from-Karl-Marx.html [Accessed 26 July 2018]

35. Karl Marx, 'A Contribution to the Critique of Political Economy: Preface,' 1859, https://www.marxists.org/archive/marx/works/1859/critique-pol-economy/preface.htm [Accessed 11 May 2018]

36. Cf Gunn, "Against Historical Materialism", 36–37, n. 12. See also Terrell Carver and Daniel Blank, *A Political History of the Editions of Marx and Engels's "German ideology Manuscripts"*. (New York: Palgrave Macmillan 2014)

37. Walter Benjamin, 'Theses on the Philosophy of History,' *Illuminations: Essays and Reflections,* ed. Hannah Arendt (London: Pimlico. 1999), 245–55 (249–50)

38. See e.g. Owen Jones, 'We should be striving to work less, not toiling until we drop,' *The Guardian*. 3 March 2016, https://www.theguardian.com/commentisfree/2016/mar/03/retirement-retiring-age-77-strive-work-less-progress-challenge-bleak-prospect [Accessed 18 May 2018]

39. Tom Peck 'Jeremy Corbyn promises to 'rebuild Britain' with digital manifesto,' *The Independent*. 30 August 2016, http://www.independent.co.uk/news/uk/politics/jeremy-corbyn-labour-leadership-democratise-the-internet-broadband-manifesto-digital-britain-a7215491.html [Accessed 18 May 2018]; Patrick Wintour, 'John McDonnell to unveil 'socialism with an iPad' economic plan,' *The Guardian*. 20 November 2015, http://www.theguardian.com/politics/2015/nov/20/john-mcdonnell-to-unveil-socialism-with-an-ipad-economic-plan [Accessed 18 May 2018]

40. Annabelle Dickson, 'Jeremy Corbyn to address challenge posed by robots, *Politico*, 26 September 2017, http://www.politico.eu/article/jeremy-corbyn-labour-leader-post-brexit-to-address-challenge-posed-by-robots/ [Accessed 18 May 2018]

41. Jeremy Corbyn, Speech to Cooperative Party Conference, 14 Oct 2017. : https://labour.org.uk/press/jeremy-corbyn-speech-to-cooperative-party/ [Accessed 18 May 2018]

42. Cf Frederick Harry Pitts, 'Paul Mason, *Postcapitalism: A Guide to Our Future*,' *Marx and Philosophy Review of Books*, 4 September 2015, https://marxandphilosophy.org.uk/reviews/8066_postcapitalism-review-by-frederick-h-pitts [Accessed 26 July 2018]

43. Paul Mason, *Postcapitalism: A Guide to Our Future* (London: Allen Lane, 2015

44. The key accelerationist text with regard to Corbynism is Nick Srnicek and Alex Williams, *Inventing the Future* (London: Verso, 2015) – the book was sent to every member of the Shadow Cabinet. See Alex Williams and Nick Srnicek, 'Three reasons why the Labour shadow cabinet should read *Inventing the Future*,' *Verso Books Blog*, 12 November 2015, https://

www.versobooks.com/blogs/2332-three-reasons-why-the-labour-shadow-cabinet-should-read-inventing-the-future [Accessed 28 April 2018]

45. See Ana Dinerstein and Frederick Harry Pitts, 'From Post-Work to Post-Capitalism? Discussing the Basic Income and Struggles for Alternative Forms of Social Reproduction,' *Journal of Labour and Society*, forthcoming.

46. Paul Mason, 'Labour must become the party of people who want to change the world, not just Britain,' *OpenDemocracy*, 26 April 2018, https://www.opendemocracy.net/neweconomics/labour-must-become-party-people-want-change-world/ [Accessed 9 May 2018]; cf. Daniel Randall, 'Why class still matters: a reply to Paul Mason,' *OpenDemocracy*, 3 May 2018, https://www.opendemocracy.net/neweconomics/class-still-matters-reply-paul-mason/ [Accessed 9 May 2018]

47. See Harry Cleaver, 'The Inversion of Class Perspective in Marxian Theory: From Valorisation to Self-Valorisation,' in *Open Marxism* Vol. II: Theory and Practice, eds. Werner Bonefeld, Richard Gunn and Kosmas Psychopedis, (London: Pluto Press, 1992): 107-144. See also Mason, *Postcapitalism*, Ch. 7

48. Michael Hardt and Antonio Negri, *Multitude*. (London: Penguin, 2005)

49. Paul Mason, 'Why it's still kicking off everywhere,' *Soundings* 53, Spring 2013

50. Norman Geras, "Post – Marxism?" *New Left Review*, 163 (1987), 40–82.

51. Frederick Harry Pitts, 'Beyond the Fragment: postoperaismo, postcapitalism and Marx's 'Notes on machines', 45 years on,' *Economy and Society*, 46:3–4, 324–345

52. Paul Mason, 'The end of capitalism has begun,' *The Guardian*. 17 July 2015, https://www.theguardian.com/books/2015/jul/17/postcapitalism-end-of-capitalism-begun [Accessed 28 April 2018]

53. Pitts, 'Beyond the Fragment'; see Karl Marx, *Grundrisse*. (London: Penguin: 1973), 704–6

54. Moishe Postone, *Time, Labor and Social Domination*, p. 35

55. Werner Bonefeld, "Negative Dialectics and Critique of Economic Objectivity," *History of the Human Sciences*, 29(2) (2016): 60–76

56. For the definitive critique of the misplaced salience of the base-superstructure model in Marxist theory, see Raymond Williams, "Base and Superstructure in Marxist Cultural Theory," *New Left Review*, I/82, Nov-Dec 1973. https://newleftreview.org/I/82/raymond-williams-base-and-superstructure-in-marxist-cultural-theory [Accessed 14 May 2018]

57. Quoted in Gunn, "Against Historical Materialism", 10

58. Cf George Comninel, *Rethinking the French Revolution* (London: Verso, 1987) Chapter 3

59. Nick Land, 'A Quick-and-Dirty Introduction to Accelerationism,' *Jacobite*, 25 May 2017, https://jacobitemag.com/2017/05/25/a-quick-and-dirty-introduction-to-accelerationism [Accessed 11 May 2018]; Park McDougald, 'The Darkness Before the Right,' *The Awl*, 28 September 2015, https://www.theawl.com/2015/09/the-darkness-before-the-right [Accessed 11 May 2018]; Shuja Haider, 'The Darkness at the End of the Tunnel: Artificial Intelligence and Neoreaction,' *Viewpoint*, March 28 2017, https://www.viewpointmag.com/2017/03/28/the-darkness-at-the-end-of-the-tunnel-artificial-intelligence-and-neoreaction [Accessed 11 May 2018]

60. Nick Land, 'A Quick-and-Dirty Introduction to Accelerationism.' Cf Park McDougald, 'Accelerationism, Left and Right,' 14 April 2014, https://pmacdougald.wordpress.com/2016/04/14/accelerationism-left-and-right [Accessed 11 May 2018].

61. Tamas, "Telling the Truth about Class"

62. Tamas, 'Telling the Truth about Class,' pp. 5–8

63. Danny Postel, discussion comment in '30 years of the Islamic Revolution in Iran'

64. Jan-Werner Müller, *What Is Populism?*

65. Carl Schmitt, *The Concept of the Political* (Chicago: Chicago University Press, 2007); Chantal Mouffe (ed), *The Challenge of Carl Schmitt* (London: Verso, 1999)

66. Hence the widely respected soft left NEC stalwart Ann Black was removed from a Momentum-backed 'left slate' for her alleged support for a cut-off date limiting new members' eligibility to vote in Corbyn's second leadership contest. Black denied the charge and claimed the cut-off had been imposed due to Corbyn and his supporters leaving a crucial meeting early and thus missing the vote. Black's place on the 'left slate' was taken by none other than Momentum founder Jon Lansman. Cf Paul Waugh, 'Momentum 'Slate' For Labour's National Executive Committee (NEC) Axes Veteran Ann Black,' *Huffington Post*, 9 February 2018, https://www.huffingtonpost.co.uk/amp/entry/momentum-slate-for-labours-national-executive-committee-nec-axes-veteran-ann-black-christine-shawcroft-not-standing-jon-lansman_uk_5a7d8a2ae4b0c6726e123624/ [Accessed 16 July 2018]

67. Maxine Molyneux and Thomas Osborne, 'Populism: A Deflationary View,'

68. Jacob Hamburger, 'Can There Be a Left Populism?' *Jacobin*, 29 March 2018, https://www.jacobinmag.com/2018/03/left-populism-mouffe-fassin-france-insoumise [Accessed 14 May 2018]

69. David Runciman, 'Tony and Jeremy,' *London Review of Books*, 20 April 2017, https://www.lrb.co.uk/v39/n08/david-runciman/short-cuts [Accessed 1 June 2018]; Chris York, 'Portland PR Company Condemns Len McCluskey's 'Ridiculous' Claim They're Behind Corbyn

Coup,' *Huffington Post*, 3 July 2016, https://www.
huffingtonpost.co.uk/entry/portland-pr-company-conspiracy_
uk_57791308e4b073366f0f2cc5 [Accessed 01 June 2018]

70. Frances Perraudin, 'Owen Smith: Corbyn is exploiting my
     former work in pharmaceuticals,' *The Guardian*, 15 August
     2016, https://www.theguardian.com/politics/2016/aug/15/
     owen-smith-corbyn-career-pharmaceutical-industry-labour-
     leadership [Accessed 1 June 2018]

71. John McDonnell, 'The soft coup is under way,' *Labour
     Briefing*, 26 February 2017, http://labourbriefing.squarespace.
     com/home/2017/2/26/the-soft-coup-is-under-way [Accessed 1
     June 2018]

72. Lee Harpin, 'Momentum founder Jon Lansman 'subjected to
     antisemitic abuse' after announcing bid for top Labour job,'
     Jewish Chronicle, 6 March 2018, https://www.thejc.com/
     news/uk-news/momentum-founder-jon-lansman-subjected-to-
     antisemitic-abuse-after-announcing-labour-job-bid-1.460102
     [Accessed 15 May 2018]

CHAPTER 6: THE RIGGED SYSTEM: CORBYNISM AND CONSPIRACY THEORY

1. Jeremy Corbyn, 'My statement on Donald Trump's victory
    in the US presidential election,' 9 November 2016, http://
    jeremycorbyn.org.uk/articles/jeremy-corbyn-my-statement-
    on-donald-trumps-victory-in-the-us-presidential-election
    [Accessed 13 May 2018]

2. Tom Mctague and Charlie Cooper, 'Jeremy Corbyn's Plan to
    Copy Trump's Playbook', *Politico*, 9 January 2017, https://
    www.politico.eu/article/revealed-jeremy-corbyn-labour-plan-
    to-copy-donald-trump-playbook [Accessed 13 May 2018]

3. Jeremy Corbyn, 'The people who run Britain have been taking
    our country for a ride', *Labour List*, 13 January 2017, https://

labourlist.org/2017/01/corbyn-the-people-who-run-britain-have-been-taking-our-country-for-a-ride [Accessed 13 May 2018]

4. Jeremy Corbyn, "It is a rigged system': Jeremy Corbyn's launch speech – in full,' *Independent*, 20 April 2017, https://inews.co.uk/news/politics/rigged-system-jeremy-corbyns-launch-speech-full [Accessed 13 May 2018]

5. Courtney Weaver, 'Trump Democrats shake up US election,' *Financial Times*. 9 March 2016 https://www.ft.com/content/4558db62-e61a-11e5-a09b-1f8b0d268c39 [Accessed 13 May 2018]

6. Jonathan Martin, 'Rift Between Labor and Environmentalists Threatens Democratic Turnout Plan,' *New York Times*. 16 May 2016, https://www.nytimes.com/2016/05/17/us/politics/democratic-turnout.html [Accessed 13 May 2018]

7. Ashley Parker and Jonathan Martin, 'Donald Trump Borrows From Bernie Sanders's Playbook to Woo Democrats,' *New York Times*, 17 May 2016 http://www.nytimes.com/2016/05/18/us/politics/donald-trump-bernie-sanders-campaign.html [Accessed 13 May 2018]

8. Donald Trump, 'Declaring American Economic Independence,' 28 June 2016, https://www.politico.com/story/2016/06/full-transcript-trump-job-plan-speech-224891 [Accessed 13 May 2018]

9. BBC News, "Drug dealers, criminals, rapists': What Trump thinks of Mexicans,' *BBC News*, 31 August 2016, http://www.bbc.co.uk/news/av/world-us-canada-37230916/drug-dealers-criminals-rapists-what-trump-thinks-of-mexicans [Accessed 13 May 2018]

10. J Lester Feder, 'This is how Steve Bannon sees the entire world,' *Buzzfeed*, 15 November 2016, https://www.buzzfeed.com/lesterfeder/this-is-how-steve-bannon-sees-the-entire-world [Accessed 13 May 2018]

11. Donald Trump, 'Donald Trump's Argument for America,' *YouTube*, 6 November 2016, https://www.youtube.com/watch?v=vST61W4bGm8 [Accessed 13 May 2018]

12. Bernie Sanders, 'A Rigged Economy: This is how it works,'
     YouTube, 20 November 2015, https://www.youtube.com/
     watch?v=pnSQVixz7wg [Accessed 13 May 2018]

13. Bernie Sanders, 'Bernie Sanders on Free Trade,' *On The Issues*,
     2016, http://www.ontheissues.org/2016/bernie_sanders_free_
     trade.htm [Accessed 13 May 2018]; Dylan Matthews, "This
     is a massive effort to attract cheap labor.' Why Sen. Bernie
     Sanders is skeptical of guest workers,' *The Washington Post*,
     25 May 2013, https://www.washingtonpost.com/news/wonk/
     wp/2013/05/25/this-is-a-massive-effort-to-attract-cheap-
     labor-why-sen-bernie-sanders-is-skeptical-of-guest-workers
     [Accessed 13 May 2018]

14. Paul Mason, 'What kind of capitalism is it possible for the
     left to build?,' *Open Democracy*, 20 June 2018, https://www.
     opendemocracy.net/neweconomics/kind-capitalism-possible-
     left-build [Accessed 27 July 2018]

15. Chantal Mouffe, 'Jeremy Corbyn's Left Populism,' *Verso*, 16
     April 2018, https://www.versobooks.com/blogs/3743-jeremy-
     corbyn-s-left-populism [Accessed 13 May 2018]

16. TOP Berlin, 'Make a foreshortened critique of capitalism
     history!: Without a radical critique every action becomes
     mere activism- reflections on the anti-G8 mobilisation 2007,'
     Shift Magazine 1, September 2008, https://libcom.org/library/
     make-foreshortened-critique-capitalism-history-without-
     radical-critique-every-action-bec [Accessed 9 May 2018]; see
     also London Wine and Cheese Appreciation Society, 'Debate
     and Analysis of 'Make a foreshortened critique of capitalism
     history!',' *Gruppen Gegen Kapital Und Nation*, 28 March
     2010, https://gegen-kapital-und-nation.org/en/debate-and-
     analysis-make-foreshortened-critique-capitalism-history/
     [Accessed 9 May 2018]

17. For neo-villeiny see Geraint Harvey, Carl Rhodes, Sheena J.
     Vachhani, and Karen Williams, 'Neo-villeiny and the service
     sector: the case of hyper flexible and precarious work in fitness
     centres.' *Work, employment and society* 31, no. 1 (2017):
     19–35.

18. Karl Marx, *Capital* Vol 1 (Penguin; 1990) p. 92

19. Philip Spencer, 'The shame of antisemitism on the left has a long, malign history,' *The Guardian*, 1 April 2018. Available from: https://www.theguardian.com/commentisfree/2018/apr/01/shame-of-anitsemitism-on-left-has-long-malign-history [Accessed 18 May 2018]; Brendan McGeevor and David Feldman, 'British Left's anti-Semitism Problem Didn't Start With Corbyn. It's Been Festering for a Century,' *Haaretz*, 9 April 2018, https://www.haaretz.com/opinion/labour-s-festering-anti-semitism-problem-didn-t-start-with-corbyn-1.5980426 [Accessed 18 May 2018]

20. Jason Cowley, 'The Last Comrade', *New Statesman*, 14 December 2016, https://www.newstatesman.com/politics/uk/2016/12/jeremy-corbyn-last-comrade [Accessed 13 May 2018]

21. Peter Dominiczak, 'Jeremy Corbyn: 9/11 was 'manipulated,' 25 September 2015, https://www.telegraph.co.uk/news/politics/Jeremy_Corbyn/11892383/Jeremy-Corbyn-911-was-manipulated.html [Accessed 13 May 2018]

22. Aufheben, 'The Rise of Conspiracy Theories,' 24, September 2017

23. For an example of the latter claim, see Makia Freeman, 'ISIS Is a US-Israeli Creation. Top Ten 'Indications',' *Global Research*, 5 April 2016, https://www.globalresearch.ca/isis-is-a-us-israeli-creation-top-ten-indications/5518627 [Accessed 13 May 2018]

24. For a testimony see Ivor Gaber, 'Why my antisemitism antenna keeps twitching', *Jewish Chronicle*, 2 Oct 2017. Available from: https://www.thejc.com/comment/comment/why-my-antisemitism-antenna-keeps-twitching-1.445353 [Accessed 18 May 2018]

25. Peter Beaumont, 'Ken Livingstone muddies history to support claims on Hitler and Zionism,' *The Guardian*, 1 May 2016, https://www.theguardian.com/politics/2016/apr/30/livingstone-muddies-history-to-support-hitler-and-zionism-claims [Accessed 16 July 18]

26. Heather Stewart, 'Corbyn in antisemitism row after backing artist behind 'offensive' mural,' *The Guardian*, 23 March 2018, https://www.theguardian.com/politics/2018/mar/23/corbyn-criticised-after-backing-artist-behind-antisemitic-mural [Accessed 13 May 2018]

27. Marcus Dysch, 'Did Jeremy Corbyn back artist whose mural was condemned as antisemitic?' *Jewish Chronicle*, 6 November 2015, https://www.thejc.com/news/uk-news/did-jeremy-corbyn-back-artist-whose-mural-was-condemned-as-antisemitic-1.62106 [Accessed 13 May 2018]

28. Rob Merrick, 'Len McCluskey dismisses Labour conference anti-Semitism claims as an attempt to 'bring Jeremy Corbyn down',' *Independent,* 27 September 2017, https://www.independent.co.uk/news/uk/politics/len-mcluskey-labour-anti-semitism-jeremy-corbyn-attempt-unite-chief-trade-union-friends-israel-a7969366.html [Accessed 13 May 2018]; Rajeev Syal, 'Diane Abbott says claims of antisemitism within Labour are smear,' *The Guardian*, 1 May 2016, https://www.theguardian.com/politics/2016/may/01/diane-abbott-smear-labour-antisemitism-problem-andrew-marr [Accessed 13 May 2018]; Seamus Milne, 'Jeremy Corbyn's surge can be at the heart of a winning coalition,' *The Guardian*, 20 August 2015, https://www.theguardian.com/politics/commentisfree/2015/aug/19/jeremy-corbyn-coalition-labour [Accessed 13 May 2018]; 'Copy of Jeremy Corbyn on Jonathan Freedland,' *YouTube*, 9 August 2016, https://www.youtube.com/watch?time_continue=68&v=ghNH14ybnUw

29. David Collier, 'Exclusive: Jeremy Corbyn with hard-core antisemites, say what about the Mavi Marmara?' *David-Collier.com*, 7 March 2018 http://david-collier.com/exclusive-corbyn-antisemitism/ link [Accessed 13 May 2018]

30. Letters, 'Stop Jeremy Corbyn's trial by media over antisemitism,' *The Guardian*, 2 April 2018 https://www.theguardian.com/politics/2018/apr/02/stop-jeremy-corbyns-trial-by-media-over-antisemitism [Accessed 13 May 2018]; Benjamin Kentish, 'Thousands of Jeremy Corbyn supporters

endorse letter saying Jewish-organised antisemitism protest
was the work of 'very powerful special interest group',
Independent, 28 March 2018, https://www.independent.
co.uk/news/uk/politics/jeremy-corbyn-labour-antisemitism-
protest-powerful-special-interest-group-jewish-a8278761.html
[Accessed 13 May 2018]

31. Michael Segalov, 'Jeremy Corbyn is no anti-Semite, but he
    did fuck up,' *Huck Magazine,* 26 March 2018, http://www.
    huckmagazine.com/perspectives/opinion-perspectives/jeremy-
    corbyn-anti-semitism-michael-segalov [Accessed 13 May 2018]

32. Sky News, 'Jeremy Corbyn apologises for 'pockets' of
    anti-Semitism within Labour Party,' *Sky News,* 26 March
    2018, https://news.sky.com/story/jeremy-corbyn-apologises-
    for-pockets-of-antisemitism-within-labour-party-11304273
    [Accessed 13 May 2018]

33. Chris Mullin (@chrismullinexmp), 'Sorry to see Jewish leaders
    ganging up on Corbyn. Far less anti-semitism in the Labour
    Party than in other parts of society and in some other political
    parties. Suspect it has more to do with criticism of Israel than
    anti-semitism,' Twitter, 25 March 2018, https://web.archive.
    org/web/20180326101618/https:/twitter.com/chrismullinexmp/
    status/978160263848394752 [Accessed 13 May 2018]

34. Campaign Against Antisemitism, 'Antisemitism Barometer
    2017,' *Antisemitism.uk*, 20 August 2017, https://
    antisemitism.uk/wp-content/uploads/2017/08/Antisemitism-
    Barometer-2017.pdf [Accessed 13 May 2018]. See also
    CST, 'Antisemitism and the Left: what does the new report
    from CST and JPR tell us?' *Community Security Trust*, 14
    September 2017, https://cst.org.uk/news/blog/2017/09/14/
    antisemitism-and-the-left-what-does-the-new-report-from-cst-
    and-jpr-tell-us [Accessed 13 May 2018]. One widely shared
    Corbyn-supporting article which used the CAA's research
    to minimise the problem of antisemitism in the party was
    Skwawkbox, 'Exclusive: proof Labour antisemitism has gone
    DOWN under Corbyn,' *The Skwawkbox*, 29 March 2018,

https://skwawkbox.org/2018/03/29/exclusive-caa-yougov-data-show-labour-significantly-less-antisemitic-under-corbyn/ [Accessed 13 May 2018]

35. Campaign Against Antisemitism, 'What CAA research really says about the Labour Party's antisemitism problem,' *Antisemitism.uk*, 24 April 2018, https://antisemitism.uk/what-caa-research-really-says-about-the-labour-partys-antisemitism-problem [Accessed 13 May 2018]

36. Moishe Postone, 'Antisemitism and National Socialism'

37. Aufheben, 'The rise of conspiracy theories: Reification of defeat as the basis of explanation,' *Aufheben* #24 (2017), 12–28

38. Theodor Adorno and Max Horkheimer, *The Dialectic of Enlightenment* (London, New York: Verso, 1979) pp. 173–4

39. Werner Bonefeld, *Critical Theory and the Critique of Political Economy*, 197

40. Catherine Neilan, 'Exclusive: Labour to meet Morgan Stanley after Jeremy Corbyn's 'threat' tweet,' *City AM*, 13 December 2017, http://www.cityam.com/277374/exclusive-labour-meet-morgan-stanley-after-jeremy-corbyns [Accessed 18 May 2018]

41. Werner Bonefeld, *Critical Theory and the Critique of Political Economy*, 237

42. Karl Marx, *Grundrisse* (London: Penguin, 1993) 164; Werner Bonefeld, *Critical Theory and the Critique of Political Economy*, 238).

43. Aufheben, 'The rise of conspiracy theories', 14

44. Bonefeld, *Critical Theory and the Critique of Political Economy*, 101

45. David Feldman and Brendan McGeever, 'British Left's anti-Semitism Problem Didn't Start With Corbyn. It's Been Festering for a Century,' *Haaretz*, 9 April 2018, https://www.

haaretz.com/opinion/labour-s-festering-anti-semitism-problem-didn-t-start-with-corbyn-1.5980426 [Accessed 20 May 2018]

46. Susie Linfield, 'Neither Master Nor Subject: Zionism, Empire, and the Balfour Declaration,' *Dissent,* Fall 2017, https://www.dissentmagazine.org/article/1917-balfour-declaration-zionism-imperialism [Accessed 20 May 2018]

47. Sienna Rogers, 'Jewish groups slam Labour's new antisemitism guidelines,' *Labour List*, 5 July 2018, https://labourlist.org/2018/07/jewish-groups-slam-labours-new-antisemitism-guidelines [Accessed 16 July 18]

48. David Hirsh, *Contemporary Left Antisemitism*, 11

49. Nick Timothy et al, 'George Soros, the man who 'broke the Bank of England', backing secret plot to thwart Brexit,' *Daily Telegraph*, 8 February 2018, https://www.telegraph.co.uk/politics/2018/02/07/george-soros-man-broke-bank-england-backing-secret-plot-thwart/ [Accessed 20 May 2018]; Leave.EU, 'The Soros Web,' *Leave.EU*, https://leave.eu/the-soros-web/ [Accessed 20 May 2018]

50. Robert Skidelsky, 'Trumpism could be a solution to the crisis of neoliberalism,' *The Guardian*, 15 November 2016, https://www.theguardian.com/business/2016/nov/15/trumpism-solution-crisis-neoliberalism-robert-skidelsky [Accessed 13 May 2018]

51. Narindar Singh, 'Keynes and Hitler' *Economic and Political Weekly.* 29(42), 1994 (2755–66)

52. Albert R Hunt, 'Trump's Big Plans on Infrastructure Will Stay Big,' *Bloomberg.* 29 January 2017, https://www.bloomberg.com/view/articles/2017-01-29/trump-s-big-plans-on-infrastructure-will-stay-big [Accessed 13 May 2018]

53. Ed Balls, 'There is an alternative – my Bloomberg speech,' August 2010, http://www.edballs.co.uk/blog/speeches-articles/there-is-an-alternative-my-bloomberg-speech-august-2010 [Accessed 13 May 2018]

54. Philip Stephens, 'Corbyn and Trump join hands against
    the liberal world order,' *Financial Times*, 31 August 2017,
    https://www.ft.com/content/a1c90412-8d76-11e7-a352-
    e46f43c5825d [Accessed 18 May 2018]; Slavoj Zizek,
    'Alt-right Trump supporters and left-wing Bernie Sanders fans
    should join together to defeat capitalism,' *The Independent*,
    26 November 2017, https://www.independent.co.uk/voices/
    donald-trump-steve-bannon-alt-right-bernie-sanders-hillary-
    clinton-anti-capitalism-together-a8076501.html [Accessed 18
    May 2018]

55. Kyrylo Tkachenko, 'How Right is the Left? The German
    radical Left in the context of the 'Ukraine crisis',' *Eurozine*, 15
    May 2018, https://www.eurozine.com/how-right-is-the-left/
    [Accessed 18 May 2018]

56. Bart Cammaerts et al, 'Journalistic Representations of Jeremy
    Corbyn in the British Press,' *Media@LSE Report*, July 2016,
    http://www.lse.ac.uk/media-and-communications/research/
    research-projects/representations-of-jeremy-corbyn [Accessed
    13 May 2018]

57. Justin Schlosberg, 'Should he stay or should he go?
    Television and Online News Coverage of the Labour Party
    in Crisis', *Media Reform Coalition*, 28 July 2016, p4, http://
    www.mediareform.org.uk/wp-content/uploads/2016/07/
    Corbynresearch.pdf [Accessed 13 May 2018]. For a critique of
    the methodology and tendentious character of these supposedly
    objective studies, see Rose Hasler, 'Bias is in the eye of the
    beholder: Understanding the truth behind the recent academic
    studies on the media and Jeremy Corbyn,' *Medium*, 25 August
    2016, https://medium.com/@rose_hasler/bias-is-in-the-eye-
    of-the-beholder-understanding-the-truth-behind-the-recent-
    academic-studies-on-cd3fd1700b76 [Accessed 13 May 2018]

58. Tom McTague and Charlie Cooper, 'Jeremy Corbyn's plan to
    copy Trump's playbook'

59. Ibid.

60. See e.g. Stuart Hall and Martin Jacques (eds.), *The Politics of Thatcherism*, London: Lawrence and Wishart, 1983; Stuart Hall, *The Hard Road to Renewal: Thatcherism and the Crisis of the Left*. London: Verso, 1988.

61. Noam Chomsky & Edward Herman, *Manufacturing Consent* (Vintage, 1995)

62. For an examination of how pro-Soviet sentiment among the new left presents precisely such a 'post-truth' sensibility, see Steve Hanson, 'The new left can be post-truth too,' *Open Democracy*, 8 August 2017, https://www.opendemocracy.net/uk/steve-hanson/new-left-can-be-post-truth-too [Accessed 18 May 2018]

63. Ashley Cowburn, 'Labour supporters hiss BBC's Laura Kuenssberg as she questions Jeremy Corbyn on EU referendum,' Independent, 2 June 2016, https://www.independent.co.uk/news/uk/politics/eu-referendum-jeremy-corbyn-bbc-political-editor-laura-kuenssberg-labour-party-a7061046.html [Accessed 13 May 2018]; Helena Horton, 'Journalist booed by Corbyn supporters at manifesto launch after asking about leader's popularity,' *Daily Telegraph*, 16 May 2017, https://www.telegraph.co.uk/news/2017/05/16/journalist-booed-corbyn-supporters-manifesto-launch-asking-leaders/ [Accessed 13 May 2018]; Nick Corasaniti, 'Partisan Crowds at Trump Rallies Menace and Frighten News Media,' *New York Times*, 14 October 2016, https://www.nytimes.com/2016/10/15/us/politics/trump-media-attacks.html [Accessed 13 May 2018]

64. Peter Walker, 'BBC political editor given bodyguard for Labour conference,' *The Guardian*, 24 September 2017, https://www.theguardian.com/media/2017/sep/24/bbc-political-editor-given-bodyguard-for-labour-conference [Accessed 13 May 2018]

65. Gavan Titley, 'Filter Bubble – When Scepticism of the Mainstream Media Becomes Denial of Atrocity,' *Wildcat Dispatches*, 14 December 2016, http://wildcatdispatches.org/2016/12/14/gavan-titley-filter-bubble-how-blanket-distrust-

of-the-western-msm-results-in-nothing-more-than-displaced-fidelity-to-its-alternative-mirror-image [Accessed 13 May 2018]

66. Evan Smith, 'How the Morning Star reported the fall of the Berlin Wall,' *Hatful of History*, 7 November 2014, https://hatfulofhistory.wordpress.com/2014/11/07/how-the-morning-star-reported-the-fall-of-the-berlin-wall [Accessed 13 May 2018]

67. Andrew Coates, 'Morning Star Hails Aleppo 'Liberation',' *Tendance Coatesy*, 13 December 2016, https://tendancecoatesy.wordpress.com/2016/12/13/morning-star-hails-allepo-liberation/ [Accessed 13 May 2018]

68. Tony Benn, 'Tony Benn on Bosnia: 'The main enemy is NATO'

69. Jeremy Corbyn (@jeremycorbyn), 'Try Russia Today. Free of Royal Wedding and more objective on Libya than most,' Twitter, 26 April 2011, https://twitter.com/jeremycorbyn/status/62790355829002240 [Accessed 13 May 2018]

70. Guido Fawkes, 'On Putin's Platform: Top Labour figures on Russia Today 40 times in two years,' *Order-Order.com*, 10 October 2017, https://order-order.com/2017/10/10/putins-platform-top-labour-figures-russia-today-40-times-two-years [Accessed 13 May 2018]

71. Haroon Siddique, 'Labour MPs should not appear on Russia Today, says John McDonnell,' *The Guardian*, 11 March 2018, https://www.theguardian.com/politics/2018/mar/11/labour-mps-should-not-appear-on-russia-today-says-john-mcdonnell [Accessed 13 May 2018]

72. RT, 'UK needs nationalist answer to globalism – Nick Griffin,' *RT.com*, 19 August 2009, https://www.rt.com/politics/griffin-uk-national-party [Accessed 13 May 2018]; RT, ''EU is in process of collapsing on itself' – Marine Le Pen to RT,' *RT.com*, 20 May 2016, https://www.rt.com/news/343715-eu-collapsing-france-lepen [Accessed 13 May 2018]

73. 'Russia Today Exposes U.S Government For False Flags!!! ~Declares 9/11 An Inside Job,' *YouTube,* 28 June 2014,

https://www.youtube.com/watch?v=fJoevAkdMpg [Accessed 13 May 2018]

74. Rory Carroll, 'Russia Today news anchor Liz Wahl resigns live on air over Ukraine crisis,' *The Guardian*, 6 March 2014, https://www.theguardian.com/world/2014/mar/06/russia-today-anchor-liz-wahl-resigns-on-air-ukraine [Accessed 13 May 2018]

75. RT, "Before NATO intrusion, Libya was African Switzerland,' *RT.com*, 25 August 2011, https://www.rt.com/news/interview-libya-nato-intrusion-127/ [Accessed 13 May 2018]; RT, 'Saving the world economy from Gaddafi, *RT.com*, 5 May 2011, https://www.rt.com/news/economy-oil-gold-libya/ [Accessed 13 May 2018]

76. Peter Dominiczak, 'Jeremy Corbyn: 9/11 was 'manipulated"

77. Adam Withnall, 'Jeremy Corbyn calls Osama bin Laden's killing a 'tragedy' – but was it taken out of context?' *Independent*, 31 August 2015, http://www.independent.co.uk/news/uk/politics/jeremy-corbyn-calls-osama-bin-ladens-death-a-tragedy-but-was-it-taken-out-of-context-10479396.html [Accessed 13 May 2018]

78. David Blair, 'Britain bans Iran's Press TV from airwaves,' *Daily Telegraph*, 20 January 2012, http://www.telegraph.co.uk/news/worldnews/middleeast/iran/9028435/Britain-bans-Irans-Press-TV-from-airwaves.html [Accessed 13 May 2018]

79. Mark Sweney, 'Iran's Press TV censured for interview with arrested journalist,' *The Guardian*, 23 May 2011, https://www.theguardian.com/media/2011/may/23/iran-press-tv-maziar-bahari [Accessed 13 May 2018]

80. Adam Payne, 'Jeremy Corbyn was paid by an Iranian state TV station that was complicit in the forced confession of a tortured journalist,' *Business Insider*, 2 July 2016, http://uk.businessinsider.com/jeremy-corbyn-paid-iran-press-tv-tortured-journalist-2016-6 [Accessed 13 May 2018]

81. 'Corbyn under new pressure for Iranian TV appearance,' *The Torch*, 11 July 2017, http://thetorch.org.uk/corbyn-under-new-pressure-for-iranian-tv-appearance/ [Accessed 13 May 2018]

82. Tom Gross, 'The truth about Iran is now of little importance to Jeremy Corbyn,' *The Spectator*, 29 January 2018, https://blogs.spectator.co.uk/2018/01/the-truth-about-iran-is-now-of-little-importance-to-jeremy-corbyn [Accessed 13 May 2018]

83. Muhammad Idrees Ahmad, 'For Russian TV Syria isn't just a foreign country – it's a parallel universe,' *The Washington Post*, 13 March 2017, https://www.washingtonpost.com/news/democracy-post/wp/2017/03/13/for-russian-tv-syria-isnt-just-a-foreign-country-its-a-parallel-universe [Accessed 13 May 2018]; James Kirchik, 'Russia's plot against the West,' *Politico*, 17 March 2017, https://www.politico.eu/article/russia-plot-against-the-west-vladimir-putin-donald-trump-europe/ [Accessed 13 May 2018]

84. Skwawkbox, 'D-notice update #Grenfell,' *Skwawkbox*, 16 June 2017, https://skwawkbox.org/2017/06/16/video-govt-puts-d-notice-gag-on-real-grenfell-death-toll-nationalsecurity [Accessed 13 May 2018]

85. Skwawkbox, 'D-notices, straw-men and MSM fake news #Grenfell,' *Skwawkbox,* 16 June 2017, https://skwawkbox.org/2017/06/16/d-notices-straw-men-and-msm-fake-news-grenfell/ [Accessed 13 May 2018]

86. Lee Harpin, 'Al-Quds Day speaker blames Grenfell Tower fire on 'Zionists',' *Jewish Chronicle*, 18 June 2017, https://www.thejc.com/news/uk-news/al-quds-day-speaker-blames-grenfell-tower-fire-on-zionists-1.440193 [Accessed 14 May 2018]

87. Dominic Kennedy, 'Antisemitic outbursts of prominent Grenfell aid organiser,' *The Times*, 11 December 2017, https://www.thetimes.co.uk/article/antisemitic-outbursts-of-prominent-aid-organiser-9qpjd0jl7 [Accessed 14 May 2018]

88. Jeremy Corbyn (@jeremycorbyn), 'I believe that homeo-meds works for some ppl and that it compliments 'convential' [sic]

meds. they both come from organic matter...' Twitter, 5 March 2010, https://twitter.com/jeremycorbyn/status/10038528258 [Accessed 14 May 2018]; Joe Pike (@joepike), 'NEW: Ahead of warnings of a flu crisis, Mr Corbyn says getting a flu jab is individual choice. Says he's not had one.' Twitter, 12 October 2017, https://twitter.com/joepike/status/918449311616323584 [Accessed 14 May 2018]

89. Craig Murray, 'Of A Type Developed By Liars,' 16 March 2018, https://www.craigmurray.org.uk/archives/2018/03/of-a-type-developed-by-liars [Accessed 14 March 2018]

90. Matt Zarb-Cousin (@mattzarb), 'I'm sure there's a perfectly reasonable explanation for why Sky News cut off the former head of the British armed forces as soon as he questioned whether Assad was behind the chemical attack,' Twitter, 13 April 2018, https://twitter.com/mattzarb/status/984833060956000256 [Accessed 14 March 2018]

91. Artist Taxi Driver (@chunkymark), 'War on the Gasman, as Theresa May follows the Orange Balloon for better rating polls an absolute joke!!! Tory Analytica. FFS!!!' Twitter, 14 April 2018, https://twitter.com/chunkymark/status/985148928101371904 [Accessed 14 May 2018]

92. Campaign Against Antisemitism, 'Chris Williamson's latest act of support for Jackie Walker met with 'utterly chilling' silence from Labour MPs and media,' *Antisemitism.uk*, 22 March 2018, https://antisemitism.uk/chris-williamsons-latest-act-of-support-for-jackie-walker-met-with-utterly-chilling-silence-from-labour-mps-and-media/ [Accessed 14 May 2018]

93. BBC News, 'BBC rejects complaints over Jeremy Corbyn's 'Russian' hat,' *BBC News*, 19 March 2018, http://www.bbc.co.uk/news/entertainment-arts-43463496 [Accessed 14 May 2018]

94. Matt Foster, 'WATCH: Jeremy Corbyn suggests non-Assad groups may have carried out Douma attack,' *Politics Home*, 15 April 2018, https://www.politicshome.com/news/uk/political-

parties/labour-party/jeremy-corbyn/news/94388/watch-jeremy-
corbyn-suggests-non [Accessed 14 May 2018]; Guido Fawkes,
'Top Corbynista MPs Attend Pro-Assad Rally,' *Order-Order.
com*, 16 April 2018, https://order-order.com/2018/04/16/top-
corbynistas-attend-pro-assad-rally/ [Accessed 14 May 2018];
Laura Pidcock (@LauraPidcockMP), 'It might not seem a huge
issue that @BBCNewsnight photoshopped @jeremycorbyn's
hat to look more Russian, or that @EvanHD denied it. But in
the broader context of media smearing of the Labour leader,
it becomes pretty unacceptable. Well done to @OwenJones84
for exposing this.' Twitter, 17 March 2018, https://twitter.com/
LauraPidcockMP/status/975139619602927616 [Accessed 14
May 2018]

95. Syrian Network for Human Rights, '207,000 Civilians Have
Been Killed Including 24,000 Children and 23,000 Females;
94% of the Victims were Killed by the Syrian-Iranian-Russian
Alliance,' *SNHR*, http://sn4hr.org/blog/2017/03/18/35726
[Accessed 14 May 2018]; Alexander Reid Ross, 'How Assad's
War Crimes Bring Far Left and Right Together – Under Putin's
Benevolent Gaze,' *Haaretz*, 17 April 2018, https://www.
haaretz.com/middle-east-news/assad-s-war-crimes-bring-far-
left-and-right-together-and-putin-smiles-1.6008713 [Accessed
14 May 2018]

96. Sabrina Saddiqui, 'Donald Trump calls Obama the 'founder of
Isis,' *The Guardian*, 11 August 2016, https://www.theguardian.
com/us-news/2016/aug/11/donald-trump-calls-barack-obama-
the-founder-of-isis [Accessed 17 July 2018]

97. Judicial Watch, 'Pgs. 287-293 (291) JW v DOD and
State 14-812,' *Judicial Watch*, 8 May 2015, https://www.
judicialwatch.org/document-archive/pgs-287-293-291-jw-v-
dod-and-state-14-812-2/ [Accessed 17 July 2018]

98. David Mizner, 'How the US helped ISIS,' Jacobin, 1 June 2015,
https://www.jacobinmag.com/2015/06/isis-syria-assad-iraq-
benghazi [Accessed 17 July 2018]

99.   Seumas Milne, 'Now the truth emerges: how the US fuelled the rise of Isis in Syria and Iraq ,' *The Guardian*, 3 June 2015, https://www.theguardian.com/commentisfree/2015/jun/03/us-isis-syria-iraq [Accessed 17 July 2018]

100.   Patrick Howley, 'Hillary Clinton Received Secret Memo Stating Obama Admin 'Support' for ISIS,' *Breitbart*, 14 June 2016, http://www.breitbart.com/2016-presidential-race/2016/06/14/hillary-clinton-received-secret-memo-stating-obama-admin-support-for-isis [Accessed 17 July 2018]

101.   George Monbiot, 'See No Evil,' *Monbiot.com*, 21 May 2012, http://www.monbiot.com/2012/05/21/see-no-evil/ [Accessed 14 May 2018]

102.   Muhammad Idrees Ahmad, 'Chomsky and the Syria revisionists: Regime whitewashing,' *The New Arab*, 5 May 2017, https://www.alaraby.co.uk/english/comment/2017/5/5/chomsky-and-the-syria-revisionists-regime-whitewashing [Accessed 14 May 2018]

103.   Andrei S. Markovits and Heiko Beyer, 'Jews and Americans as Supervillains,' *The Tablet*, 1 July 2018, https://www.tabletmag.com/jewish-news-and-politics/265365/anti-americanism-anti-semitism [Accessed 16 July 2018]

104.   N C Fleming, 'The Conservative Right, Europe and Anti-Americanism,' History & Policy, 22 April 2016, http://www.historyandpolicy.org/opinion-articles/articles/the-conservative-right-europe-and-anti-americanism [Accessed 14 May 2018]; Jacob Heilbrum, 'Germany's New Right,' *Foreign Affairs*, November-December 1996, https://www.foreignaffairs.com/articles/europe/1996-11-01/germanys-new-right [Accessed 14 May 2018]; Doug Sanders, 'Has Putin bought into these dangerous ideas?' *The Globe and Mail*, 22 March 2014, https://www.theglobeandmail.com/globe-debate/has-putin-bought-into-these-dangerous-ideas/article17610287/ [Accessed 14 May 2018]

105.   Jeffrey Goldberg, 'What Would Hamas Do If It Could Do
       Whatever It Wanted?' *The Atlantic*, 4 August 2014, https://
       www.theatlantic.com/international/archive/2014/08/what-
       would-hamas-do-if-it-could-do-whatever-it-wanted/375545/
       [Accessed 20 May 2018]

106.   As the once prominent Corbyn-supporting writer Sam
       Kriss infamously put it: 'better a 1000 honest fascists
       than some glistening sleaze who is neither left nor right.'
       Jean-Luc Melanchon, defeated in the first round, initially
       refused to endorse Macron in the final run off against Le
       Pen (Reuters, 'France's Melenchon says will not endorse
       any candidate for presidential runoff,' *Reuters*, 28 April
       2017, https://www.reuters.com/article/us-france-election-
       melenchon/frances-melenchon-says-will-not-endorse-
       any-candidate-for-presidential-runoff-idUSKBN17U2C3
       [Accessed 14 May 2018]. Cf Owen Jones, 'Don't be
       fooled by Emmanuel Macron the 'moderate',' *The
       Guardian*, 19 April 2018, https://www.theguardian.com/
       commentisfree/2018/apr/19/emmanuel-macron-moderate-
       owen-jones [Accessed 14 May 2018]; Branko Marcetic,
       'Emmanuel Macron Is Not Your Friend,' *Jacobin*, 26 July
       2017, https://www.jacobinmag.com/2017/07/emmanuel-
       macron-france-unions-workers-economics-le-pen [Accessed
       14 May 2018].

107.   Zeev Sternhell, quoted in Alexander Reid Ross, 'How
       Assad's War Crimes Bring Far Left and Right Together –
       Under Putin's Benevolent Gaze.'

108.   GM Tamas, 'On Post-Fascism,' *Boston Review,* 1 June
       2000, http://bostonreview.net/world/g-m-tamas-post-fascism
       [Accessed 20 May 2018]

109.   Tkachenko, 'How Right is the Left?'

110.   For a left critique of rising anti-liberalism see Gareth Dale,
       'Leaving the Fortresses: Between Class Internationalism
       and Nativist Social Democracy,' *Viewpoint Magazine*, 30

Nov 2017. Available from: https://www.viewpointmag.
com/2017/11/30/leaving-fortress-class-internationalism-
nativist-social-democracy/ [Accessed 18 May 2018]

CONCLUSION: A POLITICS OF PESSIMISM

1. Jeremy Corbyn, 'What I'm doing to banish anti-Semitism from
    the Labour Party,' *Evening Standard*, 24 April 2018, https://
    www.standard.co.uk/comment/comment/jeremy-corbyn-
    what-i-m-doing-to-banish-antisemitism-from-the-labour-
    party-a3821961.html [Accessed 19 May 2018]. See also
    Andrew Coates, 'Jeremy Corbyn Issues Welcome Statement
    on Banishing Anti-Semitism from the Labour Party,' *Tendance
    Coatesy*. 24 April 2018, https://tendancecoatesy.wordpress.
    com/2018/04/24/jeremy-corbyn-issues-welcome-statement-
    onbanishing-anti-semitism-from-the-labour-party/ [Accessed
    19 May 2018] [May 2018]

2. Jeremy Corbyn, What I'm doing to banish anti-Semitism from
    the Labour Party.'

3. Momentum National Coordinating Group, 'Accusations of
    antisemitism should not be dismissed as right wing smears' –
    Momentum's full statement,' *Labour List*, 2 April 2018,
    https://labourlist.org/2018/04/accusations-of-antisemitism-
    should-not-be-dismissed-as-right-wing-smears-momentums-
    full-statement/ [Accessed 20 May 2018]

4. See e.g. Owen Jones, 'The cure to 'left-wing' anti-Semitism is
    political education,' *Huck Magazine*, 30 March 2018, http://
    www.huckmagazine.com/perspectives/opinion-perspectives/
    labour-anti-semitism-political-education-owen-jones/ [Accessed
    20 May 2018]; Aaron Bastani, 'This is what I've only grasped
    in the last week,' *Twitter*, 29 Mar 2018, https://twitter.com/
    AaronBastani/status/979323159932559361 [Accessed 20 May
    2018]

5.   Daniel Finn, 'Corbyn Under Fire,' *Jacobin*, 9 April 2018,
     https://jacobinmag.com/2018/04/jeremy-corbyn-antisemitism-
     labour-party [Accessed 19 May 2018]; Phil Burton-Cartledge,
     'Corbynism, Marxism and Conspiracy,' *All that is Solid...*,
     29 March 2018, https://averypublicsociologist.blogspot.
     co.uk/2018/03/corbynism-marxism-and-conspiracy.html
     [Accessed 19 May 2018]

6.   Burton-Cartledge, 'Corbynism, Marxism and Conspiracy'

7.   Michaela Collard, 'Critiques of elite power aren't antisemitic
     or conspiratorial – they are necessary,' *Red Pepper*, 3 April
     2018, https://www.redpepper.org.uk/critiques-of-elite-power-
     arent-antisemitic-or-conspiratorial-they-are-necessary/
     [Accessed 19 May 2018]

8.   New Socialist Editors, 'Antisemitism and Our Duties as Anti-
     Imperialists,' *New Socialist*, 9 April 2018, https://newsocialist.
     org.uk/antisemitism-editorial/ [Accessed 19 May 2018]

9.   New Socialist Editors, 'Antisemitism and Our Duties as
     Anti-Imperialists'

10. See Carver and Blank, *A Political History of the Editions of
     Marx and Engels's 'German ideology Manuscripts'.*

11. Michaela Collard, 'Critiques of elite power aren't antisemitic
     or conspiratorial – they are necessary'

12. Jeremy Gilbert, 'Antisemitism, cosmopolitanism and the
     politics of Labour's 'old' and 'new' right-wings,' *Open
     Democracy*, 14 April 2018. : https://www.opendemocracy.net/
     uk/jeremy-gilbert/antisemitism-cosmopolitanism-and-politics-
     of-labour-s-old-and-new-right-wings [Accessed 19 May 2018]

13. New Socialist Editors, 'Antisemitism and Our Duties as
     Anti-Imperialists'

14. Hannah Weisfeld, 'Labour needs to realise Jews' identity is
     inexorably linked to Israel,' *Jewish Chronicle*, 13 July 2018,
     https://www.thejc.com/comment/comment/labour-antisemitism-

ihra-yachad-hannah-weisfield-1.467122 [Accessed 18 July 2018]; David Hirsh, 'Understanding Labour's disavowal of the IHRA definition,' *Times of Israel*, 18 July 2018, https://blogs. timesofisrael.com/understanding-labours-disavowal-of-the-ihra-definition [Accessed 18 July 2018}

15. Paul Mason, 'How Labour can fight back against the British establishment's attempt to destroy it,' *New Statesman*, 4 April 2018. : https://www.newstatesman.com/politics/uk/2018/04/ how-labour-can-fight-back-against-british-establishment-s-attempt-destroy-it [Accessed 19 May 2018]

16. Gilbert, 'Antisemitism, cosmopolitanism and the politics of Labour's 'old' and 'new' right-wings'

17. Richard Seymour, 'Liberalism and cruelty,' *Patreon*, 19 April 2018, https://www.patreon.com/posts/liberalism-and-18276621 [Accessed 19 May 2018]; see also Judith Shklar, *Political Thought and Political Thinkers* (Chicago, IL: University of Chicago Press, 1998); Thomas Osborne. 'Machiavelli and the liberalism of fear.' *History of the human sciences* (Vol 30, Issue 5 (2017) pp. 68–85

18. Amia Srinivasan, 'Does anyone have the right to have sex?' *London Review of Books*, 40:6, 22 March 2018, 5-10, https:// www.lrb.co.uk/v40/n06/amia-srinivasan/does-anyone-have-the-right-to-sex [Accessed 19 May 2018]

19. See Karl Marx, *Capital* Vol 1 (London: Penguin, 1976), Chapter 6

20. Mitchell Cohen, 'What Lenin's Critics Got Right,' *Dissent*, Fall 2017, https://www.dissentmagazine.org/article/lenin-menshevik-critics-right-bolshevism-stalinism [Accessed 21 May 2018]. See also A J Polan, *Lenin and the End of Politics* (Berkeley: University of California Press, 1984).

21. EP Thompson, *Whigs and Hunters* (New York: Pantheon Books, 1975) pp. 270–77; see also Daniel H Cole, "An Unqualified Human Good': E. P. Thompson and the Rule of Law,' *Journal of Law and Society*, 28(2), (2001): 117-203;

Nicos Poulantzas, *State, Power and Socialism* (London: Verso, 2014); see also Nicos Poulantzas, 'The Loss of Nicos Poulantzas – An Elusive Answer', trans. Rafael Khachaturian, *Legal Form*, 7 December 2017, https://legalform. blog/2017/12/07/the-loss-of-nicos-poulantzas-the-elusive-answer-a-translation-by-rafael-khachaturian/ [Accessed 9 May 2018]

22. Theodor W Adorno and Max Horkheimer, *Towards a New Manifesto* (London: Verso, 2011) 21, 35-6, 91-2

23. Franz L Neumann and Otto Kirchheimer, *The rule of law under siege: selected essays of Franz L. Neumann and Otto Kirchheimer*, ed. W. E. Scheuerman (Berkeley, Los Angeles: University of California Press, 1996)

24. Michael Walzer, 'Can There Be a Decent Left?,' *Dissent* (2002), http://www2.kenyon.edu/Depts/Religion/Fac/Adler/Politics/Waltzer.htm [Accessed 15 October 2017]; Michael Walzer, *A Foreign Policy for the Left* (New Haven, London: Yale University Press, 2018)

25. Claude Lefort, *The Political Forms of Modern Society*, (Cambridge MA: MIT Press, 1986); Claude Lefort, *Democracy and Political Theory*, (Cambridge: Polity Press, 1988); see also Andrew Coates, 'Miguel Abensour. 1939 – 2017. Radical Left 'Insurgent Democracy',' *Tendance Coatesy*. 28 April 2017, https://tendancecoatesy.wordpress.com/2017/04/28/miguel-abensour-1939-2017-radical-left-insurgent-democracy/ [Accessed 15 October 2017]; Robert Fine, 'The concept of totalitarianism: three comments on Claude Lefort,' *Democratiya*, 9, (2007): 187-191

26. Robert Fine, *Political Investigations: Hegel, Marx, Arendt* (London, New York: Routledge, 2001); Robert Fine, *Cosmopolitanism,* (Abingdon: Routledge, 2007)

27. Norman Geras, *The Norman Geras Reader: What's There is There*, eds. Eve Garrard and Ben Cohen (Manchester: Manchester University Press, 2017)

28. See Frederick Harry Pitts, *Critiquing Capitalism Today: New Ways to Read Marx*. (New York: Palgrave, 2017)

29. Terrell Carver, *Marx* (Cambridge: Polity Press, 2017); Gareth Stedman Jones, *Karl Marx: Greatness and Illusion* (London: Allen Lane, 2016); see also Terrell Carver, 'Review of Gareth Stedman Jones, Karl Marx,' *Marx and Philosophy Review of Books*, 24 September 2016, http://marxandphilosophy.org. uk/reviewofbooks/reviews/2016/2456 [Accessed 15 October 2017]

30. Geras, *The Norman Geras Reader*, 49-60

INDEX

Müller, Jan-Werner,
    10, 33, 196, 200
Murray, Andrew,
    5, 8, 79, 82–83

Neoliberalism, 38–41,
    152, 211, 264
Networked individual,
    5–6, 190–191
'New Reading of
    Marx', 261
New Socialist, 254
NHS (National Health
    Service), 36, 49,
    51, 135, 153–154,
    204
9/11 attacks on World
    Trade Centre
    (2001), 85, 240
Northern Ireland, 108,
    114–116
Novichok nerve agent
    attack, 243

Occupy, 38, 162–163
Orthodox Marxism,
    13–14, 23, 169, 181
Osborne, George, 33, 35,
    71, 101

Personalised (or truncated)
    critique, 214–219
Polanyi, Karl, 7–8,
    146–147, 163–164
Populism, 9–12, 33–38,
    55, 137, 157, 161,
    166–168, 196–206,
    231, 259

Position, politics of,
    106–107, 117–118,
    205, 221, 237, 244,
    248–249
'Post-fascism', 248
Post-liberalism, 15–16, 216
Postcapitalism,
    162–163, 190
Postone, Moishe, 21, 136,
    166, 193, 223
Postoperaismo, 189–190
Press TV, 228, 240–241
Preston model, 8, 135
Productivism, 35, 48–49
Pseudocritique,
    78, 85, 238, 240
Putin, Vladimir,
    87, 117, 247

'Rigged system', 1, 24,
    167, 208–217, 223,
    231, 249
RT (Russia Today), 239
Russia, 241, 243, 245–246
Russian annexation of
    Crimea, 82–83
Rutherford, Jonathan,
    14–15

Salisbury poisoning,
    243, 245
Sanders, Bernie, 24, 209,
    211, 232
Schmitt, Carl,
    164, 200–201
Sentiment, politics of,
    204, 236, 244
Shklar, Judith, 113, 258